Death by Stupidity

This edition published in 2016 by Prion
an imprint of Carlton Books Ltd
20 Mortimer Street
London W1T 3JW

A CIP catalogue for this book is available from the British Library.

ISBN 978-1-85375-971-0

Printed and bound by CPI Group (UK) Ltd, Croydon, CR0 4YY

Previously published as *1001 Ridiculous Ways to Die*

10 9 8 7 6 5

Death by Stupidity

1001 OF THE MOST ASTONISHINGLY BIZARRE WAYS TO BITE THE DUST

DAVID SOUTHWELL
& MATT ADAMS

PRION

INTRODUCTION

"To die would be an awfully big adventure" – Peter Pan

In writing this book we have come to learn that death is arbitrary – impersonal, uncaring, totally indifferent to any force you care to invoke for protection against it. Death can strike anyone at anytime. The most frightening thing is that while many of the deaths we have chronicled here occurred because of ridiculous stupidity, an equal number of them happened due to ridiculously bad luck.

Accidents happen. Wrong time, wrong place... nothing you can do to avoid it. When whatever archetypal figure of death you pull from your imagination comes calling – whether it is a classic grim reaper with scythe, or a top hat-wearing Goth girl from the pages of Neil Gaiman's "Sandman" – your number is up. In the end, the apparent arbitrariness of the universe is a lot scarier and harder to confront than the mystery of what happens to us when we die. However, you can almost understand why some cultures see death as the ultimate stalker, when you read tales of people narrowly escaping one disaster only to be struck by another within seconds.

One strange thing we have noticed about death is what some people, including authors John Keel and Andrew Collins, have called the 'Cosmic Joker' effect. At times it is almost possible to believe that there is some universal force which loves irony and playing with coincidence. What else can you do but laugh when you come across a tale like that of 18-year-old Jennifer Squelch being crushed to death by her horse, or when you notice the high number of reports of undertakers being killed by coffins.

Sometimes it is not the moment of death itself which is ridiculous, but the bizarre path that leads up to it. While many would argue there are plenty of causes worth dying for, we doubt you would find anyone who would argue it was worth dying over a can of beer, burnt toast or the loudness of someone's snoring. Yet as we have discovered, the fatal spirals that lead towards death start over the most ridiculous trivialities of life.

We have tried to ascertain the truth of each tale told here. At every turn, we have tried to rule out friend-of-a-friend stories and exclude all manner of shaggy dog tales. On some of the most unbelievable cases, we were surprised when our phone calls to the police and other authorities turned up the answer "Yes, that really happened," or "I didn't see it personally, but my colleague was on that case." Of course, for some entries the best we got was "We have heard that happened, but I can't personally verify it." It will be certainly be interesting to try to explain to the taxman why we are claiming telephone calls to everywhere from Dubbo to Uzbekistan, Henan Province and South Carolina on our expenses.

Almost every entry we have included could be tracked back to an original newspaper or broadcast media report. However, we have both been newspaper news editors and are well aware that not everything that gets reported is necessarily accurate. You would be surprised at just what a hard-pressed – or lazy – journalist will write and try to slip through a news desk. Some papers will unwittingly report urban legends as fact, only for their faux story to be endlessly repeated in other publications by those too indolent to carry out even the most cursory of checks. However, if you are ever tempted to think that any of the deaths in this book are too preposterous, just think back and remember that moment in January 2002, when George W. Bush, at the time the most powerful man on the planet, almost choked to death on a pretzel.

All death is a tragedy for someone, and even the most ridiculous death leaves the deceased's family and friends in pain. Our thoughts and sympathies are with all those who have been left behind. However, it seems to us that instead of obeying the cultural influences that see death as a taboo subject – or turn it into a complex dance of fetishes and mythology – laughing at its most outrageous manifestations is a healthier way to go. Of course, by saying that, we are now probably doomed to fall victims to the strange humour of the Cosmic Joker ourselves.

In our own lives, both of us have already faced moments when we could have exited the stage of life in manner ridiculous enough to gain an entry in this book. From falling into a bear pit to choking on a bit of carrot or getting death threats from the Albanian Mafiya, we have seen first hand that death can always lie just around the corner. The only sane response to this knowledge is to laugh, love and live as much as possible. As one of the entrants in this tome, writer Sherwood Anderson, once said: "Life, not death, is the great adventure."

RIDICULOUS DEATHS

DRINK AND DIVE

Drinking and driving is an obvious killer, but drinking and sleeping it off in stupid places can be, too. It certainly proved fatal for a mystery man whose body was recovered 500 yards out to sea, below a cliff top called Dancing Ledge.

The unknown idiot had spent the day of 30 July, 2006 alone, drinking heavily on the cliff top near Swanage in Dorest. Many holidaying walkers had observed his alcohol-fuelled behaviour. He was sleeping off his excesses close to the cliff edge when a walker's dog barked, waking him up with a start. Disorientated, he stumbled backwards off the cliff, falling more than 300ft to his death.

DEATHWISH DEREK

Derek Kieper from Nebraska led a campaign against seatbelt laws as an infringement of civil liberties. He died in 2005 when a car carrying him and two other passengers crashed – the seatbelt-wearing passengers survived, non-seatbelt wearer Kieper died.

THE DEATH SEAT

When medics arrived at the Florida home of morbidly obese woman Gayle Grinds, they found she had spent so much time sitting down, her 220-kilo bulk had fused to the sofa. She died shortly after a six-hour operation to separate her skin from the seat.

HEART OF GLASS

Patrick Quinn, a 24-year-old from Seattle, Washington, died when he placed a lava lamp on a hotplate. The lamp exploded, creating a storm of glass, shards of which embedded themselves into the walls of Quinn's apartment and also pierced his heart.

CASH FLOW PROBLEM

Security guard Hrand Arakelian was crushed to death by more than $50,000 worth of coins. He was travelling in the back of a security truck which was forced to break sharply on the highway, spilling the contents of 25 cash transit boxes all over him.

FATAL FOX HUNT

It's always worth keeping the safety catch switched on any time you're carrying a loaded shotgun, otherwise you might end up accidentally blowing your brains out. In November 2004, William Keen, 55, of Little Horsted, East Sussex, was attempting to climb over a gate when he slipped. His rifle swung round and fired its only bullet into his head. Mr Keen had set off in darkness to catch a fox which had been bothering his chickens when the accident occurred.

LOOK BEFORE YOU LEAP

Experienced skydiver Ivan McGuire leapt out of a plane 3 kilometres above Raleigh, North Carolina, in 1988, intent on filming his fall. Unfortunately, while he remembered his video camera, he forgot his parachute, with predictably fatal results.

ATTACK OF THE KILLER ROBOTS I

When the future history of man's war with the robots comes to be written, one day shall stand in infamy – 25 January 1979. For it was on that day that we have the first confirmed killing of a man by a robot. The opening casualty in what seems destined to be a long conflict was Robert Williams, a worker at a Ford motor plant in Michigan.

Williams was retrieving a part from a storage bin when he was attacked. It was actually a task meant to be done by the robot that killed him, but Williams had stepped into the robot's work area because it was too slow and was holding up production. In what could be perceived as a fit of pique over job demarcation lines, the arm of the 1,000 kilogram robot smashed into Williams' head, killing him instantly. More than a decade later, his family won a $10 million compensation payout for the inaugural robot slaying – setting a deadly pattern which would be repeated many times over the coming years.

WELL, WELL, WELL...

Only Richard Relf's boots were visible above the surface of his garden well after he fell in head first. Mr Relf, 65, was in the habit of watering his plants with water from the 20ft deep well, but slipped in after mowing his lawn in July 2005. Unable to work out where he was, his wife reported him missing and police launched a search of the surrounding area before finding him down the well at their home in Hawkhurst, Kent. There is no word regarding whether he made any wishes whilst down there.

PLONK PERIL

In 2002, Canadian winery owner Victor Manola died when he fell through a manhole into a 2,000 litre vat of wine while trying to collect a sample. He was quickly killed by carbon dioxide gas in the tank, as was his friend Frank Supernak, who tried to pull him out.

DROPPING IN, DROPPING DEAD

A 68-year-old woman from the province of Ubon Ratchathani in Thailand died in a freak parachuting accident. A parachutist whose chute had failed plummeted more than 2,000 metres and crashed through the roof of her hut, killing her.

BAND AID

Weighing in at 31 stones, super-obese landlord Nigel Brown, 45, of Louth, Lincolnshire, knew that unless he did something drastic his enormous bulk would be the death of him. He was so worried about dying young that he had a gastric band fitted to his stomach, a device to reduce the amount of food his body could consume. True enough, his weight did prove his downfall. Stitches to hold the band in place perforated his stomach and he died from peritonitis a few days later in May 2007. Maybe a diet would have been a safer option?

THE CURSE OF THE MUMMY?

In 1994, Hussein Badar, a modern day Egyptian tomb raider and an illegal dealer in stolen antiquities, was found dead atop a hill in the province of Sohag. Strangely, he had been pecked to death by crows.

TOP 10 RIDICULOUS
WORK-RELATED DEATHS

10. In September 2002, a 43-year-old worker at a food manufacturing plant in the town of Phan Tiet on the south-eastern coast of Vietnam fell into a vat of fish sauce and drowned. Four colleagues who tried to rescue him were overcome by the fumes of the fermenting fish and also fell to their deaths in the tank.

9. A cook at Tangalle Prison in Sri Lanka died when he fell into the huge pot of bean soup he was preparing for prisoners. The 27-year-old's life ended when another cook slipped on a wet floor and sent his colleague tumbling headfirst into the giant pot of broth.

8. Unlucky teen Elmer Cassellano got his first job as dough boy at a pizzeria in Newark, New Jersey, in October, 2001. The hapless Cassellano somehow managed to snag his clothes on the paddles of the industrial dough mixer and was pulled into its one-metre bowl, where he was paddled and mixed to death.

7. For those of you whose stomachs are turned at the mere thought of spinach, spare a thought for unfortunate Zacharia Conteh. The 34-year-old cook was scalded to death by 500 kilograms of spinach soup when a vat of it exploded as he added cream to it at a food factory in Harlesden, London.

6. Patricia Marcello, the chauffer for American comedienne Phyllis Diller, died on the job in 2001. She parked on a hill, left the limo she drove in neutral and got out to ask directions to a hotel. Marcello was crushed as the limo rolled over her, with Diller still in the back.

5. When shelves collapsed at a warehouse in Zhengzhou, China, in 2004, more than 30 employees were covered in hundreds of kilograms of garlic. Scrabbling and stumbling from the aftermath of garlic bulbs, shoots and broken shelving, the 29 workers eventually realized one of them was suffering from something a lot more fatal than a case of garlic breath.

4. Sicilian lemon farmer Massimo Salamita was reducing trimmings from his orchard in a garden shredder when his clothing got caught in the machine's workings. He was dragged into the shredder's blade – capable of chomping down trees up to 45cm in diameter – and reduced to a bloody pulp.

3. New York securities administrator Esther Penn became accidentally locked in the basement vault of the Depository Trust in Lower Manhattan, on 27 July 2000. She pulled a fire alarm hoping it would summon help, but instead it triggered a fire extinguishing system that filled the chamber with suffocating carbon dioxide.

2. Malaysian Hussin Sulaiman made his living by collecting coconuts with the help of a trained monkey. However, on 17 January 1995, his gathering days came to an unexpected end when his simian colleague misjudged and threw a coconut directly at his neck.

1. HEAVENS ABOVE
When it comes to dangerous workplaces, you do not expect observatories to be high on the list. However, in May 1987, astronomer Marc Arnold Aaronson found out just how deadly they can be. The 37-year-old world-renowned expert on the age of the universe was working at the Kitt Peak Observatory, Arizona, when he was crushed by the 150-ton revolving dome of the telescope. Aaronson had just stepped outside to check the weather when he got caught between the door and turning dome. Ouch!

TIMBERRRR!

Here's a bit of simple advice: when chopping down a tree, make sure you know which way it's going to topple. You would have thought experienced park ranger Hadrian Robinson, 28, of Rayne, Essex, would have sussed this out, but he was hit on the head by a falling maple tree and died on March 27 2003. Hadrian had removed several branches with a chainsaw, but when he came to chop down the remainder of the tree it unexpectedly fell towards him, whacking him on the head as it did so.

WITH FRIENDS LIKE THESE...

Pensioner Mary Russell should have caught the bus. Accepting a generous lift home after a shopping trip with a pal seemed a good idea in principle. Unfortunately, everything went wrong when she got out of the Ford Escort and went to collect her shopping from the boot. Her friend accidentally put the car into reverse, ploughing into 62-year-old Mrs Russell, of Pontefract, Yorkshire, before running through a fence into a nearby garden.

ONCE BITTEN...

Just because something works once doesn't mean it's foolproof. Motorist Richard Kay, 23, claimed he escaped death in a car crash by not wearing a seatbelt. He was then killed after being flung through the side window of his car in another smash five years later. Richard, of Harrogate, Yorkshire, died within a mile of the scene of his first accident, which had seen him dive out of his seat just before the driving compartment was flattened.

After a policeman told Richard he probably would have died if he had been wearing his seatbelt, he made it a habit not to wear one. The 100mph crash which killed him saw him thrown through his window and into the path of an oncoming car in January 2005. The coroner said he probably would have escaped with bruises had he been strapped in.

JUNK FOOD

There's a lot of publicity these days about ensuring you have the right diet. Ideally, it should be one that doesn't include cutlery, glass and throwing darts – unlike the one followed by Karen Johnson, 37, of Leeds. Years of these bizarre meals eventually took their toll and Karen eventually died in January 2007 of bronchopneumonia brought on by her unusual snacking habits.

YOU CAN RUN...

Sometimes the long arm of the law stretches further than you might think. Fugitive Thomas O'Reilly plunged to his death from the top floor of a block of flats after hiding from police by clinging to a window ledge. Thomas, 22, fell from the bedroom ledge on the 10th floor while officers searched his girlfriend's flat in Leeds in February 2008. They wanted to bring him back to jail for breach of parole, but eventually found his crumpled body at the bottom of the tower block. A life sentence, then.

TYRE TRACKS

A trucker escaped a serious accident when a wheel fell off his rig, flying 30ft in the air. He managed to pull over onto a motorway hard shoulder. But when Juliano Parker went to recover the wheel, the tyre unexpectedly exploded, causing it to catapult into the air and hit him in the head. Juliano, from Leeds was killed instantly and went to the great Greasy Spoon in the sky.

DEATH SUCKS

A 59-year-old man from California died when he sat on top of a swimming pool's improperly covered drain. The drain had a sucking power of more than 300 pounds per square inch and it pulled out his small intestine, ending his life.

DEADLY FEET

Student Sam Wilkinson's size 12 feet were the death of him. Sam, 21, of Leeds, died when he crashed his new Peugeot 205 into a wall after losing control on a sharp bend. His father Gary, 55, told an inquest he believed Sam's huge feet were the cause of the tragedy, as his chunky shoes may have become stuck between the brake and the throttle, preventing him from stopping before the fatal collision.

IT COULD BE YOU

Boris Peric must have thought his life and luck had changed for the better when he won 4.5 million euro in the Euromillions lottery. The 48-year-old Serb national had been struggling to earn a living as an immigrant worker within the French textile industry when his numbers came up in a draw in 2006.

Instantly lifted out of grinding poverty, Peric decided to return to his native Serbia to be with his wife and children, who he had been supporting by working in France. Like many other lottery winners, amongst Peric's first purchases were an expensive car and a new, luxurious home.

Peric had bought a massive villa on the outskirts of the village of Klicevac in the north-eastern Serbian district of Branicevco. A member of the 'Naša Stvar' – the Serbian Mafia – had previously owned the villa and it had enough rooms to allow its new master to house his whole extended family.

On moving day, Peric drove his wife and children to their villa in his Mercedes, getting out of the car to open the heavy metal gates that guarded his imposing residence. However, as he opened them, the gates fell on him. Crushed by their weight and impaled on their security spikes, Peric died instantly.

STAGE FRIGHT

The spectacular finale to a gig by rock band Bad Beat Revue saw lead singer Patrick Sherry, 29, jumping off the stage into the crowd. On the night of July 20, 2005, Patrick was playing the Warehouse Club in Leeds. Unfortunately, he attempted to grab hold of a lighting beam, only to lose his grip and hit the dance floor head first, sustaining fatal head injuries. No chance of an encore, then...

SPROUT STOPPAGE

Another reason to hate Brussel sprouts... Pensioner June Burton, 64, of Staffordshire, died during a Christmas meal after the vegetable cut off the blood supply to her gut. Her downfall was said to have been a failure to chew her food properly, as the sprout went down her gullet almost whole, causing a partial obstruction in her small intestine. She was taken ill 24 hours after the meal, but died in hospital six weeks later. The cause of her demise was only revealed during a post mortem.

SLEEPING IT OFF FOREVER

Letting boozed up Nichola Shanks sleep off a drinking binge in a car might have sounded like a good idea at the time... But Nichola, 28, from Seaforde, County Down, Ireland, contracted deep vein thrombosis in her left leg after spending 12 hours immobilised in the vehicle in May 2002. This led to blood clots travelling to her heart and lungs, killing her before anyone realized what had happened.

CHOKED ON HIS CHOPPERS

Pensioner Phillip Jacques, 78, choked to death on his own false teeth after they slipped down his throat while he was eating. Mr Jacques turned blue and collapsed after eating lunch in his nursing home at Bretby, Staffordshire and attempts to revive him proved futile. A post mortem revealed his teeth had become wedged at least 5ins down his oesophagus, completely blocking his airways, and not even the Heimlich Manoeuvre would have saved his life.

BEER HEAD

Lifting a beer keg over your head might sound like a good way to impress the ladies, but for Gerald "The Yank" Gallen, 20, the party trick went uncomfortably wrong. Illinois-born Gerald was showing off in a bar in Castlederg, Ireland. He lifted a full keg in the air, but then his arms buckled, sending him falling backwards. He was followed swiftly down by the keg, which landed on his head. Ouch!

DEADLY TONIC

If someone offered you a drink of cigarette butts and water, you'd tell them where to go. So why did Siobhan James-Moore, 39, of Stourbridge, West Midlands, think gulping down a two-litre bottle of tobacco-infused "tonic" was anything but a bad idea? She quaffed the sickly brew at an eco-village in Calca, Peru, during November 2005, in a bid to cleanse her system, but immediately collapsed. She started to tremble and suffer convulsions, and was dead by the time medical assistance arrived, having choked on her own vomit. This wasn't the first time she'd drunk the deadly toxin – she had been ill for three days on the previous occasion – so why she thought this bizarre tribal medicine was worth trying again is anyone's guess.

STRIKE A LIGHT!

Smoking while wearing overalls soaked with white spirit is not to be advised, as Bradley Peat, 34, found out when he turned into a human fireball. He was using the solvent to clean paint brushes after decorating at his home in Newcastle, when he decided he fancied a smoke. But within seconds he had caught alight, his clothes had burnt off him and his boots had melted to his feet. He died from his burns three days later.

IN THE LION'S DEN

An Azerbaijani man living in Ukraine died when he lowered himself into the lion's enclosure at Kiev Zoo. It was a highly misguided show of faith designed to prove that God existed.

Ohtaj Humbat ohli Makhmudov, 45, climbed down a rope into the lion's den. He then turned to the large crowd enjoying Sunday morning at the zoo and proclaimed: "God will save me if he exists." At this point, one of the four lions in the enclosure knocked Makhmudov down. It then seized him by the throat and severed his carotid artery, killing him instantly.

The pathologist found no evidence of alcohol in Makhmudov's body when it was autopsied. A local policeman commented: "From his all black clothes and actions it is very clear he was a cultist. We attribute his actions to religious zealotry."

BLIND LUCK

A blind cyclist died after failing to spot a piece of wood in the road which jammed in his front wheel. Yes, it really is as unlikely as it sounds. William Huelsman, 60 – who was registered blind but did have some partial vision – died from brain injuries after tumbling over the handlebars of his bike in South Oxfordshire. He had failed to spot the piece of wood, about the size of a small ruler. It wedged between the front fork and the wheel, locking it solid and throwing him forward onto his face.

WORKING STIFF

Egyptian civil servant Adel Nasim Gerges had waited more than a decade for advancement at work. He was so shocked to see his named finally printed on a list of promotions in 1999 that he died from a heart attack.

FLOORED!

You're in a lift which is dropping dramatically – do you try to jump out the doors or risk your chances in the falling elevator? Student Andrew Tucker, 19, chose the former, but ended up crushed between floors.

Andrew and eight friends had overloaded the lift in a student hall of residence at Reading University, Berkshire, when it started to fall. He tried to leap onto the first floor, but the lift was accelerating too fast for him to make the crossing.

He managed to get his head, shoulders and arms through the gap, but the lift roof caught him across the back, wedging him fast. Andrew's friends used a fire extinguisher, vacuum cleaner and weightlifting bar to lever the doors open and free him, but he died later of multiple injuries. Should have taken the stairs...

THE RUNAWAY DIED

Yeah, they might give the infirm a chance to get around unaided, but we hate the way motorised buggies are driven at reckless speeds along the pavement by deranged pensioners. So we're not shedding any tears for Winnifred Tapster, 86, of Tunbridge Wells, Kent, after she careered to her death down a steep hill on a motorised invalidity buggy in December 1997. Winnifred was crushed by a machine built to improve her quality of life, after a terrifying ride which saw her reach speeds of up to 15mph before flipping over. Speed demon!

TIRAMISSING YOU

A killer pudding proved to be the last supper for granny Jessie Hewitson, 98, after she ate some tiramisu at a West Cumbrian hotel. She suffered from severe food poisoning days after eating the traditional Italian pudding and died shortly after going into hospital in July 2006. The salmonella outbreak, which affected 15 people, was blamed on the use of raw eggs in the production of desserts. Nothing to trifle over.

ATTACK OF THE KILLER ROBOTS II

Kenji Urada was a 37-year-old maintenance worker at a Kawasaki motorcycle assembly plant in Akieski, Japan. In 1981, Urada ignored standard health and safety protocol and climbed over a safety gate to service a robot. As he had not used the gate, the robot did not fully deactivate. When he attempted to repair it, the robot mistook him for a component and began to try to grasp him. Using its hydraulic arm and nudging its electric cart body forward, the robot manoeuvred Urada towards a metal gear-cutting machine. Its faulty sensor still in need of repair, it kept pushing forward, forcing Urada into the metal grinder, which quickly rendered his soft human flesh into its component parts. Although officials blamed the death on Urada's stupidity for leaping into the robot's den, we are not so sure it was not another case of robot revolt.

VIDEO NASTY

You can be sure this videocam footage will never turn up on a home video TV show... Experienced parachutist Peter Leighton-Woodruff , 41, was so busy concentrating on recording his descent using a helmet camera that he didn't notice how close to the ground he was and he plummeted to his death in November 2004.

TOP 10 RIDICULOUS ALCOHOL-RELATED DEATHS

10. Builder Roderick de la Cruz became so drunk at his brother's house in Caloocan City in the Philippines that he bragged he had "a way with electricity like no other". He pulled a wire from the ceiling and began to twirl it between his thumbs and fingers. Within seconds the intoxicated idiot had managed to electrocute himself.

9. Alcohol and ex-military hardware are never a good combination. In 1999, three Cambodians from the Svay Rieng province were killed when, after a drunken night in a bar, they decided to play with a 25-year-old landmine. Witnesses who fled before the inevitable explosion reported the drunken men kicking the landmine to each other and daring each other to step on it.

8. Joan Scovell from New London, Connecticut, got so drunk in the early hours of 6 July 1985, she attempted to climb onto Freda, a 2,950 kilo circus elephant that was chained up in a parking lot. Freda did not like the drunken attention. She swiftly grabbed Joan with her trunk and smashed her down onto the concrete.

7. Yorkshireman Clifford Greenwood got so drunk on whisky when the River Wharf flooded his home in 1995 that he fell asleep on the couch in his lounge, rolled off into just 40cm of water and drowned.

6. During the annual drunken riot that some Finns call 'midsummer madness', visiting Swedish student Hjalmar Aalto got so drunk that when he dropped his mobile phone off the ferry he was on, he dived in after it and drowned.

5. A chilled ale is many a man's idea of heaven, but when Idahoan Clifton Doan went to his refrigerator in March 1992, cold beer sent

him into the next life. A crack in the bottom of a beer keg caused it to shoot upward when he opened the fridge door, striking him in the face and killing him instantly.

4. Romanian farmer, Dimitru Dumitrazcu, was making and sampling plum brandy in his barn during the 1993 festive season. Dumitrazcu became so intoxicated that he fell face first into a barrel of the potent drink and drowned.

3. Krzystof Azninski from Poland spent all day drinking in his garden with three friends. In an act of drunken bravado, he placed his head on a block and challenged one of his drunken pals to take an axe to his neck. His pal swung, with predictable results.

2. Emma Blackwell, a 31-year-old from Plymouth, was drinking for hours on a ferry between England and Spain. Highly intoxicated, as the ferry sailed past the coast of France, she struck the famous outstretched-arms pose of Kate Winslet in a scene from the movie *Titanic*. Emma lost her balance, plunged from the ninth deck and drowned.

1. PISSED AS A NEWT
In 1979, a Mexican man who had binged on vast quantities of whisky while in California died when he swallowed a newt for a dare. Unfortunately for the drunken sot, the newt he was dared to down was a rough-skinned newt. The creature's skin produces toxin so potent that just one 30th of the toxin present in the skin of an average adult newt is sufficient to kill a healthy adult human.

FOGGY JUDGEMENT

OK, so you're piloting a plane packed full of drugs and you don't want to get caught, but is trying to make an emergency landing in thick fog really that wise? Travel agent Malcolm Cook, 52, from Horsham, Surrey, crashed his single-engine four-seater plane into a field at high speed, skidding 50 metres before smashing into a hedge. Firefighters found four large holdalls containing 22kg of cannabis with a street value of almost £40,000. A witness said only a lunatic would be flying so low in such limited visibility. Maybe he was stoned?

ON THE PISTE

Facing a choice between a safe but adventurous slope and a run that offers a dangerous challenge to even the most experienced skiers, ensuring you don't make a wrong turn is pretty vital. But Duncan Gourlay, 45, of Sunderland, careered off the run and hit a tree after missing a warning sign. He accidentally took the wrong turning onto a closed, difficult black run at the famous Hahnenhamm ski slope in Austria. He struggled to make his way down one of the most challenging runs at the resort, but slipped on a sheet of ice and fell onto his back. He then hurtled head-first through a safety barrier into nearby woods and ended up hitting a tree, suffering massive head injuries as a result.

KEEP YOUR MOUTH SHUT!

Never tempt fate. Moments after saying, "This looks like being the best holiday we've ever had!" tourist Jonathan Rodwell was swept to his death from Africa's Victoria Falls in 2006.

Jonathan, 30, from Essex, had been nervously crossing rocks over the roaring Zambezi River assisted by a guide, but lost his footing and was washed 500 feet over the falls. His body was found two days later, a sad end to what was definitely not the best, but certainly the last, holiday he ever had.

FLY POSTER

What would Nicole Kidman have thought? A giant hoarding of the Hollywood beauty watched on silently as scaffolder James Harris plunged to his death in front of shocked commuters in the heart of London's West End.

James, 23, of Essex, had been perched on a six-inch ledge, 70ft above rush hour Oxford Street, taking down a massive poster advertising hit movie *Moulin Rouge* in September 2001. But he found helmets and safety harnesses cumbersome and awkward, so did not wear them. He lost his footing and fell. As Nicole sung in the film: "One day we'll fly away..." Not quite, eh James?

ANAL TRAUMA

Sometimes you just need to take it in your stride, not worry too much about tomorrow, and take each day as it comes. Unfortunately tourist Robert Cairns, 53, of Brentwood, Essex, was so worried about his hire car that his constant checks resulted in him slipping off a hotel balcony and plunging into the hotel garden below in November 2001.

He had been enjoying the last night of a holiday in Florida with his wife Janice, who said he must have been looking at where the car was parked ready for bringing down their suitcases. The moral of this story: just chill...

COOKING TONIGHT...

Few chefs can claim to have been killed by the food they were preparing. Matthew Dunn, 27, of Sussex, died from severe burns caused when he tipped a pan of boiling soup over his body. Matthew was cooking in a hotel in St Nicholas Cliff, Scarborough, when he suffered a fit, collapsing to the floor and knocking the soup all over him. The soup of the day was off the menu afterwards.

DEADLY DUNG

Michigan farmer Carl Theuerkauf was overcome in 1989 by methane gas from the manure pit on his property. Four other members of his family, and a friend, also collapsed and died while trying to retrieve his body.

BETTER DEAD IN SHED

It was a convoluted set-up worthy of *Mission: Impossible*, although most of the agents in the TV show tried to avoid blowing themselves to kingdom come. Librarian Lucien Moore, 46, of Eastbourne, created an elaborate death trap to blow himself up in his garden shed. First he connected a two-bar heater in the shed to the mains of his house using extension leads, and rigged this up to a pre-set timer switch. Then he doused the inside of the shed with petrol, swallowed booze and sleeping pills, and sat back to wait for the fireworks. This shed will self-destruct in 5 seconds...

DUCK!

If you were 6ft 4ins tall, you think you'd be used to bending down to avoid low beams. But gentle giant Andrew Carr, 29, of Scarborough, died after banging his head in a bar. He missed the notice advising people to mind their head and whacked his skull on the support beam. Andrew initially seemed fine, but died later that night from swelling of the brain.

TROUBLE AND STRIFE

Former soldier Kim Hoan accidentally blew himself up during a row with his wife in May 2006. The 41-year-old ex-soldier from the south-eastern Vietnamese province of Prey Veng had been threatening his wife, Mam Pen Sreng, with a hand grenade in an attempt to try and shut her up after hours of incessant nagging. Unfortunately for him, the explosive device went off whilst he was holding it.

Pen Pheng, the police chief for the area, said Kim Hoan had a reputation for regularly fighting with his wife and that no further investigation was needed as the grenade was a souvenir from his time in military service. Mam Pen Sreng was not injured in the explosion.

NO SMOKE WITHOUT FIRE

Starting a fire at the bottom of a tree before climbing it has to smack of total stupidity, but that's exactly what tree surgeon Richard Coates, 28, did in June 2002. Richard climbed up a partly dead 15ft Cyprus tree, in a friend's garden in Corbridge, Northumberland, after starting a fire close at the bottom to burn the branches he was trimming. But not only did this engulf him in dense smoke, but one of the branches he dropped sent sparks flying, igniting the tree. His friend went to call for help, but when the fire brigade arrived they found Richard's badly burned body at the base of the tree where he had fallen. He had broken his neck in the fall and died instantly because of the severity of his burns.

INSTANT KARMA?

A Buddhist monk cutting the grass near a peace pagoda died after falling under a mower attached to a runaway tractor on 21 August, 2007. Rev Seiji Handa, 50, had been using the machinery in North Willen Park, Milton Keynes, when he lost control of the tractor. Witnesses reported him chasing after it down a slope, but as he tried to get back inside he slipped on the wet grass and fell under the moving mower, which sliced and diced as it dragged him down the slope. Rev Handa, who built the Willen Peace Pagoda in 1980 and had maintained the 12 acres of ground around it ever since, had lost three of his fingers in a previous mowing accident.

RUBBISH DIET

Dewi Evans, 61, of Pontyclun, South Wales, had such a passion for swallowing inanimate objects that he eventually needed to undergo surgery on his small bowel in 2006. Surgeons discovered a paper towel, a screw, a pen top, a magnet and 54p in small change while working inside him. Unfortunately, he didn't recover and died shortly afterwards. Not hard to swallow really!

LOVEMORE BREATHES NO MORE

In 1991, Zimbabwean shaman Lovemore Mpofu told his tribe they must sing for 48 hours while he remained underwater to perform a cleansing ceremony. However, the ceremony was declared a failure when the singing stopped and Mpofu's body was found floating in a lake.

"I BELIEVE I CAN FLY…"

He thought he was the son of God and angels would save him from any danger. He wasn't and they didn't. Schizophrenic Douglas Knox, 32, of Milton Keynes, jumped off a railway bridge onto the West Coast Main Line on 16 October, 2006, believing he would either be saved by an angel or would actually become one. Instead he died from multiple injuries after plunging onto the track.

KILLER SHOPPING TRIP

Shopping should be a relatively safe activity, lacking in any obvious dangers. But Kenneth Farr, 37, of Penarth, Wales, died in May 2002 during a trip to the supermarket. An unsecured car park barrier smashed through his car windscreen as he drove out of the store in Cardiff Bay, because staff had failed to padlock it open. He had gone to buy a garden shed, when he was hit on the head by the steel barrier as a gust of wind blew it into the path of his car.

NAKED TRUTH OF LUNE-ATIC

A man walks into a pub, takes all his clothes off, jumps into the River Lune and drowns. No, this isn't a joke, but the story of bricklayer Brian Woodcock, 45, from Lancaster, who had a habit of taking his kit off and jumping into water.

A week before his death in June 2007, he had been for a swim after a funeral and had previously stripped off in a pub after getting drunk. On the day he died he walked into the Wagon and Horses, ordered a drink and said he was going to swim to another pub on the other side. He walked across the road, took his clothes off and dived into the river, but got into difficulties because of the strong tide and drowned. Coroner Carolyn Singleton said: "Mr Woodcock was a man with a drink problem who was not averse to taking his clothes off and going in the canal or river."

ALARMING TALE

Nobody likes being woken up by a ringing alarm clock, but it rarely proves fatal. However, nurse Lisa Browne, 27, died from heart failure brought on by the sudden shock of her 6am alarm call. It turned out that Lisa, from Cheshire, England, suffered from an undiagnosed heart abnormality and the alarm stress caused her heart to stop beating on the morning of 10 January 1998.

MORTAL MICKEY

Roseann Greco from New York State was so convinced that the spirit of Mickey Mouse had taken over her husband's body that she repeatedly drove their car over him. She was sentenced to 15 years in jail for his death.

HOLIDAY BLUES

Imagine the scene... You're relaxing on the beach, immersed in a good book, when all of a sudden a speeding car crashes through a beach hut, hurtles over a 6ft wall and lands on top of you. Enough to spoil your holiday really. But that was how Professor Harvey Flower, 58, was killed in August 2003 whilst enjoying a break on the Isle of Wight.

WINDS OF DOOM

Tornadoes aren't exactly commonplace on the south coast of England, so the odds of granny Pamela Hudson, 57, being killed by one are probably off the scale. But Pam was killed while on a family break in Corfe Castle, Dorset, when a freak mini-tornado suddenly sent winds of up to 70mph tearing through the village. They brought down a large pine tree, which crushed her to death. The tornado left a five-mile trail of damage on 28 October 2004, but Pam was the only fatality.

SENILE SUPERMARKET SWEEP

In most cultures, old age is usually associated with wisdom and a certain degree of decorum – or least a little restraint in behaviour. No one seems to have bothered mentioning this to 80-year-old Dennis Wiltshire from Neath in South Wales, whose death was captured on the CCTV of his local supermarket.

The octogenarian former railway worker attracted stares from fellow shoppers in August 2005 when he stood on the back of a shopping trolley, and rode it up and down the store's aisles. As if that wasn't enough to make people take notice, he also serenaded his friend Julie Brinkworth, who was with him shopping for cat food, whilst zooming around on the back of the trolley. He was certainly noticed by the security staff at the store, who were busily engaged in recording his exploits on their CCTV cameras.

Emboldened by his earlier freewheeling fun, Dennis Wiltshire decided to ride one of the supermarket's trolleys down a ramp whilst leaving the store. Shouting out, 'Wheee!' as he picked up speed, Dennis found his joyride coming to an abrupt end. A wonky wheel on the trolley caused it to spin out of control, throwing its passenger headfirst onto the tarmac of the store's car park. He was killed instantly.

Ms Brinkworth commented: "Dennis was always larking about. He was always joking, singing or doing dances."

EVERYBODY NEEDS GOOD NEIGHBOURS

A long-running dispute over a garden hedge ended with one man gunned down in his doorway and his murderer swinging from a noose in his prison cell. George Wilson, 66, was blasted with a revolver by next-door neighbour Robert Dickenson, 52, following a row over a tiny privet hedge which separated their gardens. George claimed "Dicko" had chopped the two and a half feet high row of shrubs down to a few inches, and a bitter argument followed. Several days later, on 13 June 2003, a drunken Dicko turned up on George's doorstep and shot him four times. Dicko was arrested and held in Lincoln prison on remand, but he hung himself exactly a week later. Two lives lost and all over a hedge...

BUT IS IT ART?

Student Helen Dobson, 22, of Southampton, was a big fan of modern artist Damien Hirst, who famously embalmed half a cow in a tank of formaldehyde. She was using the chemical, used as an embalming preservative, for her own art projects – also involving animal organs – in 2002. Maybe she ran out of inspiration, because she decided to drink a glass of the poisonous liquid. She then thought better of it and phoned the emergency services, but sadly she died before paramedics could help her.

KISS OF DEATH

Bank worker Douglas Marwick had rather an emotional reunion with his girlfriend after meeting her for the first time in four months. Douglas, 24, from Edinburgh, suffered a massive seizure after kissing Rebecca Downey in a hotel room in Southampton on 18 April 2002. A post-mortem examination revealed an abnormality in his heart. Must have been some kiss!

BLOOD ON THE TRACKS

During an argument with his girlfriend, Brandon Julius Funches, a 21-year-old from Los Angeles, drove his 2005 Dodge Magnum onto train tracks and stopped it as a high-speed Metrolink train approached his car.

According to initial reports made by his girlfriend, Michelle Wright, to the police, Brandon deliberately placed them in the path of the train with the aim of killing them both. However, just before the 450-ton Metrolink hit the car at 128 km per hour, Brandon got out. As he fled, he was struck by flying debris from the smash which killed him instantly. Despite the Dodge being broken into so many pieces police initially could not identify the model of car, Michelle Wright miraculously survived the impact.

THE CASE OF THE STRANGLED SHERLOCK HOLMES FAN

Ironically, mystery surrounds the death of the world's (former) leading expert on fictional detective Sherlock Holmes. Richard Lancelyn Green, 50, who wrote a biography of Holmes' creator Sir Arthur Conan Doyle, was found garrotted with a shoelace tightened around his neck using a wooden spoon. He was said to have been growing paranoid about a conspiracy surrounding the auction of Conan Doyle's diaries in May 2004, which he believed should go to the British Museum. Mr Green was found to have died from asphyxiation, but it proved impossible to determine whodunit.

ANOTHER ONE BITES THE DUST...

Who wants to live forever? A Queen fan who legally changed his name to Freddie Mercury died on the tenth anniversary of his idol's death. It's a hard life and Freddie, 49, was obviously feeling under pressure after rowing with his girlfriend on the A3M road near Portsmouth. They say too much love will kill you, and he died in hospital on 24 November 2002, four days after falling off the bridge. The real Freddie died on the same day in 1992.

ARE MOLES ELECTRIC?

Uma Werner, a 63-year-old German from the town of Zingst, north of Berlin, was enraged by moles continually digging up his garden. He decided to use extreme means to eradicate the pests. The former construction site supervisor went as far as rigging up a high-voltage cable from his house to the garden and ramming a series of metal spikes from it into the ground. He was found dead next to it.

A police spokesman investigating Werner's death said: "The 380-volt cable supplied enough electricity to run an industrial cement mixer or other heavy machinery. Mr. Werner appears to have died while trying to hook up the cable to the spikes. The moles appear to have survived unharmed."

CLEAN LIVING?

Recluse Jacques Niemand, 42, died after becoming obsessed with cleaning himself and his home with the disinfectant Dettol. Jacques' over-exposure to the cleaning agent resulted in a fatal lack of oxygen in his system. His sister visited his flat in Didsbury, Lancashire, after his death in July 2006 and found a suitcase crammed with 100 bottles of Dettol, empty bottles littering the flat, and several buckets containing the fluid.

DIVINE JUSTICE?

Convicted of stealing from a church in Tanzania in 1990, Salimu Hatibu managed to escape from the courthouse and fled into the bush. To evade pursuing police, he waded into a river and was promptly chomped by a crocodile.

EVERY ROSE HAS ITS THORN

Keen gardener Jeanne Harris died days after being pricked by a rose thorn at her home in Gloucestershire in June 2002. The 61-year-old was pruning the flowers when she caught her finger. Within a matter of days, her elbow had swollen, and she was rushed to hospital after vomiting and growing increasingly weak. Her condition deteriorated and she eventually died six days after being pricked, due to a combination of septicaemia and necrotising fascilitis.

TRUNK PACKS A PUNCH

William Sharp from Texas tried to force a 470-kilo baby elephant into a shipping crate in 1984 by prodding it with an axe handle. The elephant responded by smacking him in the mouth with its trunk so hard he fell onto concrete and split his head open.

STUDENT SUPERMARKET SWEEP

Student Martin Filder, 22, should have known riding a shopping trolley down a hill was bound to end in tears. He had been drinking all afternoon in a bar in Bournemouth on the last day of term before Easter 2005 and decided to ride down the hill in the trolley with two pals. But it hit a kerb and overturned, and Martyn suffered a fatal blow to the head as he fell out.

DEATH BY PAINTBALL

Grown men running around muddy woodland playing at soldiers – the worst injury you can expect from paintballing is to lose your eye, right? But Kenneth Costin, 39, from Bedfordshire, actually became the first known person to die from a paintball injury in 2001. Ken was hit in the back of the neck from a distance of about eight feet and took a funny turn immediately after the competition. The trauma to his head and neck had forced his arteries to go into spasm, and he collapsed at home, dying in hospital 10 days later from a stroke.

CATAPULT CATASTROPHE

Using a medieval-style catapult to throw yourself 100ft through the air is nothing short of idiotic. So why Oxford University student Kostydin "Dino" Yankov, 19, thought it was an intelligent idea is a mystery he took to his grave. Dino died from multiple injuries and serious spinal damage when he fell short of the safety net.

Tragedy struck in November 2002 while Dino was on a day trip to an extreme sports club in Somerset. He volunteered to have a go on the machine, which was based on the medieval trebuchets used to hurl rocks and dead animals over castle walls during sieges.

WIFE FOR THE CHOP

Plunging a chainsaw through your wife's neck is one way of shutting her up. Retired company director Roland Pudney, 56, virtually decapitated wife Pauline, 57, after falling from a ladder and plunging the power tool through her neck. She had been supporting the base of the ladder as he cut branches off apple trees in their garden in London in June 2004, when the couple's dog jumped up and caused him to tumble.

GROSS POINT BLANK

Bedridden Karen Chandler, 48, spent her last few weeks living in her own waste in what a coroner described as "appalling squalor" at her home in Mold, North Wales. She had received a catheter while being treated for a broken leg, but cancelled an appointment to have it changed. This brought on a serious and rare bladder infection, which led to gangrene and subsequently killed her on 5 December 2006.

She was found covered in faeces on a rotten mattress on the living room floor. Dr Andrew Dalton, who conducted a post-mortem examination, said living in her own filth for weeks had caused her catheter to become infected: "The gangrene had meant the walls of her bladder had become incredibly thin and fragile. It was a dead bladder. It is so rare that I have never seen it before."

HIC HIC BANG

High school student David E. Duquette crept up on his friend Nicholas Lovel while holding a handgun in an attempt to cure his pal's hiccups. However, instead of inducing a fright-based cure, the gun went off, accidentally killing the hiccupping Lovel.

SNOW HOPE

A woman on a snowmobile charged recklessly across a dangerous road, careered into a pick-up truck, and was thrown into the path of a 50-tonne logging lorry while on a business trip in Quebec, Canada, in January 2002. Carole Ferguson, 56, from near Bury St Edmunds, Suffolk, failed to stop at the road, ignored cries from witnesses to stop, and carried on going without looking left or right. The pick-up truck sent her flying into the air and straight under the wheels of the lorry. She had never ridden a snowmobile before and had had just 15 minutes' basic safety training, which didn't include anything about stopping at roads.

THE TOOTH HURTS

A lesson in why it's important to visit the dentist... A priest died after overdosing on paracetamol for a painful abscess on a wisdom tooth. The Rev William Keyes, 34, of West Bromwich, was found collapsed in his flat in March 2002.

WASTED

If janitor Eoghan Power, 42, really had the luck of the Irish then he was dead before he fell into a tank of effluent at a factory in County Tipperary. Eoghan had suffered a heart attack and fallen into the tank, which was used to hold waste products from butter, in October 2005.

BLOCK PARTY

An unsupported, freestanding 1.7 ton wall blew down in high winds and dropped dozens of 15kg concrete blocks onto granny Sandra Jones, 56, like some horrific version of Tetris. Sandra had been pushing her bike down a street in Rugby when gales of up to 55mph sent the wall crashing down on top of her in 2002. The wall had been put up in the 1980s to deter squatters and was only held up by its own weight, failing numerous building regulations.

MAGIC TRICK?

Whether TV magician Kevin Reay had something more magical in mind when he fell 150ft off a railway viaduct outside Hartlepool is an enduring mystery. Kevin, 61, had appeared in front of millions when he featured in BBC magic show *Paul Daniels' Secrets*. Whatever led him to fall off Crimdon Dene viaduct in May 2003, it proved to be the one trick he didn't pull off.

TOP 10 RIDICULOUS DEATHS FROM HISTORY – ANTIQUITY TO THE DARK AGES

10. A scroll discovered in a burial ground and dated to 876BCE gives an account of the death of Lin Wan Pai. He was suffocated by his own tent when the pet oxen he doted on knocked into its frame and caused it to collapse.

9. Zeuxis of Heraclea was a famous artist in Greece during the 5th Century BCE. He died after laughing so hard at his own painting of an old woman who had paid him to portray her as Aphrodite that he burst a blood vessel.

8. Agathocles, the Tyrant of Syracuse, was a military despot who overthrew the democratic constitution of Syracuse during the 4th Century BCE. After murdering 10,000 citizens he went on to become King of Sicily. His reign and life were ended in 289 BCE when he choked on a toothpick. It could not have happened to a nicer guy.

7. Chrysippus of Soli, 280-207 BCE, was one of the founders of Stoic philosophy. He died from laughter after watching his drunk donkey, which he had given wine to, attempt to eat some figs.

6. Poet and critic Philitas of Cos is regarded as one of the most influential thinkers in the early Hellenic world. However, thinking led to his demise when in 270 BCE he became obsessed with solving the paradox contained in the statement: "A man says that he is lying. Is what he says true or false?" He eventually wasted away from insomnia.

5. Arius, 256-326CE, was a Christian priest whose views were considered so heretical and threatening to the church that they led to the calling of the Council of Nicaea in 325CE. In 326CE, in what many saw at the time as divine judgement, he died when he passed wind and in so doing "evacuated his smaller intestines and portions of spleen and liver, which brought such an effusion of blood he almost immediately died". Judgement passed.

4. Given his tough villain image it is surprising to learn that when Attila the Hun died in 453CE, it was not on the battlefield, but as a result of the nosebleed he suffered on the night of his wedding to the young Gothic maiden Ildico. He was so drunk, the nosebleed led to him drowning in his own blood.

3. Li Bai, 701-762CE, is one of the greatest poets in Chinese literary history. Part of a group known as the Eight Immortals of the Wine Cup, it is fitting he died from falling into a river after drunkenly trying to kiss the moon's reflection in the water.

2. Al-Jahiz, one of the most famous scholars in the early Arab world, died in 869CE. An author of books on literature, zoology, Mu'tazili theology and history, Al-Jahiz's end came when he was crushed as the bookshelves in his library fell on him.

1. WHAT HAS HISTORY TAUGHT US?
If there is one lesson for survival we can derive from tales of ridiculous deaths in ancient history, it is to watch the skies as danger often comes from above. In 456 BCE, renowned Greek playwright Aeschylus – whose works included *Agamemnon* and *Prometheus Unbound* – died when an eagle dropped a tortoise on him, after confusing his bald head with a stone. It is reported that the tortoise survived the ordeal.

GRAIN GRAVE

All that could be found of farmer David Capon, 71, were his Wellington boots sticking out of the bottom of a grain silo. Employee Edward Holden said: "My first reaction was to think someone had dropped a welly. I grabbed hold of it to pull it out and there was something in it. There was a foot in it. I panicked."

David, of Bedfordshire, had climbed into the silo and walked on the grain to check its quality. Some got inside his wellies, however, and he was pulled under. He was dragged beneath the surface and drowned in grain on 7 April 2004.

CUT OFF MID-FLOW

Alexander Bains' mobile phone conversation with his girlfriend came to a premature end when he stumbled onto train tracks and was electrocuted. Alexander, 21, from Aldingbourne, West Sussex, was walking home from a nightclub in October 2006. He got lost in a field and tripped over some barbed wire before calling his girlfriend and then eventually reaching the tracks. At least he didn't reverse the charges!

WAGONS ROLL!

Pensioner James Hunt followed in the footsteps of his racing driver namesake when he crashed his motorised scooter as it rolled off the back of a bus. James was shopping in Hartlepool on 16 January 2005 and decided to catch a lift on a Dial-A-Ride bus. He reversed his scooter onto a platform used to raise such machines from the pavement onto the bus. Unfortunately, a barrier came loose and his scooter rolled back, throwing him to the ground and fatally smacking his head on the pavement.

ATTACK OF THE KILLER ROBOTS III

Tyron Watson was a 48-year-old worker for the J.R. Wheel Company in Cleveland. In December 2001, Tyron was working an early Saturday morning shift when a de-energised assembly robot, which should have been immobile and incapable of any function, suddenly sprung back to life. Once reactivated, the robot mistook the unfortunate human for a wheel that it needed to work on and with one almighty fatal blow flung Tyron onto a conveyor belt.

One of Tyron's fellow workers commented to the press: "You can't blame the machine, it was human error. He should have known better than get into the robot's cage." Having seen *Terminator* enough times, all we can say is never trust a robot!

HIDDEN HOLE

A labourer died after falling down a manhole concealed by rotten wooden boards. Kevin Horner, 19, of Hartlepool, was working at a nuclear power plant in Finland when he fell 35ft down the hole in September 2007. He suffered a fractured skull which later killed him. Quite why anyone was attempting to hide the hole under bits of old wood was never explained.

JOB DONE!

Decorator Steven Worville decided he'd had enough and he was going to take an overdose to end his life. But Steven, 36, who lived in Buckinghamshire, was going to make sure he did it properly. Quite how he managed to acquire such a vast quantity of painkillers hasn't been revealed, but he died on 26 February 2002 after taking a phenomenal 576 ibuprofen tablets. Wonder if he rattled afterwards?

TRIP ON THE OLD BLOCK

What good are rules if you don't follow them yourself? Coach trip organiser Joyce Dibden, 66, enforced a strict policy of ensuring passengers remain seated. Unfortunately, she ignored her own guidelines to give out mince pies on a Christmas trip to Salisbury, Wiltshire, in November 2006. When the coach driver was forced to brake suddenly she was thrown backwards into the air, hitting her head and dying instantly. That was one trip she probably wished she hadn't taken.

TOO COOL

Catching some killer waves is every surfer's dream, but 24-year-old Michael Ruinet didn't really take the expression literally. He headed out into the sea off West Wittering, West Sussex, on 13 October 2002, wearing a modified winter wet suit. Sadly, he didn't realize there was a wind chill of around 13°C and sea temperatures of around 10°C. His body temperature plummeted during the four hours he was surfing, but he didn't realize and spent a normal evening with girlfriend Juliet Bell. But despite feeling warm and comfortable, he had already caused major damage to his internal organs and died in his sleep from hypothermia. Surf's up dude.

SELF-DECAPITATION

Tree surgeon Scott Donnison almost sliced his own head off while working on a tree 40ft above the ground. He died instantly after his chainsaw kicked back from a branch and hit him on the left side of the neck, but his body was left hanging from a harness until it could be freed using a cherry picker. Friend Phil Wilkinson said after the tragedy in March 2008: "It is a dangerous job, statistically the most dangerous job in Britain."

NO SECOND CHANCES

Changing your mind midway through a suicide attempt is a risky gamble, as unfortunately it doesn't always pay off. Matt Wodhams, 28, was on the top of a car park in Worthing on 29 August 2007 when he decided to give life another shot. But as he tried to climb back over railings installed to prevent suicides, he slipped and fell to his death. If it's meant to be...

"LET'S GO FLY A KITE..."

Kite flying on a clifftop might guarantee you a good breeze, but you've got to watch your footing... Barry Ripley, 38, from Newhaven, East Sussex, was showing off with a kite at nearby Seaford Head in September 2005 when he stepped off the cliff into space, plunging 150ft to the ground below. Hiker John Betteridge had tried to warn him of the danger: "I resolved to speed up my pace to warn him how close he was to the cliff edge. The kite dropped and he pulled on the kite string, took a half step back and he was gone."

DON'T MIX YOUR DRINKS

Sometimes death is nothing more than the result of complete and utter incompetence. How carers at a nursing home in Hastings confused corrosive dishwasher fluid with diluted orange squash beggars belief. But that's exactly what they did in June 2002 and served up the fatal concoction to 95-year-old Kathleen Challis. They only realized something was wrong when her lips started peeling away as they wiped them afterwards. Staff escaped a manslaughter charge due to lack of evidence, but it was discovered the deadly cleaner was stored alongside almost identical containers of fruit juice – "a complication of errors" according to the coroner.

BLAME BILL

Illinois resident Michael S. Allen so hated actor and comedian Bill Cosby that when his mother insisted watching his TV show in July 1986, Allen took out a revolver. First he shot the television and then he shot his mother in the head.

BLOODY MINDED X-PERIENCE

Moped rider Richard "Boyley" Ball might have been the seventh best BMX rider in the world, but perhaps even he was chancing it riding with one foot in plaster and his crutches resting between his legs. Richard, 24, of Hastings, had been smoking cannabis and drinking prior to riding his bike in the early hours of 30 May 2002, but lost control and crashed into two parked cars, suffering fatal internal injuries. Sussex Police accident investigator PC Brian Welsh said carrying the crutches impeded Richard's ability to control his machine.

OLD FATHER DEATH

Strange deaths – often alcohol related – are not uncommon on New Year's Eve. However, drink was not a factor when Brian Spink failed to see in 2007. The 46-year-old from Murton, County Durham, went out whilst most people were celebrating the end of the old year, to indulge in his favourite hobby – digging up antique bottles.

In an effort to add to his 3,000 strong collection of old glassware, Murton was busy excavating at the bottom of an earth embankment. He was last seen alive a few minutes before midnight. The embankment collapsed and the fall of the soil above him crushed Murton to death. A fellow bottle collector, digging in ground disturbed by the collapse, found his body the next morning.

OUT WITH A BANG

Writer Aimee Stephenson, 45, from Hastings, suffered serious burns when a box of powerful fireworks smuggled under the seat of a Peruvian bus exploded in front of her, but that wasn't what killed her. She did not receive specialist treatment for her 48 percent burns for more than a day, because paramedics would only take Peruvians with private medical insurance to hospital. She was eventually airlifted back to Britain, but died at a specialist burns unit in November 2001. Her death prompted an investigation by Peruvian authorities into the illegal trade in dangerous fireworks.

IT'S ALL GONE DARK...

It's all very well and good looking cool and mysterious in your motorbike helmet, but surely it defeats the object if you can't see where you're going. Ex-professional footballer Steve "Smudger" Smith died days before his 37th birthday in June 2007 because his tinted visor only let in 20 percent of the light. He couldn't see where he was going and crashed his bike into a van in Kent.

STAG NIGHT STAGGER

After stripping a bridegroom naked and dragging him around the village of St Leonards, East Sussex, you'd expect it to be plain sailing for 51-year-old Anthony Read to get home following a riotous stag night. Unfortunately, in his drunken state he fell over onto his knees, rolled forward and smacked his head on the pavement. He ended up in a position where his airways were restricted and died from asphyxiation. He was found by a dog walker in this unusual position in a resident's front garden on the morning of 15 June 2003. Not sure how the groom got on.

THIS JOB'LL KILL YOU

If you can't beat them, join 'em. Psychiatric nurse Emma Gibson, 35, from Brighton, was so depressed about her work with mental health patients that she poured petrol over her body and set herself on fire. She died from 96 percent burns on 3 March 2003. Having suffered from depression since she was 17, it's possible she was in the wrong line of work...

DANCE OF DEATH

Morris dancing can be condemned for many things, not least amongst those being the fact that it is an idiotic opportunity for beardy men wearing bells and ribbons to hit each other with sticks. But is it really a killer? Company director Peter Hardy, 53, died from a previously unknown but underlying heart condition after taking part in a Morris dance near Newmarket in 2005. Thankfully his premature passing brought the excruciating dance to an early end.

TOURIST TRAP

Alberto Silveria was passing under a bridge in Genoa in 1986 when a tourist accidentally dropped a video camera on his head, instantly killing him. The tourist narrowly missed being charged with manslaughter.

SINKING HABIT

It's all very well having a routine, but you've got to be flexible. Artist Eamonn Cahill, 55, of St Leonards, East Sussex, enjoyed a daily swim in the sea at Hastings. Unfortunately, he didn't consider knocking it on the head for once as gale force winds battered the coast in November 2006. He was swept away by the huge waves and drowned.

BIG WHEEL RIDE

Pensioner Hilda Weston, 83, was catapulted into the air when a wheel flew off a passing lorry in October 2000. She was standing at a bus stop just yards from her home in Cross-in-Hand, East Sussex, when one of eight rear wheels of a 32-tonne tipper truck came loose and hit her head on. She was thrown into the air by the full force of the impact, dying instantly from massive chest injuries. Coroner Alan Craze said Miss Weston was standing in an unfortunate place when tragedy struck.

CROWDED SKIES

Parachutist Phillip Cheasley, 24, from London, jumped out of a plane only to collide with the left wing of a passing glider, piloted by Jon Crewe, 69, from Oxford. The glider then crashed to the ground, killing both men. The freak accident took place above Hinton Airfield, near Brackley, Northamptonshire, England, on 1 June 2002.

PIPE NIGHTMARE

Widow Annie Mitchell, 81, from Oxford, died following a bizarre series of events as she tried to fix a leaking pipe in her airing cupboard. DIY enthusiast Annie attempted to stop the leak by flattening the pipe with a shoe, but cracked it and sent 10 gallons of water spraying over her from the attic tank. But the water also caused the carpet to swell and the cupboard door to expand, trapping her inside the 3ft square cupboard. She was found dead from hypothermia two days later, in February 2002.

Oxfordshire coroner Nicholas Gardiner said: "The circumstances of her death, to put it mildly, were most unusual." He said Mrs Mitchell would have been trapped in the cold, drenched and claustrophobic cupboard until she died.

TILLIKUM THE KILLER WHALE I

You would think the fact that the other name for an Orca is Killer Whale would give the authorities a big clue it was not a safe and suitable animal to keep in captivity. However, it was not a big enough neon danger sign to stop three Orcas called Haida, Nootka and Tillikum being kept in a pool at Sealand in Victoria, British Columbia. In 1991, the whale's trainer, Keltie Byrne, was walking around the edge of pool when she slipped and fell in. Immediately Haida and Tillikum took turns to seize her legs and pull her under the water.

Alerted by Byrne's scream, other trainers rushed to her aid and tried to distract the whales. However, Haida and Tillikum were not going to put off, and continued to drag her under again and again until she finally lost consciousness and drowned. Debate still rages as to whether the Orcas were just playing with what they thought was a new toy or were out for revenge. Ironically, translated from the Chinook, Tillikum's name means 'friend'.

HOWZAT!

Cricketer Derek Newman died from an undiagnosed heart condition whilst trying to make a catch in a match between Porthleven and St Just, in Cornwall, on 21 July 2007. Derek, 45, was struck on the chest by the ball while fielding close to the boundary, triggering a heart attack.

Pathologist Dr Robert Marshall said: "I play cricket myself, and fielding where he was fielding, I would be surprised if the ball was travelling with enough force to cause death in someone with a healthy heart. It was a blow that someone might have survived, but it fell on a heart that was diseased."

BARMY BOMBSHELL

Mechanic's workshops are not naturally the safest places. Heavy machinery combined with a momentary lapse of coordination has unfortunately caused the loss of many lives over the years. However, it is hard to have any sympathy for the mechanic in one of Rio de Janeiro's many favelas who managed to kill himself while trying to open a rocket-propelled grenade with a sledgehammer.

The explosion that resulted from hammering the grenade destroyed his workshop and several parked cars outside caught fire. Another man who was also in the garage at the time later died in hospital of severe burns. Police investigating the incident, which happened in July 2006, reported scavengers wanting to sell the ammo as scrap metal had brought it there.

WARNING SIGNS

Known chancer and loveable rogue Stephen Mayho, 50, ignored warnings about overhead power cables. He was frazzled when he hit the cables with a crane he was using, sending 6,500 volts pumping through his body. Stephen, of St Osyth, Essex, had been told not to use the lorry's crane when delivering a log cabin. He had snubbed both this advice and the homeowner's warnings about power cables on 3 July 2006, leading to his highly-charged demise.

GYPSY CURSE?

A gypsy warned biker Shane Webb that he would die while riding a red motorcycle, and for this reason he always avoided riding red bikes. But when the opportunity arose to purchase his dream machine – a red and black Suzuki GSX 1300 RX Hyabusa, said to be the fastest production bike ever made – he was unable to resist. He actually told his partner, and the mother of three of his children, Joanna Mellows, "It will kill me."

Shane, 44, from Falmouth, Cornwall, died on his way to an anger management class in Truro on 5 December 2006, when he lost control of his bike and crashed into an oncoming vehicle. Destiny foretold by a psychic, or just a case of Shane riding a bike too powerful for him to handle? You decide.

LAST RIDE OF HER LIFE

A student was killed when two rollercoaster cars collided at a theme park in North Yorkshire. Gemma Savage, 20, of nearby town Wath, suffered head and neck injuries in the collision on the ride in June 2001. Computer safety devices built into the rollercoaster to ensure two cars were never on the same section of track together had been disabled and Gemma's car was hit at a speed of around 45mph, causing severe whiplash injuries.

NEEDLESS NEEDLE NIGHTMARE

Many people suffer from a phobia of needles, but few would let it kill them. Jane Rice, 19, was admitted to Addenbroke's Hospital in Cambridge, on 20 June 2005, suffering from a severe sore throat and high temperature. She refused to be treated with an injection of penicillin, and died the next day from acute tonsillitis. An injection was the only option, because she could not have taken the required dosage orally.

DEMONIC POSSESSION?

A trustworthy, reliable and friendly man suddenly became violent and aggressive, told his fiancée he was the Devil, and jumped from a railway bridge to his death. Tony Levett, 42, from Mexborough, South Yorkshire, started acting out of character the day before his death on 2 September 2007. His fiancée, Jean Thompson, said he became confused and panicky, and she sent him to hospital, only for him to violently attack ambulance staff. The following morning he told her: "You don't know me, I am the Devil!" before grabbing her by the throat and leaving, heading to a nearby railway bridge and jumping onto the railway line below.

He was still alive when PC David Simpson arrived on the scene and his last words were: "I am the Devil and we are going to all die today." He died in hospital a short time later.

PANCAKED

Steam engine enthusiast Derek Cox was squashed to a pulp after slipping under the wheels of a five tonne machine. The 71-year-old, from Huntingdon, England, was sitting on top of the engine when the seat broke, he plunged into the road and disappeared under its massive iron wheels. Horrified Richard Coulson, who was driving the Bluebell steam engine, was unable to stop the vehicle in time, and flattened Derek at the steam fair in Walgrave, Northamptonshire, on August 20, 2006.

ROCKET TO THE CRYPT

Village headman Chom Incham supervised the lighting of homemade rockets during the annual Bun Bang rocket festival in the Thai province of Chantaburi. However, the rockets went up fine, only to crash back down upon his head, killing him instantly.

TRUCK STOP

A mechanic was killed when a 15-tonne lorry held up on jacks fell on top of him. Steven Parsons, 18, was working under the vehicle at Truck Craft in Doncaster, England in March 2000, when it fell off the jacks and crushed him dead. A colleague said he'd never seen a truck supported with two jacks. Probably won't again either, after this calamity.

LEFT DEFLATED

A woman was trying to inflate her car tyres using an electric pump when the vehicle rolled backwards, knocked her over and squashed her. Barbara Towers, 77, of Chiswell Green, London, was killed immediately in the freak accident on February 29, 2008.

TOP 10 RIDICULOUS CRIME-RELATED DEATHS

10. Brooklyn burglar Terrence Adams died in 1999 while trying to break into a clothes store. Breaking in through the roof, his sweater got caught on a metal support, strangling him. Ironically, the name of the store was the Dum Dum Boutique.

9. Shoplifter Mary Terrell fled from the Value Village store in Detroit clutching two pairs of shoes in May 2000. To escape pursuing security guards, she hid in a garbage compactor. Not knowing she was there, when workers returned from lunch they started the machine, crushing her to death.

8. Andreas Plack, a 23-year-old Italian from Merano, bled to death after persuading his cousin to cut open his leg with a chainsaw in an attempt to cash in on a $600,000 insurance policy.

7. Takahisa Igarishi, a 19-year-old Japanese Bosozoku biker gang member, was evading police in a high-speed chase through the streets of Tokyo. He turned to flip the finger to police officers in a car behind and did not the see red light he ran or the taxi he smashed into which killed him.

6. James Mhlanga held up an entry kiosk at the Rhino and Lion Reserve at Krugersdorp in South Africa. Fleeing from pursuing staff he climbed a high fence and found himself facing a pair of tigers. Police spokeswoman Milica Bezuidenhout said: "First they grabbed and played with him. Then they bit him. He died of a broken neck and a fractured skull."

5. In 2001, thief Edward McBride ran into the Arkansas River in Tulsa, Oklahoma, to try and evade chasing police officers. Unfortunately a 50-kilogram bag of swag, including stolen cameras and CDs, weighed him down and he was drowned before reaching the other side.

4. Chicken thief Henri M'Bongo was chased by an angry mob in Donuala, Cameroon, in 1998. When they caught him, the enraged vigilantes forced Henri to eat one his ill-gotten gains in its entirety. He choked to death on a mixture of chicken feathers, beak and bones.

3. Not just villains die ridiculously as a result of criminal activity. Giacario Burramti was so infuriated after 10 break-ins to his shop in Milan that he rigged up a bomb as a security system. Unfortunately, he forgot to disarm it one day in 1992 and blew himself to bits.

2. Vandal Matthew David Hubal met his end at 3am on 2 February 1998 as he slid down a ski run at the Mammoth Mountain resort in California. He was riding on a makeshift sled formed out of yellow foam safety padding he had ripped off a ski lift tower. He died when he crashed into exactly the same ski tower he had removed the foam from.

1. A RIGHT STUFF-UP
Robert Puelo ran into a 7-Eleven in St Louis, grabbed a hotdog, stuffed it into his mouth and ran out without paying. He managed to get a couple of metres away from the scene of his crime before collapsing onto the sidewalk in a choking fit. When police found his unconscious form, his fingertips had turned blue and there was a six-inch piece of uneaten frankfurter lodged in his throat. Puelo was pronounced dead at hospital, where a further three chunks of unchewed sausage were found in his oesophagus.

BUTTON MAN

Knowing the difference between up and down can be a matter of life and death.

Lorry driver Glyn Clarke trapped his head in hydraulic lifting equipment because he pushed the wrong buttons on a tailgate lifting machine. For some reason Glyn, 28, from the West Midlands, pressed the up button instead of the down one, and was crushed to death at a petrol station on the A10 in Cambridgeshire in July 2006.

KILLER MOVES

Dancing with her family in front of the TV shouldn't have proved fatal for mother-of-two Grace Ward, 41, of Milton Keynes, England. Sadly, during the course of her boogying, she banged her leg on the same spot she had hit it earlier in the day. Her health deteriorated rapidly and she died from a blood clot a couple of days later on May 21, 2007.

WHEN HIPPOS ATTACK I

Menes – also known as Hor Aka – was the Pharaoh who has gone down in history as unifying the kingdoms of Upper and Lower Egypt between the 31st and 30th centuries BCE. Of more interest to us is the fact the 5th century BCE historian Manetho reports that when he was 62 years old, Menes was attacked and killed by an enraged hippopotamus while walking alongside the Nile.

It is not surprising, then, that some ancient Egyptians saw the hippo as the representative of the god Set, the embodiment of all that was evil. Apologists for hippos have tried to suggest Manetho was merely recording a metaphorical myth. However, anyone who has studied the habits of the excrement eating, cannibalistic, human-killing machines that hippos clearly are will beg to differ – although they look silly, they are savagely aggressive and extremely strong, and kill more safari tourists each year than any other animal.

'CHUTE SHOT

A spectator at the European Drag Racing Championships died when a car's parachute opened and sent debris flying into the stand. Roger George, 64, from Norfolk, was watching the finals of the event at the Santa Pod race track in Porington, Bedfordshire, in September 2006. A car opened its rear parachute and sent a fatal chunk of shrapnel shooting into his chest in a million-to-one accident.

GREENHOUSE EFFECT

We're always warned not to leave dogs in hot cars, but what about leaving drunk holidaymakers? Friends of Andrew Lewin, 18, of Rushden, Hertfordshire, left him in their hire car to sleep off the booze after a night's drinking at a Marbella nightclub on 29 July 1997. But several hours later they found him dead in a pool of sweat. The car had reached temperatures of up to 50C (122F), literally cooking him alive.

TRACK TREK TRAGEDY

Walking along rail tracks isn't a good idea, but if you're going to do it, you should at least be aware of the prospect of trains occupying the same space. Michael Carrig, 30, somehow failed to notice a train speed past him in the opposite direction and then moments later didn't hear another train approaching from behind. He was killed on the line at Waltham Cross, England, on the night of 26 May 2007.

Michael, from nearby Waltham Abbey, had been out drinking since midday and decided to take a shortcut home along the tracks. He was hit by the 55mph train. Coroner David Pidgeon said: "It seems clear to me that he was not aware of the presence of the oncoming train behind him. The driver had no chance of breaking to avoid a collision."

STYLE BEFORE SENSE

Fashion proved fatal for 20-year-old Shane Solon, of Telford, Shropshire, who plunged to his death in a Spanish gorge, because he had not been properly dressed for a trek in the mountains. Shane wore tracksuit bottoms, a football shirt and smooth-soled Lacoste trainers when he and two pals embarked on a trek around the Pyrenees on 21 April 2007. Although it was perfect weather when they started off, as they reached the snowline it began raining and hailing. Shane had been constantly slipping in his trainers, and ended up somersaulting off a ledge and falling onto rocks below.

SLIPPING UP

Cornish-born Bobby Leach defied death in 1911 when he became only the second man to survive going over Niagara Falls in a barrel. However, the Cosmic Joker had the last laugh. Leach died during a publicity tour to New Zealand, when he slipped on some orange peel.

ONE LAST DRINK

A reformed alcoholic spent six months dry, but died after falling off the wagon and drinking one can of lager. Builder George Irving, 42, of Clacton on Sea, Essex, had the solitary drink with a pal on 11 April 2001, but died after going for a lie-down afterwards. Had he known what to expect, you can be sure he'd have had another.

STAKE KEBAB

Vampires aren't the only creatures to die when impaled through the heart with a stake made of ash wood. It's just as fatal for mortal humans as well! The managing director of Birmingham International Airport was impaled by the wood after fierce storms brought down an ash tree near Bridgnorth, Shropshire, on 18 January 2007. Richard Heard, 49, who lived in the village, died instantly after being skewered by the wooden stake.

LONG ROAD TO RUIN

It's not the fact that jilted lover Robert Maich stabbed his girlfriend in the head with a screwdriver, it's the way he drove 250 miles to top himself afterwards. Maich, 42, of Wokingham, Berkshire, lost the plot after finding out Kate Sefton-Jenkins, 32, was having an affair with a former colleague. He attacked her at their home, before driving all the way to Cheshire where he threw himself under the wheels of a high-speed train in November 2002. Surely he didn't need to waste so much petrol? Think of his carbon footprint!

DRYING OUT

Giving up the booze should be good for your health, but it led to a shock reaction for alcoholic Nicholas Buttle, 25, of Reading, Berkshire. He had been referred to a community alcohol service because he regularly drank up to 150 units a week – the equivalent of 75 pints – and they helped him quit drinking. But he suffered a fit from alcohol withdrawal, and collapsed and died on May 8, 2005. Oh the irony.

WHALLOP!

A huge branch from a 300-year-old oak tree snapped off the trunk and fell on 53-year-old Christopher Imison as he prepared to go for a bike ride. The freak accident occurred because the 40cm thick, 15 metre long branch had rotted from the inside due to a fungal infection, and there was no way anyone could have known it was a hazard. Christopher, from Sandhurst, near Windsor, died a week later in August 2007.

LOOK BEFORE YOU LEAP

Student Toby Mann, 19, fell 150ft down a lift shaft because he failed to check the lift was actually there. Toby, from Salisbury, Wiltshire, planned to take the service lift from the 14th floor of an apartment block in Buenos Aires, Argentina, but a fault caused the safety door to open on its own. He entered without realising the lift was still on the ground floor – a long way down...

MINE SHAFTED

What are the chances of anyone being poisoned by gases from a long abandoned mine beneath their home? James and Molly McDonald, both 74, died from carbon monoxide poisoning in July 2005. Drilling operations nearby disturbed an old mineshaft under their house in Dudley, in the West Midlands, in a one-of-a-kind tragedy.

WATER TORTURE

We all know water can be deadly, especially if you cannot swim, but death by water intoxication is rare enough that you can be forgiven for not knowing about the phenomenon. It is shame that Jennifer Lea Strange had never heard of how deadly it can be.

The 28-year-old mother of three from Rancho Cordova in California entered local radio station KDND 107.9's January 2006 competition 'Hold Your Wee for a Wii' to win a Nintendo game console for her children. Contestants were all given 8fl oz bottles of water to drink every 15 minutes of the first hour and then progressively larger bottles of water after that. The winner was the one who could control their urge to urinate for the longest possible time. Despite being one the last three people to pee, Jennifer Lea Strange did not win a Wii and drove home empty-handed.

On the way, Jennifer rang one of her work colleagues. She was in tears and complaining of severe head pain. Her body was found at home shortly afterwards by her mother.

The coroner declared that she had died from water intoxication, a problem caused by the fact that healthy human kidneys can only excrete up to three pints of water per hour. Any greater volume can lead to death by lowering the concentration of sodium in the blood to levels that causes cells to rupture, swollen by osmosis. KDND 107.9 sacked 10 staff, including three DJs, in the wake of Jennifer's death.

THAT SINKING FEELING...

Helen Hogan, 30, drove her car off a ferry slipway following a row with her boyfriend, but enjoyed a last cigarette as she waited it to sink. It took up to five minutes before the vehicle sank nose-first beneath the waves at Poole, Dorset, on 13 November 2005. She managed to escape her watery grave, only to be found floating in the sea later that evening. She eventually died from hypothermia the following morning.

NO MAN OF STEEL

Another lesson to be learned here: unless you're Superman, don't try and manually stop a three-and-a-half-ton runaway van by sticking your arms out and hoping for the best. Michael Tipton, 21, from Birmingham, threw himself in front of his works van to stop it crashing into a factory in May 2008. Unsurprisingly, he wasn't strong enough to stop it from hitting him and the wall, causing just as much damage as it would have done anyway.

DEAD DUNK

At a 1979 village fete, an English vicar sat atop a tank of water and if punters hit a target with a ball he would be tipped in. Unfortunately, he was holding a live microphone when he got his inevitable dunking, leading to a flash of fatal holy smoke.

BOMBER BARNES

A 20-year-old man obsessed with explosives blew himself up after putting a homemade pipe bomb in his mouth and accidentally lighting the fuse. Kevin Barnes, 20, stuffed a four-inch length of copper piping with firework gunpowder before sucking on it. Then he chanted: "Grenade! Grenade!" before laughing and saying: "Tick, tick, boom!" and flicking a lighter, a smirk on his face. His friends watched in horror in his flat in Daventry, Northamptonshire, as the bomb suddenly ignited, blowing up in his face. Ka-boom!

A SLIGHT OVER-REACTION?

Mixing guns and alcohol at a party proved a lethal combination which ended with the death of a Welsh soldier and his killer's suicide. Drunken banter between Sergeant Robert Busuttil, 30, from Swansea, and Corporal John Gregory, also 30, from North Yorkshire, deteriorated nastily. Finally, Gregory stormed off to fetch his gun, pumped 10 rounds into Busuttil's body and then blew his own brains out. The two soldiers had flouted a ration of two cans of beer each at a farewell barbecue in Kabul, Afghanistan, in August 2003.

RUBBED OUT

Despite having an obsessive fear of rubber, Andrew Cunningham, 22, died after secretly swallowing a rubber glove. Autistic Andrew's phobia was so bad he had thrown away up to 200 rubber bath plugs at the residential home where he lived in Llandeilo, Wales. But he was also obsessive about a watch that he owned, and would regularly pull out the strap pins and throw them away so he could buy new ones. The rubber glove was found to contain one of the watch pins, which had perforated his small intestine and poisoned him in November 2002. The motivations for his actions died with him.

WEIGHTY JUMP

A 20-stone student proved too heavy for a bungee jump and crashed into the ground. Chris Thomas, 22, from Llanelli in Wales, leapt from a 180ft crane in the car park of a pub in Swansea in 2004. Unfortunately, the rope holding him had a maximum load of just 90kg, compared to his 132kg weight. It should have slowed him down when it reached full stretch, but instead he was thrown out of the harness when it snapped, hitting the ground at speeds of up to 31mph.

MAKE MINE A STRONG ONE!

Mystery surrounds the reason why Liverpool dentist Margaret Cunniffe, 56, decided to knock back a drink of pure alcohol on 7 September 2005. The ethylene glycol – one of the main components of antifreeze – proved too much for her to handle and killed her.

NO DODGING DEATH

After a tough battle amongst teens from across America, 17-year-old Michael Doucette was proclaimed 'The Nation's Safest Teen Driver' in a 1989 competition organised by the Chrysler Corporation and an American veterans' group. Among Doucette's prizes was a $5,000 scholarship and use of a brand new Dodge for a year. After winning the contest Doucette told the press: "Good driving means you need to concentrate on a lot of things. Not everyone can do it."

A few months later, in February 1990, Doucette was driving the Dodge he had won in Concord, Massachusetts. He drifted over the centre line and ploughed into the oncoming car of Shannon Ann Link, killing them both. State police said: "It looks like he may have fallen asleep at the wheel."

KING OF THE WORLD

An Oxford University student died after climbing a 200ft crane to re-enact a scene from the movie *Titanic*. Kai Dawson, 21, who had been drinking at a friend's birthday party, inched his way along the jib before standing with his arms outstretched.

Anthony Partridge, the landlord of a pub near the crane, said: "He was standing at the end of the boom, bolt upright, arms outstretched in a DiCaprio and Winslet sort of thing." But then Kai lost his balance and fell, crashing through a tree and landing on a bicycle. His body was found in the back garden of the house the next day following the stunt in 2001.

JESUS WEPT!

Devout Christian Rosaline Gilbert died after undertaking a 40-day religious fast during which she only drank water. Rosaline, 34, of Hackney, London, had apparently tried to emulate Christ's 40 days and 40 nights of starvation in the wilderness, but died 23 days into her effort in April 2006. Her mother Gloria, 66, said: "I had no idea it would end like this. She would only have water and when people from her church offered her food she refused, saying the Lord would provide for her." Sorry Rosaline, but He didn't.

ROUGH GUIDE

Hikers Christopher and Jennifer Parratt confidently chose a route up Mt Tryfan marked 'easy' in a guidebook. They got lost in low cloud, and Christopher, 32, slipped and fell 30ft to his death. At an inquest into the tragedy in June 2007, experienced mountaineer Det. Insp. David Lloyd said the route was impossible to follow and slated the guidebook as extremely misleading.

GUNS OF BRIXTON

What did he really expect to happen? Derek Bennett, 29, waved around a gun-shaped cigarette lighter, claiming it was a real weapon, outside a block of flats in Brixton, south London, on 16 July 2001. He ended up being blown away by armed police.

BARRED

Keeping fit is a dangerous game. Owen Smith, 17, of Cardiff, Wales, died in a freak accident while exercising at the gym. He was doing chin-ups when he hit his head on a metal bar, fracturing his skull in 2002. But the injury was not spotted in two visits to his doctor and another to hospital, and he died 19 days later after an infection spread to his brain. Pathologist Derek James said: "I can't recall seeing an injury before caused by anything like this. He must have pulled himself up with some force."

WHO ATE ALL THE CAKES?

Student Adam Deeley, 34, choked to death while taking part in a fairy cake eating contest. Adam, from Birmingham, died in February 2008 following an impromptu competition to see who could scoff the most cakes left over after a buffet at a bar in Swansea, Wales.

DEAD DODGER

Egyptian Mohamed Abderrahman decided to avoid paying for a rail ticket into town by riding on a train's roof. Unfortunately he forgot to duck when going under a bridge, so while his body pulled into Cairo's main station, his head did not.

TOP 10 RIDICULOUS DEATHS FROM HISTORY – THE MIDDLE AGES TO THE 16th CENTURY

10. Edmund II, king of England, earned the title 'Ironside' for his stout defence of his kingdom from invasion by the Danish King Canute. On 30 November 1016, King Edmund died when he was stabbed in the anus by a soldier hiding inside a latrine.

9. Henry I was an English king known as the 'Lion of Justice'. His reign ended on 1 December 1135 after a feast held at Denis-en-Lyons in Normandy. Henry gorged on so many lampreys – a jawless fish, his favourite food – that he died from digestive problems.

8. Martin of Aragon was not only the ruler of the Aragon, but also King of Valencia, Sardinia and Corsica, Count of Barcelona and, from 1396 until his death in 1409, King of Sicily. The title-hungry monarch eventually died from overeating complicated by a bout of uncontrollable laughing.

7. Al-Musta'sim Billah was the Caliph in Baghdad, ruling from 1242 to 1258. After the Mongol invasion of his territory by Hulegu Khan, the captured Caliph was wrapped in a Persian rug and trampled to death by a horse, as Hulegu did not wish to be seen as spilling royal blood.

6. King Edward II of England was deposed from the throne and imprisoned by his French wife Isabella and her lover Roger Mortimer. To add fatal injury to insult, in 1327 they killed him by inserting a red hot plumber's iron through a tube in his anus so that it "burned the inner portions beyond the intestines". Nice.

5. The English Marcher Lord Fulk Fitzwarine IV was the son of the man who may have partly provided the inspiration for Robin Hood. In 1264, Fitzwarine was fleeing the Battle of Lewes when the weight of his and his horse's armour bogged them down in a marsh, suffocating them both.

4. Pope John XXI had a reputation not just for holiness, but for scientific inquiry into fields as diverse as medicine, physics and astronomy. His passion for science led to him having a new laboratory wing added to his palace at Viterbo. However, the builders did a poor job and the laboratory collapsed on the Pope, killing him as he slept in it on 20 May 1277.

3. Long before the Guinness Book of Records, Austrian Hans Steininger had achieved renown throughout Christendom for having what was considered to be the world's longest beard – measuring at least 1.4 metres. In 1567, as he was fleeing a burning tower, he tripped over his beard, fell down the stairs and broke his neck.

2. Humphrey VIII de Bohun, the 4th Earl of Hereford, was an important nobleman and powerbroker in Norman England. As he was crossing a wooden bridge on his horse in Yorkshire on 16 March 1322, a pikeman hidding below rammed his weapon between the planks and skewered old Humph through the anus.

1. THERE WAS AN OLD POPE WHO SWALLOWED A FLY
Pope Adrian IV – born Nicholas Breakspeare – is the only Englishman to have ever become Pope. In 1159, Breakspeare delivered a violent speech in Rome, excommunicating reigning Emperor Frederick I. While in full thundering force, a fly flew into his open mouth, causing the Pope to choke to death.

MORNING AFTER CHILL

A one-night stand became a nightmare for Lesley Patterson when she woke to find her lover ice-cold dead in bed beside her. Lesley, 22, from Cardiff, Wales, had enjoyed a night with 35-year-old Darren Owen in August 2006, but realized she only knew him by his nickname of "Kinder" from the few hours they spent together. She had to explain to police that she hardly knew him when they came to investigate, but insisted they hadn't had full sex because both had been too drunk.

Lesley said: "We were both too wasted and we just crashed out in bed. I woke up once in the night at about 6am and I realized he was snoring. But when I woke at 9am I found he was dead. It was the most terrible shock."

She got an even bigger one when police traced Darren's identity, only to find he had left behind a long-term partner, the mother of three of his five children, and had just been released from jail following six months on remand.

The cause of Darren's death could not be established, but Lesley has since calmed down her boozy lifestyle: "I'm certainly not the wild girl I once was. I don't go knocking back the pints like I used to, I'm too frightened of what might happen."

WASTE OF LIFE

Father-of-four David Griffiths ended up crushed in a recycling plant in Middlesbrough, England, on 26 April 2002. He had climbed into a skip to sleep off a night's boozing in the town. He was found dead among piles of rubbish, with extensive crush injuries, having been emptied into a refuse wagon.

SLIPPING AWAY

Pensioner Brigid O'Callaghan was strangled by the seatbelt of her wheelchair after sliding down in her sleep. The 74-year-old had been left in the chair by staff at a Birmingham nursing home when she refused to go to bed, only to be found with the seatbelt round her neck the following morning, 28 October 2005.

STEVENSON'S ROCKET

Fitter Andrew Stevenson, 51, was rocketed 30 metres into the air after a spark from his angle grinder ignited a gas storage tank he was working on, at a water treatment works outside Derry, Northern Ireland, on 2 June 2005. Pal Peter Thompson suffered a broken leg in the explosion, and coroner John Lecky said: "It seems that they were not aware of the danger of the hydrogen gas beneath where they were working. In many ways it was like working on top of a bomb and the spark was the detonator."

COINING IT IN

Royal Mint worker John Wynne, 50, was crushed to death by a six-ton furnace carrying metal to be made into coins. John died after the furnace fell on top of him from a damaged crank hook at the Mint in Llantrisant, South Wales. He was only in it for the money.

LAST RAP

The Eminem song "Stan" reveals how an obsessive fan of the rap star kills himself and his girlfriend after fixating on his idol. David Hurcombe, 17, from Teignmouth, Devon, didn't go so far as to drive off a bridge with his pregnant fiancée in the boot of his car. However, it appears he may have been sufficiently inspired by Marshall Mathers' lyrics to run in front of a train in October 2000. His suicide note quoted from the song "Rock Bottom" from the singer's *The Slim Shady* album – "Cause when you die you know we are all going the same way." He signed off, "Anyway got to go, miss my train, see ya'll in hell."

A CHOP OFF THE OLD BLOCK

A 24-year-old German man living in Cologne brutally stabbed his elderly father to death and then cut off his own head with an electric chainsaw in May 2007. Police arrived at the bloody crime scene at the pair's apartment after receiving an emergency call from the father that was cut short by the attack from his son. The first things officers saw when they forced entry was the headless corpse lying beside the chainsaw.

One of Cologne's most senior prosecutors, Alf Willwacher, said: "We are not looking for any third party in relation to the deaths."

A neighbour of the dead father and son said: "The mother committed suicide some years before and after that the pair were like hermits. They were clearly a family with problems."

DRILLER KILLER

DIY fan Zoe Turner, 28, loved working on the £400,000 home she shared with her brother in Brixton, south London. They had been renovating the three-storey terraced house for five years. Unfortunately it proved her downfall – an electric drill she was using caught her hair and strangled her with the cable in November 2004.

HEAD FIRST

Soccer legend Jeff Astle died from brain injuries caused by repeatedly heading the ball. The former West Bromwich Albion centre forward, who died in January 2002, aged 59, had complained to his wife that heading a wet leather football was like heading a bag of bricks. Consultant neurosurgeon John Firth warned that even heading a modern football is the equivalent of having a house brick smashed into your skull.

SPINACH EXPLOSION

It's unlikely that even spinach-munching sailor Popeye would have survived the fate of chef Zacharia Conteh, 34, of Deptford, London. Zacharia was scalded to death when half a tonne of spinach soup exploded over him as he opened a pressure cooker at a factory in Willesden, London, in 2002.

SEEING THE LIGHT

DIY worker James Gobey, 26, was electrocuted in 2005 as he tried to change a light bulb while the power was on. James, from Burnley, London, had been helping a friend repair a boiler when water splashed on an inspection lamp, causing the bulb to explode. But when he went to change the bulb he suffered a massive electric shock and died instantly.

ANOTHER NAILED BY A COFFIN

French undertaker Marc Bourjade died when a stack of coffins at his workshop collapsed on top of him in 1982. With fitting irony, he was buried in one of the same coffins that had crushed him to death.

SEEING STARS...

Amateur astronomer Paul Linnington was driven over and killed whilst lying in the road stargazing in Kingham, Oxfordshire, in 2003. The driver continued home, unaware that he had run over 42-year-old Paul, who often lay in the road to look at the stars after a night down the pub. Charges against the driver were dropped.

WHAT'S THE PUNCHLINE?

The father of British alternative comedy, Malcolm Hardee, 55, fell into the River Thames in London following a marathon drinking session in January 2005. A police diver told an inquest that Malcolm was still clutching a bottle of beer when his body was brought up three days later. He'd been trying to make his way home by dinghy to his houseboat in Rotherhithe when he lost his balance and fell into the river.

HANDBAG FAUX PAS

If only partygoer Lydia Martin, 21, had decided to accessorise, she'd still be alive today. Lydia, from Exeter, Devon, left her keys in her back garden because she didn't want to carry a handbag. She died from head injuries after a 6ft wall collapsed as she tried to climb over it on 13 December 2003.

COULDN'T TAKE ANY SNORE

Nightclub DJ Colin Vincent killed himself after being driven out of his home because of his grossly loud snoring. Colin, 33, who played salsa music in London's West End, had sought specialist medical treatment after the problem caused a split with his girlfriend and arguments with his neighbours. He gave up his flat and moved back in with his mother, but found it all too much and hanged himself from a tree on Tooting Common on 24 September 2002.

DROWNED ON DRY LAND

A woman who drowned while on holiday on a Greek island had actually got out of the water first. Harriet Newton-Clare, 58, of Hampshire, had clambered out of the sea onto a jetty after running into problems swimming off the coast of Fiskardos in 2003. She staggered about for a while, sat down and then fell on her back, and by the time a doctor arrived 20 minutes, she later was dead. She had suffered a little-known phenomenon called secondary drowning, in which a lack of oxygen damages the lining of the lungs, but victims often survive long enough to get onto dry land. Harriet was effectively a dead woman walking.

DON'T TRY THIS AT HOME!

When TV's various extreme stunt programmes broadcast a warning to viewers not to attempt any of the stupid things they do each week, it's likely they do this for a reason. But for some reason Jackass fan Robert Appleton, 20, thought it didn't apply to him. Robert, from Cornwall, electrocuted himself after taping wires to his chest and connecting them to a 12-volt car battery adapted to deliver a 240-volt current, in 2003.

His dad William said: "The only reason I can think this happened is they did something similar on Jackass and he tried to copy it. On that show they do stupid things and Rob watched it frequently. I think it was a stunt that went wrong." Johnny Knoxville was unavailable for comment.

DEATH BY UFO

According to scientists, the chances of being killed by a meteorite are astronomically small. However, scientific opinion will be of no comfort to the relatives of three nomads who died in a remote area of Rajasthan, India. The three men were sitting in a field in February 2007 when they were struck by an ulkapind – Hindi for unknown flying object. Their relatives who rushed to the scene heard the resulting explosion.

Two of the nomads died on the spot and the third on his way to hospital. From the crater left in the field, some local officials believe there is good reason to believe a meteorite hit the men, though a full police investigation could not decide conclusively what had caused the big bang.

NO POWER, NO AIR

A woman who relied on a portable ventilator to breathe died after workmen accidentally cut off power to her home. Kathleen Russell, 77, who suffered from the lung disease emphysema, had been totally dependent on the machine for the last two years. Power to hundreds of homes in Radstock, Somerset, was cut off in 2005 when workmen drove a metal spike through an electricity cable, but for the majority the worst thing that happened was they missed an evening's TV. Kathleen, however, was also switched off as a result.

HOT DIP

A rare condition that reduced skin sensitivity led to a teacher burning to death after stepping into a bath of near-boiling water. Anne Garnett, 45, was found by husband David with 70 per cent burns following the tragedy at their home in Lancashire, England, in 2007. Water hitting 90C from a full-on boiler caused horrific injuries, but she didn't notice until it was too late.

HIS AND HEARSE

Undertaker Jose Agustin Noh and his lover Ana Maria Camara Suarez from Mexico succumbed to carbon-monoxide poisoning as they slept after having sex in a hearse. The engine had been left running to keep the air-conditioning going.

OPEN AND SHUT CASE

A salesman suffocated after climbing into his car boot to sleep off Christmas drinks. Charles Courtier-Dutton, 34, of Surrey, England, had been to a pub bash with workmates in December 2006, and decided to kip in the boot afterwards rather than catch a taxi home. But he was trapped in the dark, when the keys – with the fob to spring the lock – slipped out of reach in the boot, and tried in vain to frantically claw his way out. Police found his body when they prised open the boot 14 hours later.

LARD LUCK

Butcher David Jones, 46, suffered a massive brain haemorrhage after slipping on lard. David, who worked in Kilburn, West London, picked up a film of animal fat on the soles of his shoes and fell over in a nearby supermarket in 2007. He died in hospital a month later.

BRUSHING TWICE A DAY DIDN'T KEEP THE UNDERTAKER AWAY

Francesca Sanna, 19, is thought to have died from a severe allergic reaction to brushing her teeth. The accounts clerk, from Lancashire, was plagued by a string of allergies and was very careful about what she ate. She always used the same toothpaste, but the design of the squeezy tube changed not long before her death from anaphylactic shock in October 2007. Although no direct link to the toothpaste could be proved, a pathologist could not rule out a connection.

A RUBBISH WAY TO GO

Oddball John Jones, 62, crammed his house in Aberystwyth, west Wales, with tons and tons of rubbish over the course of 20 years. He was forced to build a network of tunnels to get around. Unfortunately the 20-stone weirdo died when part of the massive hoard fell on top of him in 2007. Police had to clear out four tons of junk through his bedroom window before they could reach his badly decomposed remains.

DARE DEVIL MISSES TARGET

Teacher Mark Dare, 21, set out to make 100 parachute jumps, but crashed to his death on the 99th. Sky-diver Mark, of Sussex, attempted a risky series of mid-air aerobatics and left it too late to pull his cord, hitting the ground after a fall from 4,000ft in the French Alps in 2007.

HORSING AROUND

It was like a scene out of horse-love play Equus, or maybe one of those dodgy DVDs you can only buy under the counter. Somehow Derek Carmichael, 56, of Bristol, ended up half-naked in a field of horses without his trousers or underpants in 2003. Derek was discovered face down wearing just his shirt and socks, his trousers nearby with his pants in a pocket. He had died of a heart attack. What exactly he was doing stripped below the waist in a field of horses is a mystery he took to his grave.

KICKED THE BUCKET I

A window cleaner drowned in his own bucket of water after suddenly collapsing at work. Mark Fairhurst, 35, of Wigan, was found with his head in the pail he used for his rounds in June 2006. A latent heart condition had caused his collapse, but the cause of death was drowning because his head became submerged in the bucket's water and he was unable to save himself.

MOTORWAY MADNESS

Dad Peter Mourier, 50, of Worcestershire, was killed when he let his seven-year-old son David drive at 70mph on the M5 motorway on 4 March 2005. He offered the wheel to the youngster despite the pleas of his two older boys Joseph, 15, and Isaac, nine, in the back seat. Front passenger David leaned over to help steer from lane to lane. But the Rover 216 hit an object in the middle lane, veered off the road and hit a tree, killing Peter as the crumpled bonnet crushed his skull. Fortunately, his sons all survived.

TIP OF THE ICEBERG

The body of a missing woman missing was found in the back of a truck delivering vegetables to a grocery store depot. The coroner in the case was quick to rule out foul play, explaining the death was lettuce related.

Sheila Kay Ross of Des Moines, Iowa, had been in the truck's trailer, checking its contents against some paperwork when she was struck by falling lettuces that knocked her unconscious. According to Dr John Kraemer, director of forensics for the Iowa medical examiner's office, her unconscious body was then covered by lettuces, which had led to compressional asphyxiation. Ross' husband reported her missing to the police in January 2007, but she was not discovered until the truck was emptied of its cargo of killer lettuces during a delivery three days later.

MIND THE GAP!

Robert Starke, 29, tried to squeeze through a six-inch gap in a window, only to become wedged and unable to breathe properly. Slender Robert was visiting a friend's flat in Farnborough, Hampshire, on 3 November 2007. Although he buzzed several flats he was unable to get in. Instead he took out a pane in a narrow louvered window and tried to get in that way. He died from a rare condition caused pneumathoraces, which meant he could take air into his lungs but couldn't exhale. He also suffered puncture wounds from glass.

TOP 10 RIDICULOUS DEATHS FROM HISTORY – THE 17th & 18th CENTURIES

10. Tycho Brahe was a Danish nobleman famed for his accurate planetary and astronomical observations. He is also notorious for his ridiculous death in 1601, when he ruptured his bladder because he thought it the height of bad manners to leave the table during a royal banquet.

9. John Whitson was an English merchant adventurer who became Mayor and MP for Bristol. He was known locally as 'Iron John' after he survived a murder attempt in which he was stabbed in the face. In 1629, he fell from his horse while in a blacksmith's yard and his skull was impaled on a huge iron nail.

8. Thomas May was an English poet and historian whose debauched lifestyle saw him pile on the pounds. By the time of his death in 1650, he had gotten into the habit of holding up his multiple chins with strips of cloths. After a night of too much drink, he forgot to untie them and they caused him to choke to death in his sleep.

7. 17th century English dramatist Thomas Otway had once enjoyed success and renown with plays such as *The Orphan*. However, by 1685 he was reduced to begging for food. A passer-by, learning who he was, gave him a guinea, with which Otway ran to a baker to buy bread. Unfortunately, he ate too hastily and choked to death on the first mouthful.

6. In 1687, Jean-Baptiste de Lully was conducting a concert in front of the French King Louis XIV to celebrate the monarch's recovery from illness. He banged the staff he was using to keep time so hard on his

foot that it created an abscess, which turned gangrenous and led to his death.

5. On 17 February 1673, renowned French playwright and actor Molière died from a coughing fit that brought on haemorrhaging whilst performing one of his plays, also in front of King Louis XIV. The title of the play was *Le Malade Imaginaire* – the imaginary invalid or hypochondriac.

4. Polymath Scottish aristocrat Thomas Urquhart has achieved a position in history for being the first man to translate Renaissance writer Rabelais into English. Although he sounds deadly dull and serious, Urquhart met his end from fatal hilarity. He laughed himself to death when he heard news that Charles II had retaken the throne of England.

3. François Vatel was cook to French king Louis XIV. The inventor of Chantilly cream, the perfectionist chef was so distraught at the late arrival of an order of seafood that he needed to prepare for a banquet that he ran himself through with a sword. His body was discovered by the delivery boy who came to announce the fish had arrived.

2. There is no doubting philosopher Francis Bacon was one of the most influential minds of his age. In 1625, he observed a snowstorm and was struck by the brilliant thought that ice might be used to preserve food instead of salt. Buying a chicken, he then stood outside in the snow to test his theory. In the process he became so cold he suffered from hypothermia and eventually died from a chill.

1. THE KING WHO ATE HIMSELF TO DEATH
   Alfred Frederick was king of Sweden until his ridiculous death in 1771. He died of digestion problems after eating a meal made up of lobster, caviar, sauerkraut, kippers and 14 semla pastries – all topped off with huge quantities of champagne. Not surprisingly, in Sweden he is known as "the king who ate himself to death".

DO THE TWIST

You'd never expect something as trivial as a twisted ankle to kill you, but unfortunately for shop manageress Leanne Harris, 37, that's exactly what happened. The fit and healthy furniture store supervisor suffered a fatal blood clot after having her injured ankle put in plaster. Leanne, from Llanelli, South Wales, collapsed and died the day her plaster was due to come off, 12 August 2005, after the clot travelled to her lungs and blocked an artery.

KICKED THE BUCKET II

How did 87-year-old widower Ken Norsworthy end up on his knees with his head submerged in a bucket of water? A coroner could not decide whether Ken, from Rotherham, South Yorkshire, meant to kill himself or if it was a bizarre accident. A visiting district nurse found him kneeling down with his head in a bucket, which in turn was in the bath, in 2007.

BOLT OF BAD LUCK

David Mushikle from Namibia was lucky to have survived being struck by a bolt of lightning while walking along a Windhoek street. However, as the dazed man picked himself up, he was struck and killed instantly by a hit and run driver.

FATAL FACIAL

A relaxing massage proved too much for 77-year-old Catherine Loverdos-Typaldos, who became confused after nodding off and slipped off the couch. The Greek pensioner, who was in England to spend Christmas 2003 with her family in Kensington, London, had fallen asleep with a facemask on. She woke up in a panic and fell off the table at a posh store in Piccadilly. She suffered internal bleeding which proved difficult to spot and died on the operating table a week later as surgeons tried to repair the injury.

CHICKEN LICKED 'IM

Warehouse worker Paul Langford was crushed to death by a ton of frozen chicken at the factory where he worked in Lincolnshire, England. Paul, 17, from South Yorkshire, was unable to dive out of the way as a huge pallet of the chilled meat toppled off a forklift truck. He was pinned beneath shrink-wrapped pieces of chicken equivalent to hundreds of birds in 2002.

WHAT A BORE!

Surely it took rather an unpleasant amount of time for graphic designer Dragan Radoslavjevic, 42, to kill himself by boring a hole in his head with an electric drill? His horrified wife Dawn found him in the bedroom of their home in Devon, in 2003, with blood splattered across the walls. Unless he was trying DIY trepanning?

SLASH AND BURN

A lesson in going to the toilet before you leave the pub... Boozy builder Ian Critchell, 27, of Dorchester, was driving back to work with colleagues after a lunchtime pint when he suddenly heard the call of nature. Pals watched in horror as he opened the door of the Transit, despite the fact that it was moving at 25mph, only to fall out of the van and smash into the road surface in 2003. Coroner Michael Howells said: "It is difficult to imagine anything more foolish."

DYNAMIC DEER

In some sort of bizarre ricocheting incident, a driver was killed when a deer bounced off the bonnet of an oncoming car and was catapulted through his windscreen. The animal was hit by one vehicle before being bounced onto the glass of Leslie Kingham's Subaru hatchback with such force it ended up in the boot. Civil servant Leslie, 50, died from head injuries following the accident in Somerset, in 2003. The other driver escaped alive.

WHAT AN ARSE!

Student Alexander Edwards, 18, was run over and killed after standing in the middle of the road mooning at passing cars. Alexander and three pals were exposing their backsides while walking to a party in Somerset, in 2004, when motorist John A'Court was blinded by headlights and ploughed into the lads like skittles.

WHEN HIPPOS ATTACK II

Jean Duguin, a director of Zoo de Bordeaux at Pessac in south-western France, died when he was knocked off his bike by an agitated hippo. Duguin was well-known to Comir – the 20-year-old hippopotamus that charged him – as he had been involved in the animal's care at the zoo for nearly two decades. One old poster promoting the zoo even featured Duguin petting Comir.

Speaking on 1 November 1999, Jean-Caude Marchais, director of public relations for Zoo de Bordeaux, said: "Comir had escaped and the director was trying to lead him back to his cage. For no apparent reason the beast charged him and killed him instantly. We do not want to keep Comir at the zoo any longer and it is up to the authorities to decide whether they put him to death."

GAS SHOWER

The naked bodies of Rosalyn Harris, 22, and boyfriend Karl Bissett, 31, were found dead in the shower by her adoptive dad when he became worried she had been in there for too long. Rosalyn had sneaked Karl into the bathroom of her parents' bungalow in Cresselly, Pembrokeshire, for a steamy morning romp in 2004, but the pair were overcome by deadly carbon monoxide fumes from a faulty gas water heater. Dad John said: "The water had been running for 30 minutes so I knocked on the door, but couldn't get an answer. I thought they might both be in there and too embarrassed to answer."

ARMLESS BUT NOT HARMLESS

Jonathan Bennison used a circular saw power tool to chop off his arm in a bizarre suicide ritual. Jonathan, 37, from Swansea, Wales, went into his garage and severed his left arm while wife Sandra was out with their young baby in 2003. He was found with the blood-splattered tool nearby. Exactly why he decided chopping his arm off was a good idea, even as a means to kill himself, remains a mystery.

WEIGHT OF THE WORLD

What gets us about some of these stories is the convoluted and bizarre way in which people choose to end their lives. Rather than just taking an overdose or slitting their wrists, some of our protagonists go to extreme measures to set up the perfect suicide operation. Case in point: retired solicitor's clerk William Leach, 81, of the Isle of Wight, drowned in a half-buried old bath full of stagnant water which he kept in his garden in 2003. He had placed a mattress in the bottom and tied an iron and a lump hammer round his neck to weigh his head down before lying down face first.

BONFIRE NIGHT

It's an age-old source of frustration, but no matter how hard it is to light your bonfire, don't use flammable liquids which are likely to blow up in your face. Grandad Richard Stratton, 61, was trying to torch garden prunings in the garden of his home in Radwinter, Essex, in 2004. The retired engineer decided to use paint thinners to get his bonfire going, but there was a sudden explosion as the fuel vapour ignited and he was engulfed in a ball of flames, suffering 80 percent burns.

DECREE ABSOLUTE

Samantha Taylor, 33, was thrilled to receive her final divorce papers, and bought a bottle of vodka and some lagers to celebrate the fact she was free to marry boyfriend Steven Farrell. But after a few glasses of vodka and orange she trod on a nail at the flat they were decorating in Blackburn, Lancashire, lost her balance and fell down the stairs. She died from her head injuries in 2002, her new start cut prematurely short.

BAD VIBES

Belgian Aloys Wouters died in 1986 from peritonitis. This was brought on when his wife sodomised him with a 14-inch vibrator designed, according to the manufacturers, to "bring you to the edge of heaven". But sadly, not back from it.

FLASH GARY

Drunken joker Gareth Mason, 22, dropped his trousers and yelled, "Who wants some of this?" out of an open window. He then stumbled and fell 12ft onto railings, impaling himself through the neck and chest. Gareth had been on a pub crawl with friends in Aberystwyth, west Wales, in 2005, and was four times the drink-drive limit when he made his scantily-clad plunge to his death.

'DEM BONES

Burglars called the cops after discovering the skeletal remains of Sally Shearing, 52, when they broke into her home in Liskeard, Cornwall, in 2006. It is believed she was last seen alive in January 2003, but nobody seemed to have missed her in the years since she disappeared. Whether the burglars took the opportunity to raid her house before dialling 999 wasn't established.

THE TEXT LIFE

"Sorry mate, I just killed myself!" was the text message John Hull received on his mobile from pal Steven Harris in 2004. It was followed up with the confirmation: "No joke, jumped. Can you inform da police?" But John still didn't believe his friend, because he was known for his weird sense of humour. He was still smiling when the police called to tell him Steven, 19, had leapt from an electricity pylon in Toddington, Bedfordshire. "Even then I couldn't wipe the smirk off my face. I thought he had caught somebody else out," John said sheepishly afterwards.

FLYING KILLERS I

Garage worker Simon Elliot, 38, from Hook, Hampshire, took a swig from a can of drink only to swallow a wasp. The insect stung his mouth and triggered an anaphylactic shock, swelling his throat and neck, and causing him to hyperventilate. Colleagues tried to resuscitate him, but he died later in hospital on 18 August 2004.

LOST IN TRANSLATION

Tycoon Reg Penny might be alive today if a Lithuanian prostitute had spoken English and known how to dial 999 for an ambulance. Reg, 65, died from a heart attack after having sex with a call girl in Cardiff, Wales, 2004. The 30-year-old used nail clippers to keep his airways open and put him in the recovery position before running away. Police found Reg's body after reports of a scantily-clad woman running from his £750,000 house late at night. A bottle of sex stimulant amyl nitrate was found next to Reg's naked corpse. At least he went with a smile on his face.

IN AT THE DEEP END

In August 1985, the New Orleans Recreation Department threw a pool party for its lifeguards to celebrate their first drowning-free year in the memory of everyone at the department. However, with the sort of perfect timing that makes you almost believe that there is a Cosmic Joker at loose in the universe, tragedy struck. Towards the end of the party, the body of 31-year-old Jerome Moody was found at the deep end of the department's pool. The Recreation Department's director, Madlyn Richard, told the press that Moody was not a lifeguard and it was not known how he had managed to drown under the noses of the four lifeguards who were on duty at the pool during the party.

WHEN SEX GAMES GO WRONG I

The estranged wife of David Baron, 58, found her former partner wearing women's clothing and hooked up to a dental anaesthetic machine pumping out nitrous oxide. Carol discovered him wearing tights, a grey pleated skirt, black bra, blue jumper and a clear plastic apron, in his dressing room at the family home in Gloucestershire, in September 2004. He was surrounded by pictures of scantily-clad women with anaesthetic equipment. The machine should have pumped out an oxygen-nitrous oxide mix, but was faulty, leading to David's rather ignoble death.

COP KILLER

Sometimes there are good reasons for not wanting to get the police involved when you have a problem – especially if the cop you call on is anything like Clouseau-esque Belgian policeman Marc Fagny. When a woman in Arlon asked the local police to deal with a rabid German shepherd that had broken into her garden, Fagny was dispatched. He attempted to put the dog out of its misery with his shotgun, but ended up hitting the woman who had called him out, killing her instantly. When questioned about the death at a subsequent trial for manslaughter, Fagny explained: "The bullet went wide. They should not have sent me. Everyone knows I am a lousy shot."

FLYING KILLERS II

Camper Terry Phillips, 61, from South Wales, tried to walk off the effects of being stung in the face by a bee while in holiday in Italy during 2007, but started feeling stiffness in his legs. He dropped dead from coronary and respiratory failure shortly afterwards.

THE SHOW MUST GO ON I

Johnny Ace was one of the stars of US rhythm and blues, responsible for a string of hits including "My Song", "Please Forgive Me" and "Never Let Me Go". His career came to a premature conclusion after a performance in Houston's City Auditorium at Christmas 1954. Breaking between sets and high on PCP, he decided to play a game of Russian Roulette with girlfriend Olivia Gibbs and her pal Mary Carter. Aiming a .45 calibre revolver at each of them in turn, he pulled the trigger, only for the hammer to fall on an empty chamber. He then pointed the gun at himself and blew his brains out. End of concert, end of Johnny Ace.

FLYING KILLERS III

This story isn't one of the usual bee-related deaths, but what else can you blame for the deaths of David and Sheila Johnson, 66 and 65, from Greater Manchester? The couple were killed in a head-on crash when the driver of a minibus veered into their car after being stung on the crotch by a bee. Andrew Workman, 26, lost control after being stung on his privates, ploughing into the Johnsons' approaching Volvo, in 2007.

SICK TO THE HIND TEETH

An off-duty bus conductor swallowed his dentures and choked to death as he was taking a nap on the back seat of his vehicle as it travelled across Malaysia to the city of Seremban.

SOMETHING TO REALLY WORRY ABOUT

Egyptian taxi driver Abdul Aziz's habit of chewing on his worry beads really gave him something to worry about. His cab was rear-ended and he choked on the supposed stress relievers.

THE SHOW MUST GO ON II

Jon-Erik Hexum was a co-star of the TV series *Cover Up*, which was based on the unlikely premise of a fashion photographer and his model (Jennifer O'Neill and Hexum) who lead a secret life as CIA agents. While taping an episode in 1984, Hexum jokingly put a prop gun to his temple and pulled the trigger. Wadding from the blanks were driven into his skull and he later died of brain damage.

According to a crew member on the set: "Jon smiled and pulled the trigger. There was a loud bang and a bright flash, then black smoke. Jon screamed in agony, then looked kind of amazed as he slumped back onto the bed with blood streaming from a severe head wound. It was horrible." Like its co-star, *Cover Up* was also short-lived and was cancelled in 1985.

THE SHOW MUST GO ON III

Yoshiuki Takadi was a member of an avant-garde dance troupe called Sankai Juku. The troupe were practioners of style of dance known as Butoh, typified by grotesque imagery and white body make-up. Sankai Juku had developed a reputation for staging shows in which its dancers were often suspended upside down by ropes.

The upside down man motif of a Sankai Juku production was even extended to when they performed outside shows. In September 1985, Sankai Juku gave a performance called *Homage to Prehistory* in which four dancers, hanging upside down from the top of the Mutual Life building in Seattle, were slowly lowered to the ground. During the element of the show known as The Dance of Birth and Death, the rope holding the inverted Yoshiuki Takadi suddenly snapped. In front of hundreds of spectators and news crews filming the event, Takadi plunged six storeys to his death.

THE SHOW MUST GO ON IV

Hoseph W. Burrus was an amateur magician, escape artist and recovering drug addict from San Francisco. He took part in a benefit gig in 1990 for a rehab clinic, with an act which saw him bound with chains and handcuffs, placed into an acrylic glass coffin of his own construction and then buried under 6ft – and seven tons – of dirt and wet cement. But when Burrus had practiced the stunt he had only used dirt, meaning he failed to estimate the higher weight of wet concrete versus dry earth. The coffin collapsed and he was buried alive. By the time rescuers reached him, that had changed to definitively dead. Even the great Houdini couldn't have got out of that one.

FLYING KILLERS IV

A country estate manager died within 25 minutes of being stung 22 times on his legs by wasps at the end of a day's grouse shoot. Guy Canby, 53, ran the 17,000-acre Fitzwilliam Estate, near Rotherham. He had been out on Strines Moor in South Yorkshire, in August 2003, where he was attacked by a swarm of the striped devils. He died shortly afterwards.

THE SHOW MUST GO ON V

Rob Harris was a stuntman and sky-surfer who also held down a successful career as a DJ and musician in Los Angeles. None of this helped him when he was filming a commercial for Mountain Dew soft drink in 1995, which saw him playing a James Bond-style hero whose parachute is lost early in the jump. Unfortunately his secondary parachute became tangled and his reserve parachute also failed, leading to him plunging to his death. Contrary to an urban legend, footage of his death was not shown in the commercial, as all shots were from earlier takes of the jump.

DRINKING TO DEATH I

Bank worker David Reid, 22, and his pal James Lynch decided to recreate a scene from a movie in which two men have a drinking competition until one of them drops – known as "last man standing".

They knocked back bottles of tequila, gin and whiskey in less than 45 minutes, until high flier David couldn't stand any more and was put to bed. He was found dead a few hours later, seven times the legal drink-driving limit.

DRINKING TO DEATH II

It's your first party and, with 22 stones of weight behind you, you're pretty confident you can down everything on a table laden with booze, especially as the prize for doing so is a cool £1,000. Unfortunately for 18-year-old Anthony Rand, of Braintree, Essex, it would also be the last party he attended. Already very drunk, Anthony managed to get through most of a bottle of vodka before collapsing and drowning in his own vomit in May 2001. Bet void.

DRINKING TO DEATH III

For alcoholics Dermot McConnell and Irene Kelly of the Isle of Man, off the English coast, the demon drink claimed their lives in particularly bizarre fashions. Irene, 55, died after getting into a bath while drunk on three-quarters of a bottle of whisky. She scalded her feet and banged her head, before sliding under the water. Boozed-up Dermot thought she was rinsing shampoo out of her hair, pulled out the plug and left her to drown on 30 October 2001.

Later that year on 6 December, the 53-year-old hit his head after a drinking session, turning up to give evidence at Irene's inquest three days later with a black eye. But the injury caused a subdural haemorrhage and he passed out in his flat. He lay there unconscious for so long the electricity ran out, cutting off the heating and resulting in his death from hypothermia.

Coroner Michael Moyle said: "There is no doubt about it that in my view the real cause of his death was the fact that he was addicted to alcohol." Hey, you booze, you lose.

DRIVE-THRU DEATH

Marshall Gambrell from Virginia came a cropper when he lost control of his car whilst driving in 1992. His vehicle ploughed through a hedge at high speed into a graveyard, hurling him headfirst through the windscreen into a tombstone.

DRINKING TO DEATH IV

The drinking culture on the Isle of Man, as on many small islands, encouraged men to drink as much alcohol as possible, because it was considered macho. So when 21-year-old Jim Kelly consumed 25 drinks in 45 minutes at a local pub on 14 October 2001, he was seen as one of the lads.

The massive drinking binge saw him down nine pints, 13 whisky and cokes, and a strong Polish vodka. He died from alcohol poisoning, with seven times the drink-drive limit of alcohol in his blood, having literally drunk himself to death. Not much of a man really, but at least his death prompted a review of drinking habits on the island.

DRINKING TO DEATH V

Knocking back 13 pints on a bar crawl through York proved too much for student Robert Ailwood, 22, to handle. He ran off and abandoned his friends, subsequently falling in the river and drowning. Housemate Wenche Gunderssen said after the death in 2007: "He tended to run off when drunk. He didn't know why." Now we'll never find out.

PLAIN NUTS

Willie Murphy was working in an American peanut processing plant in Georgia in 1993 when he was crushed to death by an avalanche of unshelled nuts.

KILLER COCK

Arnel Torres, a 47-year-old from San Isidro in the Philippines, became the victim of a freak fatal accident in 2002 when acting as a setensyador – a cockfight referee. He was officiating at a charity cockfight designed to raise funds for the family of a deceased neighbour when he fell foul of one of the fowls. The bird was wearing tari-a blades – spurs attached to the cock's legs so they can pierce and slice to kill their opponent – when it flew up and attacked him. In his struggle with the bird, Torres was repeatedly pierced by the blade in his left armpit and chest, severing an artery which caused him to bleed to death. Unfortunately for the killer cock, Torres' family meted out revenge by hacking it to pieces with machetes.

DRINKING TO DEATH VI

Downing pints of spirits might have saved Shane Fitzpatrick a few quid, but it cost him in the long run. Shane, 31, from Stockport, took advantage of a two-for-one drinks deal while on a holiday pub crawl in the Grand Canaries in 2004. He had already drunk six glasses of vodka and Red Bull before downing a pint of mixed spirits in one go – after being offered a second pint free. He took a sip from the second and then passed out on a chair. He was helped to bed and found dead the following morning from alcohol poisoning.

DRINKING TO DEATH VII

Social club chairman Dave Onions, 47, drank himself to death after being challenged to a drinking contest by his mates. He binged on pints of beer, six shots of whisky, two Pernods and a double rum in Bournemouth, Dorset, in December 2004. Then he started swaying and fell off his bar stool. He was helped home by some friends who laid him down in the hallway. His girlfriend Carol Meikle, who had ironically been serving behind the bar that night, covered Dave with a duvet, but found him dead the next morning.

TOP 10 RIDICULOUS DEATHS FROM

HISTORY – THE 19th CENTURY

10. The vile labour-union-busting spy and founder of the United States' first detective agency, Allan Pinkerton, died from biting his tongue when he slipped on a Chicago pavement in 1884. The wound became infected and doctor-hating Pinkerton refused to seek treatment until it was far too late.

9. In 1818, Nancy Hanks Lincoln – the mother of United States President Abraham Lincoln – died when she drank milk from one of the family's dairy cows that had eaten poisonous mushrooms.

8. Clement Laird Vallandigham was an Ohio politician and lawyer who came to prominence during the American Civil War. In 1850, Vallandigham was defending a man in a murder trial when he tried to prove his theory about how the victim had killed himself while drawing a pistol. He duplicated the event in the courtroom. Unfortunately, the gun was loaded and his theory was right, so he killed himself during the demonstration. At least his client was acquitted.

7. A spectator watching an airship created by Croatian engineer David Schwarz make its inaugural flight at Tempelhof field in Berlin in 1896 was so fixated with what was happening in the sky that he stepped backwards into a huge hole and died.

6. English MP, statesman and financier William Huskisson had narrowly escaped death on his honeymoon when his horse fell on him. However, he was not lucky on 15 September 1830 when he became the first person in history to be killed by a train. Huskisson stepped onto the track during the first journey by Stephenson's Rocket – the steam locomotive he had helped finance – and was crushed to death by it.

5. Horace Wells was an American dentist who pioneered the use

anaesthesia in dentistry through the use of nitrous oxide (laughing gas). However, Wells became addicted to another pain-blocking gas – chloroform – and began a delirious crime spree in which he attacked prostitutes. Sobering up, Wells decided to take his own life by slitting an artery in his leg with a razor, after inhaling an analgesic dose of chloroform to blot out the pain.

4. In the early days of travel by steam train, there were genuine fears that travel above 40kph would cause instant death to the human body. These might have been stoked by the demise of Nicholas Chapman in 1834, whose death doctors diagnosed as being due to "excessive strain on the heart caused by rapid movement of steam locomotive".

3. Russian revolutionary and poet Kondraty Ryleyev was sentenced to be hanged. However, when he was strung up, the rope snapped. This was seen as divine intervention and he was released. Ryleyev remarked: "You see, in Russia they don't know how to do anything properly, not even how to make rope!" This so angered the Czar his pardon was torn up and he was executed the next day.

2. Matthew Vassar, the founder of Vassar College in New York, died in mid-speech delivering his farewell address to the College Board of Trustees in 1868. He had just delivered the 11th page of the speech, in which he mentioned how lucky it was that the college had not had to contend with a death or serious illness among the board or the student body since its opening.

1. A FOOL AND HIS GOLD
Renowned Turkish wrestler Yousouf Ishmaelo came to the United States in 1897 and defeated every opponent he faced. Returning to his homeland in 1898, his ship collided with a British vessel off Nova Scotia. Although a strong swimmer, Ishmaelo drowned because he refused to take off his money belt. The weight of the gold coins it contained made it impossible to float and he sank down to death in Davey Jones' Locker.

DRINKING TO DEATH VIII

Rugby player Matthew Loveday, 19, knocked back 20 shots of ouzo in a drinking game based on a *Dirty Dancing* song. He downed a shot of the Greek aniseed-based drink every time the word "hungry" was sung in Eric Carmen's "Hungry Eyes", from the 1987 Patrick Swayze movie, at a New Year's Eve party in Bletchley, Buckinghamshire, in 2004.

After necking the 20 shots, he finished off the rest of the bottle before collapsing unconscious. His friends carried him to bed, covered him in shaving foam and cat litter, shaved off one of his eyebrows and wrote "I went to bed at ten to ten" on his stomach. Their laughter came to an abrupt end when they realized he was dead. He certainly had the time of his life.

DRINKING TO DEATH IX

For student Gavin Britton, 18, binge-drinking was his life. It also proved to be his death. He was found dead in the city centre of Exeter, Devon, England, on a Tuesday morning. He was still wearing the black wig and fancy dress he had donned for a night out the previous Sunday. It was later revealed he had downed a cocktail known as a Jackson Five – containing up to 12 shots of alcohol – during an evening of pub golf, where drinks are sunk in a 'par' number of swigs. Hampshire-born Gavin's MySpace web page featured assorted photos of him drinking shots or swigging wine, and gave his motto as: "If you're not living on the edge, you're taking up too much space." Guess that was one edge he fell off.

ANIMAL TRAGIC I

We've never trusted sheep. Oh they might come across all woolly and stupid, but we've always had a suspicion that beneath the merry, bleating exteriors beat the hearts of cold, calculating killers. Our suspicions were proved correct in 1999 when 67-year-old farmer Betty Stobbs delivered a bale of hay to her flock on the back of a motorcycle. Sensing weakness, 40 of the flock rushed Ms Stobbs, knocking her over a cliff into a 100ft deep quarry. Miraculously she survived the fall... so the evil ovines finished the job by pushing the motorcycle down on top of her.

ANIMAL TRAGIC II

Animal lover Carol Povey, 46, was probably feeling a bit more than just hoarse when she was killed after one of the beasts fell on her at a farm in Cheddleton, Staffordshire. It is thought the animal may have been spooked by something at the time of the accident in February 2008, falling onto Carol and killing her instantly. A lifelong lover of horses, she had been involved with the animals since the age of 10, but sadly they were to prove the end of her 36 years later.

DRINKING TO DEATH X

Worker Raymond Archer, 30, downed a carafe of wine in one – and then followed it with two more – as workmates at a Christmas 2001 company bash chanted his name. But after knocking back the free booze at a hotel in the Lake District, he collapsed in a corner and was rushed to hospital. Medics found Raymond, from Cumbria, England, had consumed the equivalent of four bottles of wine on top of several pints of beer at the party.

ANIMAL TRAGIC III

A pigeon killed biker Paul Askew, 49 in what a coroner called "a million-to-one chance". It flew into his helmet, causing him to lose control of his motorcycle. The bird exploded in a cloud of feathers, sending Paul veering off the road he was riding along in the Yorkshire Dales. He collided with some trees. The fate of the bird was unknown, but Paul later died in hospital from his injuries in September 1996.

HITLER STRIKES BACK

American theatre critic and commentator Alexander Woollcott died while taking part in a live radio roundtable broadcast in 1943. Woollcott enjoyed a high level of fame at the time of his demise. He had already been immortalised as both the inspiration for the main character in the play *The Man Who Came To Dinner*, and the detective Nero Wolfe in a series of books. Another claim to renown rests in his death being one of the most bizarre and tangential killings ever attributed to the Führer.

The show he was taking part in was designed to mark the tenth anniversary of Hitler's appointment as chancellor of Germany. Woollcot was so worked up discussing whether it was Hitler's fault for all the world's woes or whether it was Germany's fault for creating Hitler in the first place that he suffered a massive heart attack. The other speakers carried on despite his slipping into unconsciousness before them.

ANIMAL TRAGIC IV

Pets and booze don't mix, as alcoholic Martin Hine found out to his peril. He died after falling down a staircase at his partner's home after tripping over her dog. Martin, 62, who suffered from a drink problem, was found by Julia McClaggin at the home they shared in Wellington, Somerset, on 26 November. She thought he accidentally fell over the dog on his way out to the garage for a cigarette. Personally we'd be bringing the mutt in for questioning...

THE SHOW MUST GO ON VI

They say it ain't over until the fat lady sings, but for famed opera singer Leonard Warren the end was nigh after he performed his aria in the second act of *La Forza del Destino* at the New York Metropolitan Opera on 4 March 1960. Just as he was about to launch into the section beginning "Morir, tremenda cosa" ("to die, a momentous thing"), he began coughing and gasping. He then pitched face-forward onto the ground, having suffered a massive heart attack.

ANIMAL TRAGIC V

A playful scratch from a pet cat resulted in Maureen Ulph, 51, from Carlisle, dying from the flesh-eating bug necrotising fasciitus. The cuddly kitty scratched her tummy as she tried to give it a pill for a skin infection and, although she was given antibiotics after feeling ill a few days later, it was too late. The horrific virus had taken hold and, despite surgery to remove infected tissue from her abdomen, she died within a matter of weeks. A catastrophe for sure.

ONE IN THE EYE

Circuses can be dangerous and deadly places. However, one job in the big top you might think was fairly safe would be as a musician with the circus orchestra. Yet for Polish trumpeter Krysztof Baschuz, tooting at an evening show in Ardéche in France in August 1982 took a deadly turn. The circus owner's son, 22-year-old Tony Bertolazzi, mistimed his crossbow marksmanship act. With his crossbow tensed to 80 kilos, he let loose a bolt and, instead of connecting with a small ball his assistant was holding, he managed to hit Baschuz squarely in eye. Not surprisingly, Baschuz died later in hospital from damage to the brain.

PILL POPPING PRATT

Annoying Belgian alternative health promoter, Franz Heinan, used to lecture his friends on the benefits of taking mega-doses of vitamins – the same vitamin pills he accidentally ended up choking to death on in 1994.

ANIMAL TRAGIC VI

A spoilt sheepdog was so excited to see owner Caroline Adams, 41, that he ploughed into her, sending her tumbling down the stairs to her death. Passionate pooch Sam sent Caroline somersaulting backwards after whacking into her knees, and she repeatedly hit the back of her head on a metal staircase at her home in Tilehurst, Berkshire. Despite her fatal injuries, Caroline's first thoughts were for the dog she treated like a child and she kept asking paramedics how he was. Plotting his next victim probably...

ANIMAL TRAGIC VII

A woman died from an extreme allergic reaction when she stepped on a fish while on holiday in Crete. Lyn Buckley, 54, of Doncaster, had been swimming with her husband in the Mediterranean in June 2000 when something sharp stuck in her foot. She thought no more of it, but after sitting by her hotel pool later that day she suddenly felt tired and returned to her room to rest, only to die in her sleep. It was thought she had been bitten by a weaver fish, provoking an anaphylactic shock which caused paralysis of her respiratory muscles, a freak reaction which killed her.

ANIMAL TRAGIC VIII

A gas explosion which demolished a house and killed 80-year-old Moira Dickson was caused by rodents gnawing through pipes under the floorboards. Rats had chewed through pipes to the cooker, causing a build-up of gas which eventually exploded, reducing the house in South Shields to nothing more than rubble in the blast in May 2006.

ANIMAL TRAGIC IX

Most people's closest encounter with a hearse comes after they die, but for Brian Murdy, 61, it proved the means to his end. The dedicated traffic manager was working on a road repair job in Ponteland, near Newcastle Upon Tyne, in March 2006 when a runaway horse-drawn hearse careered towards him.

The horse had got loose following problems at a nearby funeral and galloped towards the roadworks, smashing into a trailer and knocking a barrier towards Brian. As he jumped out of the way, he injured his leg, and it was later put into plaster. But he suffered a blood clot and died at home five days after the horse hearse horror. His funeral arrangements are unknown.

ANIMAL TRAGIC X

Veteran angler Stanley King, from Hertfordshire, drowned in London's River Thames when a powerful fish tugged on his line and dragged him into the water in the early hours of 6 August 2003. The 3.5lb fish tore the 60-year-old's new rod off its tripod and when he grabbed hold of the line he was dragged down the loose shingle bank into the water, becoming tangled in the line of another rod and sinking underwater. Another fisherman raised the alarm and emergency services launched a full-scale search, but his body wasn't found until the next morning.

ANIMAL TRAGIC XI

A lot of people hate spiders, but few would go to dangerous lengths to kill the things. Pensioner Arthur Oliver, 70, climbed onto his sofa to squash a scuttling arachnid on the wall with his slipper, but slipped, hit his head and died in September 2003. His daughter Kirsten said: "We found him lying on the sofa with his head in the corner. He did not like insects and he was wearing one slipper and clutching the other. He used to do this all the time – try and hit spiders or whatever other insects were annoying him."

ANIMAL TRAGIC XII

Jan Linton, 56, jumped out of her bedroom window after suffering paranoid delusions caused by an insect bite. Independently wealthy Jan was bitten by a tick while staying on a friend's rural estate in France. Within six months, she began acting strangely, claiming the police were out to get her, before plunging three storeys from her flat in West London in January 2008. It is believed she had contracted Lyme disease from the tick. This is notoriously hard to diagnose and it had caused psychosis and delusions.

ANIMAL TRAGIC XIII

Business consultant Matthew Wareing, 36, died after being bitten by his kids' pet rat, Roger. The father of three was fit and healthy until Roger nipped his right hand, infecting his blood with unknown bacteria. But Matthew, of Uckfield, West Sussex, ignored advice to visit his doctor because he had an important business meeting to attend and his condition deteriorated rapidly. Just over a fortnight after he was bitten in July 2007, he was dead from blood poisoning.

HAYRIDE TERROR

A man died when his head slammed into the side of a hay-cart trailer when he bungee-jumped out of tree to scare people on a Halloween-themed hayride. Frank Pfister was taking party in the annual Trail of Spooks Hay Rack Ride on Saturday 28 October 2006. Several hundred people were attending the event in South Coffeyville, Nowata County, Oklahoma. In an attempt to frighten the children and parents below him, Pfister leapt out of his perch in the tree. However, things did not go according to plan and a man who wanted to scare others to death ended up dead himself.

"The cable that kept him suspended snapped," said Kassie Johnson, who was on the ride when the accident occurred. "At first I thought it was just a dummy falling out of the tree. The trailer bumped up in the air when he hit. Then everyone started screaming."

Pfister was among more than 100 volunteers working on the annual event. One of the organizers of the Trail of Spooks Hay Rack Ride said: "It is tragic. Who would have thought scaring people would lead to this? We have been doing this for 11 years and never had an accident before. It has always been fun and the money raised has bought a lot of trucks and safety equipment for the Fire Department."

ANIMAL TRAGIC XIV

A funeral procession spooked a camel carrying garden designer Valerie Hewitt, 61, and it threw her onto the pavement. Valerie, from Terrington, near York, was with her family near the Pyramids in Egypt enjoying a sunset camel ride in 2003. Her mount became frightened by the funeral traffic and bucked, throwing her into the air. She died from a brain haemorrhage 11 days after the camel catastrophe.

ANIMAL TRAGIC XV

Janice Stoneley, 51, loved her springer spaniel Lilly and feared her husband would get rid of the dog if he found out she had bitten her. So she kept quiet about the injury, only to collapse and die from multi-organ failure and severe septicaemia four days later. Janice, of Gawsworth, Cheshire, blamed the injury on a knife-cut while washing up and, although she treated the wound with medication, it became infected. In the event, her husband Edward, 51, had Lilly rehomed anyway following his wife's death in April 2001. He said: "She was only protecting the dog because she knew I would have made her get rid of it."

ANIMAL TRAGIC XVI

The Maas family didn't blame the family cat for killing dad Michael, even though it was directly responsible for his death. Michael, 61, was scratched on the left hand as he played with the pet at home in Swindon. The injury became infected and he died a few days later from septicaemia, on 10 December 2005. A family friend said afterwards: "The cat is still going strong and the family does not hold any grudges. It's just one of those things."

ANIMAL TRAGIC XVII

Whilst cats have a tendency of landing on all four paws when they fall from a great height, humans tend to end up as pavement pizza. Unfortunately for cat lover Richard Hall, 31, he slipped as he tried to rescue his pet from a window ledge, plunging 30ft from his first floor flat in South Yorkshire in 2006. He died at the scene and, although the cat fell with him, naturally it survived.

ANIMAL TRAGIC XVIII

A tiny spider led to the death of mother Brenda Sharpe, 67, on the day before her son's wedding. Brenda, from Knodishall, near Saxmundham, Suffolk, lost control of her Peugeot 106 when she saw the arachnid coming down a web between her sun visors and smashed head-on into a bus. She died from multiple injuries, but the wedding went on anyway, in September 2006.

GOING TITS UP

Ample-breasted Berbel Zumner, a 23-year-old from Vienna, Austria, died in 1994 when she was struck by lightning. Doctors said she would have survived had it not been for the substantial metal underwiring in her bra.

ANIMAL TRAGIC XIX

A Muslim with a pathological fear of disease-carrying dogs plunged 150ft from a cliff as he tried to escape a Labrador bounding towards him. Asif Bharucha, 17, from Blackburn, Lancashire, panicked and ran away from the mutt in the direction of the cliff edge near Lizard Point, Cornwall, in June 2004. He lost his footing and plummeted onto rocks. An inquest was told he regarded dogs as "unclean" and was afraid of being bitten by one.

ANIMAL TRAGIC XX

Zookeeper Richard Hughes, 34, lost an argument with a bad-tempered elephant. Four-ton Kumara smashed him against a wall by swatting him with her trunk and then butted him with her head at Chester Zoo in February 2001. The animal suffered from a painful foot condition which made her grumpy.

LAST GASP

After years of smoking heroin and cigarettes, 49-year-old Scott Dempster was lucky to be alive. Even when he began to suffer from severe emphysema he still hung on, quitting the cigs and vowing to fight to the end. Struggling to breathe and gasping for air, he was taken into hospital on 10 January 2007 and rigged up to a ventilation machine, but still promised not to give up until he took his last breath. Unfortunately for Scott, of Bognor Regis, while his nurse was taking a toilet break a pipe came loose from the machine. He died shortly afterwards from a heart attack brought on by a lack of oxygen.

TOAST TO ILL-HEALTH

Is eating toast a basic human right? According to nurses looking after sick Martin Jennings, 36, it is, even though it caused his untimely demise. Martin, who lived near Coventry, was recovering from kidney disease and on a strict "soft food diet" because he was suffering problems with swallowing. But healthcare assistants broke the rules by giving him toast for breakfast five days in a row to stop him getting upset, claiming it was their patient's basic human right to have toast if he demanded it. But on the sixth day, this political correctness gone mad proved the end of Martin, as he was left unattended and choked to death on a slice.

TIPS NOT WELCOME

Pensioner Ada Stokes, 85, was happily sitting in her wheelchair as she embarked on an ambulance journey for a hospital check-up, only to be catapulted head over arse onto the floor. The driver had failed to secure her chair using special clamps and as he pulled over to avoid an oncoming car, Ada, of East Finchley, London, was tipped over and smacked onto the ground. She died the following day, 1 July 1999.

SLOW PUNCTURE

Crescenzo Maffei shot himself in the chin with a crossbow bolt, but was sent home by his doctor and amazingly didn't die until almost a month later. On 26 April 2007, 47-year-old Crescenzo, of Kidderminster, was found by his wife lying on their bedroom floor with a wound to his chin next to a crossbow bolt. He appeared to have removed the bolt himself and was taken to hospital for treatment. However, no major injuries were found and he was sent home, only to return on 30 April for another fruitless examination. His GP was dissatisfied and demanded he went back to hospital for a third time, when doctors discovered the crossbolt bolt injury had actually entered his brain to a very small extent. Unfortunately it was enough to allow air into the brain and this caused him to eventually die from multiple organ failure on 20 May.

TUMOUR TRAUMA

When doctors told 78-year-old Carrie Measures they thought she had a cancerous tumour in her bowel, she reluctantly agreed to undergo surgery. But nothing was found with the operation, at Doncaster Royal Infirmary in June 2002. She subsequently developed gangrene and breathing difficulties, dying a few weeks later from bronco-pneumonia. Consultant surgeon Dr John Bagley said he had only known of one or two cases in his career in which a tumour was diagnosed, but not found during surgery.

THE SHOW MUST GO ON VII

Jerome Rodale was a pioneer of organic farming in the US and a self-professed expert on longevity. He was a guest on the *Dick Cavett Show*, on 8 June 1971, and bragged: "I'm in such good health that I fell down a long flight of stairs yesterday and I laughed all the way ... I've decided to live to be a hundred," as well as "I never felt better in my life!"

After his interview, Cavett turned his attention to *New York Post* columnist Pete Hamill. Rodale slumped over in his seat and let out a snort. Cavett asked whether they were boring him, but didn't realize Rodale had actually died of a heart attack until after filming concluded. The episode was never aired.

NOT A LEG TO STAND ON

Blundering doctors put a knee joint in the wrong leg of Annie Carter, 59, from South Wales, in 2003. She died of a heart attack 11 days after an operation to put it in the right place.

FED UP

Stroke patient Thomas Towler, 79, died after a care home feeding machine stuffed him with five times the right amount of food. A faulty regulator on a machine that fed him directly through his stomach meant he was pumped with food at the home in Sheffield, in 2003. He was unable to reach an alarm buzzer before it was too late. He was found lying in his own vomit 90 minutes later.

TUBE BOOB

After a successful operation to remove a cancerous tumour from his throat, former pub landlord Roy Hodgson, 66, should have had a good chance of recovery. That is, if incompetent medical staff had noticed a feeding tube wasn't correctly inserted into his stomach, and he was being both starved and poisoned to death. Roy, from Cleator, West Cumbria, was suffering such hunger pangs that he tried to flee the hospital. A nurse had incorrectly fitted the tube so whenever he was fed with liquid nourishment he was not only deprived of food, but poisoned internally. Senior staff failed to spot the error, leading to his death in November 2004.

THE THINGS WE LEAVE BEHIND

Sheer medical incompetence killed 19-year-old Karen Murray after doctors left swabs rattling around inside her. Karen, of Southport, Merseyside, collapsed and died after complaining of stomach pains while holidaying in Corfu with her boyfriend in May 1998, eight years after an operation. Five nine-inch square medical swabs had been gradually strangulating her bowel since 1990.

DUCK!

A combination of drink and drugs led student Thomas Clarke, 18, of Plumpton, East Sussex, to try his hand at train surfing. After smoking cannabis and boozing until he was more than three times over the drink-drive limit at a party in November 2002, Tom climbed out of the window of the train and got onto the roof. He started walking towards the rear carriage, only to collide with a bridge at speeds of around 70mph. Messy.

THE DRUGS DON'T WORK...

Surprisingly, it wasn't heroin which killed junkies Julia Bradbury and Timothy Kenny in June 2007. The couple were killed in a fire sparked when Tim, 43, lit an alcohol-based wipe given to drug users to help prevent infection when injecting. He was attempting to "cook" heroin. He accidentally set fire to a foam-filled chair he was using as an improvised table, which began giving out thick smoke. The pair attempted to drag it out of the front door, but it became wedged in the doorway, cutting off their escape route and trapping them to die in the blazing flat.

CHANCING THE ODDS

Driving a moped in harsh weather conditions while doped up on a cocktail of booze and drugs is a danger to yourself and others. However, if you wore a crash helmet and stayed on the correct side of the road at least you'd stand a fighting chance of making it home alive. But Carina Bennett, 50, of Hailsham, East Sussex, decided to knock back bottles of vodka, cans of Special Brew lager, and take cocaine, cannabis and methodone, and then drive off on her bike, without a helmet, in high winds and driving rain. She veered onto the wrong carriageway and ploughed straight into an oncoming car on 6 March 2007. Hardly unexpected, definitely stupid.

TOP 10 RIDICULOUS DEATHS FROM HISTORY – THE 20th CENTURY

10. English critic and poet Lionel Johnson achieved literary immortality for poems such as "Destroyer of a Soul" and "The Dark Angel". He died in 1902 at the age of 35 when he cracked his skull after falling from a bar-stool when someone told him a drunken joke.

9. A newspaper report from 1903 tells the story of Patrick Burke from Missouri dying in hospital as a result of being given his first bath in years. His death is recorded as due to "injuries sustained from scrubbing, a chill caught while wet and shock at being clean".

8. Italian poet Severino Ferrari was never the most stable of individuals, so it was little surprise to his friends that his emotional volatility and depression eventually saw him committed to a lunatic asylum. Whilst there in 1905, he received a telegram telling him he had just been appointed as Professor of Literature at the University of Bologna. The shock caused him to keel over and die.

7. Composer of frankly appalling music Arnold Schonberg died due to triskaidekaphobia, the fear of the number 13. He became so convinced that he would die on Friday 13 July 1951 – his 76th year, which he reasoned would be fatal because 7+6=13 – that he spent the whole day in bed. He was in such a state of anxiety that it was no surprise when the strain killed him at 13 minutes to midnight.

6. American film actress Martha Mansfield burned to death on the set of her film *Warrens of Virginia* in 1923. Mansfield went up in a ball of flames when a match, tossed by a smoking cast member, ignited her Civil War costume of hoopskirts and flimsy ruffles.

5. Alexander Aleksandrovich Bogdanov was a Russian doctor, philosopher and science fiction writer who believed in the possibility of human rejuvenation through blood transfusion. He died in 1928 as a result of one of the experiments, when he caught both malaria and tuberculosis from a transfusion of blood taken from one of his students.

4. Inventor and chemist Thomas Midgley Jr's discovery of CFCs has led at least one modern scientist to say of him: "He had more impact on the atmosphere than any other single organism in Earth history." However, Midgley's other claim to fame is the ridiculous manner of his death – he accidentally strangled himself with the cord of a pulley-operated mechanical bed of his own design.

3. English author and theatre critic Arnold Bennett had a reputation for being arrogant and opinionated. While living in Paris in 1931, Bennett died from typhoid. He contracted the disease from a glass of water he drank in a café to prove to visiting friends that the local water was perfectly safe to drink.

2. Austrian tailor Franz Reichelt invented an overcoat designed to function as a parachute. In 1912, to demonstrate its effectiveness, Reichelt leapt from the first deck of the Eiffel Tower, falling more than 60 metres to his death. The event was recorded on film and can still be watched to this day on YouTube.

1. WHAT A JACK ARSE
   In the 21st century, Jack Daniels is an internationally recognised name thanks to the Tennessee whiskey which carries his name. Mr Jack himself died in 1911 when he got a fatal blood infection from a toe that he injured while kicking his safe when he could not remember the combination for it.

SUN RISE, FALL DOWN

A student was enjoying an ecstasy trip so much that he decided to climb to the top of a 60ft gas tower in Bath to watch the sunrise, only to slip and fall to his death. Not a frequent drug user, James Fiddes, 20, from Cambridge, had bought two pills in a club and spent the evening dancing before deciding to get the best view for the dawn. Unfortunately for James, he took the quick route down.

YEAR'S END

As one year ended, so did the life of reveller Hayden Bowers after a night spent bingeing on drink and drugs. Hayden, 27, took cocaine, ecstasy and cannabis and swigged champagne during a night of wild celebrations at a New Year's Eve party in trendy Bayswater, London, on 31 December 2006. Despite pleas from his friends to stop, the ridiculously arrogant Bowers decided to carry on telling them he could "smoke, snort or drink anyone under the table". He then stripped down to his boxer shorts and climbed into a hot tub, and was still drinking champagne in there at 9am the following morning. But within half an hour the night's excesses had caught up with him and he was dead.

RUBBED OUT

Fetish fan Robert Garnett, 35, died from excessive overheating after taking a huge amount of cocaine while wearing a rubber body suit. The store manager, from Kennington, South London, was found lying dead on his bed in the rubber outfit after he failed to turn up to work in December 2005. A post mortem examination revealed his brain had swollen, and this was attributed to a combination of the coke and the rubber leading to him overheating.

TUMBLING TOILET

Miami-based construction worker Ramon Jose Rodriguez was well-trained in building site safety. The 23-year-old had a perfect accident avoidance record until the fateful and fatal day in April 1998 when death came from above. High winds blew a portable toilet off of the fourth floor of a building and it fell straight onto poor Ramon. Police spokeswoman Lucy Fitts said: "The toilet was on rollers so it did not take much wind to send it down. He never saw it coming."

RAVE ON GRANDAD!

Britain's oldest victim of the dance drug ecstasy was pot-smoking gramps Eric Whittle, 63, who died after popping four of the pills in conjunction with cannabis, cocaine and alcohol. His grandson Stephen said Eric, from Warrington, Cheshire, would boast about how many Es he took at any one time. The happy drugs proved the end of him in 2002 when he was found convulsing on the floor of his home. He died in hospital three days later of a heart attack.

COKE-CRAZED COOK

A leading chef went on a crazy rampage through a block of flats after losing the plot. He took a bunch of cocaine, and started breaking windows with a golf club and leaping between window ledges before falling to his death from the second floor. David Dempsey, 31, from Glasgow, died weeks after becoming head chef of the Michelin three-star Restaurant Gordon Ramsay in Chelsea, London. His death in May 2003 was blamed on "excited delirium syndrome" caused by all the cocaine.

PILL POST

Student Liam Brackell, 24, had an unusual hobby – prescription drugs. He ordered stacks of opiates and other medication online, and at one point received 300 anti-depressants in the post every day at his home in Wanstead, east London. But Liam also took illegal drugs like ecstasy, cannabis and magic mushrooms, all of which combined to flick a switch in his head. In the summer of 2002 he narrowly survived after deliberately running in front of a bus, only to finish the job on 7 June by walking in front of an oncoming train. By the time of his death he had tried 23 different types of prescription drugs, which is probably something of a record.

GODLIKE STUPIDITY

Bhupendra Paudal from Nepal became so convinced he had the powers of the god Shiva that he killed his wife, believing he could resurrect her in a form as beautiful as that of the goddess Parvati, consort to Shiva. Of course, he could not.

EAR TODAY, GONE TOMORROW

German Werner Shenke bit off another man's ear during a violent and brutal bar room brawl in the city of Bremen in 1998. However, his opponent had the last laugh as Shenke choked to death when part of the lobe stuck in his throat.

DOOM RAIDER

A lapdancer who dressed as computer babe Lara Croft to please her lover died after drink and drug-fuelled sex which saw her down a lethal mix of wine, ecstasy, cocaine and GHB. Chana Ravenscroft, 28, and boyfriend Christopher Hall enjoyed experimental sex which left her with intimate injuries at his flat in Sheffield in May 2006, but it was the drink and drugs which killed the Tomb Raider imitator. Game over.

BISCUIT SNAPS

A dad who ate cannabis biscuits to boost his bedroom performance died in a police cell after wrestling semi-naked with officers. Malcolm Flockton, 41, of North Tyneside was frolicking with fiancée Sandra Stringer and pretending to be a sheep with a sheepskin rug on his back when he suddenly flipped out. Storming off semi-nude, he threw a brick through the window of her ex-husband Jimmy and had to be restrained by several police officers. But he suffered a sudden heart attack when taken to a cell, and died shortly afterwards.

ANOTHER BRICK IN THE WALL

"If you don't eat your meat, you can't have any pudding..." Pensioner Thomas Johnson, 81, of Armley, Leeds, was left in a pool of blood for two days after being attacked by his wife for not eating his Sunday dinner. Dorothy, 83, eventually called a medical centre and told a doctor: "He wouldn't eat his bastard Sunday dinner! He's been there on the floor ever since."

Police found Thomas lying face down on the living room floor wearing just a T-shirt and underpants, covered in scratches and bruises, with blood splattered around the room. He developed hypothermia, and died in hospital four months later, claiming he didn't remember anything about the attack in 2002. His wife also said her memories were unclear and was placed into an old people's home without any charges being brought.

CLEAN MOUTH

Ex-sailor James Cross, 83, swallowed a denture cleaning tablet after mistaking it for an extra strong mint. He had found a pack of the caustic tablets in a room at the care home where he lived in Walker, near Newcastle, and was rushed to hospital when he started foaming at the mouth after drinking some water. He died of lung damage following the mix-up in 2003.

THE TOOTH OF THE MATTER

Removal of a wisdom tooth isn't pleasant, but it shouldn't prove fatal. But Robert Braber, 59, bled to death overnight after an extraction. The wisdom tooth had been removed without complications in August 2004 and Robert went to bed thinking the bleeding had stopped. But he was found on a blood-soaked mattress, with one litre of blood in his stomach and a further three in his bowel. Something to chew over eh?

THE GUN OF A PREACHERMAN

On Sunday 24 September 1998, before his family and more than 200 parishioners at the Christian Fellowship Church International at Jacksonville, Florida, preacher Melvyn Nurse gave a sermon. Melvyn liked to enliven his sermons with the use of props. On this occasion, to illustrate how flirting with the any of the seven deadly sins was like playing Russian roulette with your spiritual life, he used a .357 Magnum revolver with a blank in one of the chambers.

He put the gun to his head, pulled the trigger and fell backwards. Everyone watching thought it was part of the sermon until they noticed blood on the carpet. Unfortunately for Melvyn, no divine hand had intervened to prevent the cardboard wadding from the blank piercing his temple. The shot inflicted brain injuries which would claim his life five days later.

THE SHOW MUST GO ON VIII

Some reporters will do anything for a scoop. A news anchor on Sarasota's Channel 40 morning show, *Suncoast Digest*, Christine Chubbuck made the ultimate protest over the station owner's editorial focus on graphic imagery. On the morning of 15 July 1974 Christine told her audience: "In keeping with Channel 40's policy of bringing you the latest in blood and guts, and in living colour, you are going to see another first: an attempted suicide." She then drew out a concealed revolver and shot herself behind her right ear. Fade to black.

VIDEO NASTY

A sleepwalker who often dreamed about films he had watched may have hanged himself while re-enacting a death scene from Steven Spielberg's WWII holocaust movie *Schindler's List*. Michael Cox, 37, from Tresham, near Bristol, who had been a sleepwalker since childhood, told a friend he was going to watch the film, which has a hanging scene at its climax. He was found hanging from banisters from his trouser belt in January 2001, but there appeared to be no other explanation why he killed himself. Psychologist Jonathan Bird said he couldn't rule out sleepwalking as a cause of death.

CHILLING DIP

Thousands of people swim in the English Channel every summer, well accustomed to the fact that it's never going to be as warm as the Med. But for professional windsurfer Andrew Funnell, 21, the temperature proved his downfall. On 11 June 2004, one of the hottest days of the summer, he left his wet suit behind and went jet-skiing wearing only shorts, off Seaford, East Sussex. But when he fell off, the 11°C water caused a rare condition called vagal inhibition and he died of shock as a result.

FRIED BY FRIDGE

Apparently the chances of winning the lottery are the same as being killed in a fridge-related incident. Perhaps holidaymaker Richard Fisher should have bought a ticket? Richard, 19, from Burghfield, near Reading, was working as a lifeguard near Bodrum, Turkey, in 2004, when he entered a kebab shop soaked to the skin after attending a foam party. But as he leaned across the counter to order food he came into contact with a rusty old fridge, which sent a live current through his wet clothing. Staff carried on serving customers and refused to switch off the appliance, thinking he was just another drunken tourist. The shop owner was later charged with causing death by negligence.

READY FOR THE CHOP

A builder spent three months assembling an 8ft-high guillotine which he used to decapitate himself in an extremely impressive manner. Boyd Taylor, 36, from Milborne, Northumberland, put together an ingenious timing device to release the blade, dosed himself up on 12 sleeping pills, and then lay on his bed under the home-made death trap on 8 January 2003. An electric jigsaw plugged into a timer switch cut through a block of wood and released the wire holding the blade, sending it plummeting down and completely severing his head, before being switched off by a secondary mechanism. Coroner Eric Armstrong said: "A good deal of thought had gone into the construction and timing device, which was ingenious, if applied to a somewhat bizarre purpose."

CONVERSATION WITH A DEAD MAN

It was almost a call from beyond the grave when computer expert Eugene Kapustynski, 40, of south London, dialled 999 to report his own suicide in 2001.

The call, which had all the hallmarks of a black comedy sketch, went as follows:

Eugene: "I would like to report a suicide."

Operator: "Who is it? Do you know?"

"Yeah, it's me."

"Well I'm speaking to you. So it can't be you, can it?"

"I have committed a crime. I have stolen software from my company. I have ruined my life."

"It can be sorted out, can't it?"

"It will be sorted out shortly," he said, before putting a shotgun to his head and blowing his brains out. The line went dead...

THE SHOW MUST GO ON IX

A guitarist in several Scottish rock bands of the late 1960s and early 1970s, Les Harvey initially escaped death as a member of the Blues Council after their tour van crashed, killing their vocalist and bassist. Unfortunately for Les, he was living on borrowed time. While playing in Swansea with new group Stone the Crows on 3 May 1972, he touched an unearthed microphone with wet hands and was electrocuted. Live in concert, eh?

MIST OF DEATH

Popping along to the garden centre and checking out the spa baths sounds like the most harmless way of whiling away a few hours. But it cost 61-year-old Roger Russell his life when he contracted killer Legionnaires' disease after a salesman's demonstration in Bagshot, Surrey, during June 2001. Roger, from Berkshire, and his wife Wendy, 59, had only intended to collect a brochure, but the salesman offered to show them a bath in operation. As the taps were switched on, jets of air sprayed Roger with a fine mist. Two days later he began suffering flu-like symptoms, but his health rapidly deteriorated and he died of multiple organ failure 17 days later, doctors having diagnosed Legionnaires' disease. Tests found the deadly bacteria still present in the spa bath water more than three weeks later.

CONSPIRACY THEORY

Potboiler novel *The Da Vinci Code* might have sold bucketloads of copies and led to a blockbuster movie, but at the end of the day it's a load of poorly-researched hokum and certainly not worth killing yourself over. But Benedictine monk Abbot Alan Rees, 64, leapt 30ft to his death from a balcony at Belmont Abbey, Hertfordshire, England, after reading Dan Brown's novel in October 2005. His successor Father Paul Stonham said the abbot was depressed over the contents of the book, which claimed Christianity is a sexist conspiracy.

FOR WHOM THE BELL TOLLS

The body of 79-year-old Italian priest Carmine Capuani was discovered in the tower of his church on Easter Sunday morning in April 1998. He had been crushed to death by ringing his church's 1000-kilo bell.

BLIND FAITH

Sometimes you have to accept it's time to call it quits, but one-eyed 92-year-old motorist George Pyman certainly didn't reach that conclusion. George, from Norfolk, drove into the path of another vehicle in 2007, killing himself in the crash.

FROZEN IN TIME

When council officials called on the house of 40-year-old Joyce Vincent, she was surrounded by Christmas presents, the television was on and the heating in her bed-sit in Wood Green, north east London, was keeping the place nice and warm. The only odd thing was that she'd been dead for three years and was now little more than a skeleton. Police believe she probably died of natural causes in 2003 and she was only discovered when housing officials went to recover the thousands of pounds in rent arrears that had accumulated since her death.

WHEN HIPPOS ATTACK III

If this book serves no other purpose, it will hopefully bring to the attention of its readers the fact that hippos, far from being the sweet and pleasant animals that their portrayal in stuffed toys, numerous cartoon films, ads and children's stories suggests, are actually vicious bastards. When 50-year-old Heibrecht Beukes was walking her dog in a Transvaal nature reserve, its constant barking attracted unwanted attention from a bull hippo. In its attempt to get at the annoying canine, the hippo successfully charged an electrified fence. When Beukes tried to run away from the hippo it ploughed straight into her and, when it had brought her to the ground, trampled her to death. The hippo was eventually shot by game wardens. Beukes' yapping dog survived unscathed.

CALCULATED FATE

A chemistry student worked out the exact number of caffeine tablets needed to kill himself, before popping hundreds of them. James Bird, 20, from Hereford – a student at Cardiff University – researched the effects of caffeine and left behind handwritten notes calculating the deadly dosage. He carried on his scientific suicide in the hours leading to his death on 31 January 2002, with a note besides his body reading: "It does not seem to be having too much of an effect yet. Dead by 12pm Saturday, hopefully."

TOP 10 RIDICULOUS DIY DEATHS

10. John Baldwin was on his roof carrying out DIY repairs on his home in Norfolk in 1984 when he was mobbed by a flock of seagulls. Despite his wife and sons trying to distract the birds, they refused to leave him alone and he tumbled to his death.

9. Tim Mulvaney from Belfast was a former rock musician who had performed on three albums with heavy metal band Judas Priest. In 2007 he hit himself in the nose with a claw hammer while doing some carpentry. The blow activated the flesh-eating disease necrotizing fasciitis, which killed Mulvaney within three months.

8. Jason Burton from London was so desperate for a nose job that he attempted to perform one on himself, using a chisel and a piece of chicken bone as replacement cartilage. Unfortunately – and unsurprisingly – his DIY plastic surgery led to complications and a fatal infection.

7. Charles Cooke from Watsonville, California, spent 18 years building a DIY plane. However, within minutes of its take-off, the plane crashed to the ground in a screaming ball of flame, killing Cooke in front of friends and family who had come to watch its maiden flight.

6. German couple Achsen and Sigrid Wilberg used their DIY skills to build themselves a sauna. However, as temperatures soared to 180° in their self-built hothouse, they found themselves trapped. Neighbours eventually came to their rescue, but it was too late for the fatally cooked Mr Wilberg.

5. If there is one aspect of property maintenance more deadly than DIY, it is gardening. In 1991, Michael Davis from Dorking hired a corkscrew drill to bore holes for tree planting. However, his clothing

got caught up in the drill, which then proceeded to bore right through him and left his corpse screwed into the ground.

4. Belgian Luc Darcourt was attempting a DIY conversion of his attic into a home office in 1989 when he stepped through the ceiling. Mr Darcourt only sustained a broken wrist and ankle from his fall. However his wife, whom he landed on, died from a broken neck.

3. In 1983, Cliff Morton from Wisconsin lifted the guard on a motorised saw while cutting timber to build a DIY porch, in order to better see his pencil marks. He accidentally cut off his left hand. Staggering around in shock, Morton tried to go into his house to ring for medical attention. However, faint from loss of blood, he tripped on the stairs and broke his neck.

2. James Maine from Tonbridge was so proud of building a DIY Lotus Seven kit car that as soon as he had finished it, he took it out onto the road. Unfortunately he was not as good a mechanic as he thought he was, and as soon as the car hit 130 kph it broke up, killing him.

1. ALL WRAPPED UP
There is no more ridiculous DIY-related death than the strange and fatal fate of Austrian Hans Pender. In 1985, the 50-year-old was trying to redecorate his Salzburg home when he became entangled in a 25-metre roll of flock wallpaper. When his family returned home from a shopping expedition they found him totally wrapped up in the soggy mess. According to a police spokesman: "The glue-coated paper stuck to him and the more he tried to pull free, the more entangled he became. He eventually suffocated to death."

CLEAN FINISH

On 22 November 1990, Alfredo Castro, a 31-year-old laundry worker, was trying to fix an industrial dryer at the Hospital Laundry in Dorchester, Massachusetts. As he prepared to install a new timer mechanism, a conveyor belt carrying more than 100lbs started, knocking him into the dryer. As the lid slammed shut, the dryer started automatically. For the next six minutes he was tumbled within the machine at temperatures of 120 degrees.

Lt John Sullivan of the Dorchester police said: "A co-worker heard thumping, but did not investigate the source." The first anyone knew about the accident was when the co-worker saw Castro's cooked and battered corpse amid the clothing coming out the dryer on the conveyor belt.

BAKED

Two bakers were cooked in temperatures of more than 100C after being carried through a giant oven on a slow conveyor belt. David Mayes, 47, of Leicester, and Ian Erickson, 43, of Walsall, were slow-roasted after trying to retrieve a broken part from the 75ft oven at a bakery in Leicester, in May 1998. The firm admitted breaching safety regulations.

LAST PRICK FOR RED SONIA

The human body just isn't made to be riddled with metal. Lesley Hovvells, known as Red Sonia because of her flaming red hair, had an ambition to have 100 body piercings, but died shortly after reaching her target when her body became overwhelmed by infection.

Lesley, 39, from Llanelli, South Wales, actually had 118 piercings by the time she succumbed to blood poisoning – 28 earstuds, 13 earrings, 11 bellybars, 18 bars, six liprings, 36 bodyrings and six nose studs – but failed to keep them all sufficiently clean. She collapsed on Millennium Eve and died 11 days later from septicaemia. Better hope she wasn't cremated, all that metal would have taken ages to burn...

BAGGED AND BOXED

Teacher Christy Onwordi, 38, often wore a plastic bag over her newly dyed hair to stop products staining her pillow. All very sensible, but in June 2002 she inadvertently suffocated herself in her sleep at her home in Chorlton, Greater Manchester, when the bag slipped over her head.

OFF WITH A LIMB

After attempting suicide by lying in front of a train, farmer's wife Wendy Fairburn, 46, was horrified to find the engine had only severed her arm. So she picked up the detached limb and jumped 80ft over a viaduct to finish the job properly, on 10 December 2005. Her fate was only discovered six weeks later when divers found her arm in a river adjacent to the viaduct in Alnmouth, Northumberland.

OH KILL ALL YE FAITHFUL

In 1998, a Catholic priest at Tam Heip in Vietnam was killed in front of his congregation when a storm caused a stone crucifix on the outside of his church to crash through the roof. Eight of his parishioners were also injured in the horrific 'act of God'.

FINAL CURTAIN

Theatre worker Gloria Dawson, 69, loved to present flowers to the leading ladies when the curtain came down – an act of kindness which would claim her life. A crumbling fire safety curtain at a theatre in Reading, Berkshire, released clouds of asbestos into the air. She developed the asbestos-related cancer mesothelioma in 2005, sadly dying in June 2006.

LAST SMOKE

Smoke alarms are wonderful inventions, except when you want to enjoy a cigarette. William Wood, 50, of Newcastle upon Tyne, covered his device to have a relaxing smoke, only to die in a fire some time later, in 2007, because he'd left it muffled.

STRIKE OR SPLIT?

It was all over for Ferdinand Dela Cruz, 34, as he was cleaning a tenpin bowling machine at Hollywood Bowl in Barking, East London, in July 2006. The technician, from East Ham, was trapped and crushed to death. With life, you don't get a spare.

ROAMING IN ROME

British tourist Christopher Owen, 25, was probably sleepwalking when he fell to his death from the fourth-floor balcony of a Rome hotel in December 2006. His mother said the family was always worried about his sleepwalking and would lock doors for safety. He would also sleep in his clothes when away for fear of wandering around naked – not that it makes much difference when you fall from that sort of height.

THE PRICE OF FAME

Isabella Blow, 48, knocked back a fatal dose of weedkiller Paraquat in Gloucester on 6 May 2007. She had previously tried overdosing on sleeping pills, jumping off the Hammersmith flyover in London (breaking both ankles), driving her car into the rear of a truck, trying to buy horse tranquilizers, overdosing on a beach in India and drowning herself in a lake. She was bound to get it right in the end.

BOLT FROM THE BLUE

A tourist was blown off his feet by a bolt of lightning from an almost clear blue sky, seconds after he had climbed out of a swimming pool. Michael Haffenden, a 49-year-old recruitment consultant from Exeter, died instantly when he was struck at a pool near Siena, in Tuscany. The flash, which may have come from a rogue cloud in the otherwise empty sky, also set fire to a thatched summer house, injured a family friend and damaged a hearing aid belonging to Michael's wife.

DON'T LOOK BACK

Businessman George Schwartz was working late in his office one night in 1983 when a blast destroyed the factory he owned. He staggered from the smouldering wreckage and amazed fire fighters attending the blast rushed the lucky survivor straight to hospital. After being treated for minor injuries, Schwartz rushed back to the site of what remained of his factory to search for files and vital paperwork. While scrabbling through the rubble in his frantic search, one of the remaining walls collapsed on top of him, killing him instantly.

CHORES CHOKER

It's nothing new, kids hate doing household chores, so why dad of two David Smart decided to hang himself after a row with his children over who should lay the dinner table is unfathomable. David, 38, lost his temper with his daughters, 10 and 12, at their home in South Marson, Swindon, on 25 September 2004. The row continued the next morning over who should make breakfast and that afternoon David was found hanging from the loft hatch. Something of an over-reaction.

STAIRWAY TO HELL

Emma Niskala, a 35-year-old accounts clerk for the New York Telephone Company, was pulled into the workings of an escalator in the office block leased by her employer. The escalator had been installed in 1974 and had a track record of causing accidents, including one in 1982 where 36 employees were injured when it unexpectedly went into reverse. When Emma stepped onto the escalator at 7:45 A.M. on 16 September 1987, a step collapsed beneath her and she fell feet first into the machine. The escalator's conveyor belt then pulled her further into the workings and her colleagues were unable to get her out. By the time the police arrived to assist in rescuing her, Emma had already been crushed to death.

ANYONE FOR A SLICE OF WEDDING CAKE?

It's not the ideal start to married life, but let's hope the fact that best man Adrian Fletcher went mental at the wedding didn't ruin things too much for the bride and groom. Phone salesman Adrian, 34, from Bolton, drank an enormous amount of alcohol and took stacks of cocaine at the wedding in Cancun, Mexico, in February 2007. He then began arguing with girlfriend Lisa Miller and swept the pair of them off the balcony of their 14th-floor hotel room. Fortunately for Lisa they landed on a ledge below, but Adrian then stood up and stepped off it, plunging to his death below.

IN THESE SHOES?

Student Emma Morecombe bought a new pair of shoes for her graduation from Newcastle University in 2007, only to break her ankle in a tumble down the stairs while trying them on. Emma, 23, from Hayes End, Middlesex, underwent surgery, but three weeks later she collapsed and died from a blood clot to the lungs – the odds of which were one in 10,000. Coroner David Mitford made the unusual comment: "I think we have all put on a new pair of shoes at some stage. This is very unfortunate and tragic."

DEAD STREAMING

The internet holds all manner of opportunities for those with unusual fetishes to find special friends. For some reason, Kevin Whitrick, 42, from Wellington, Shropshire, visited an 'insult chatroom', where he was abused by other users while on a live webcam. Perhaps this wasn't the best of sites for someone suffering from depression, especially when forum users started egging him on to carry out a threat of suicide. Up to 60 people watched as Kevin strung himself up with an electrical cord on 21 March 2007 – some took the sensible decision to alert police, but others laughed it off as a practical joke.

DUMB DUMB BULLETS

Haitian vodoo doctor Jacquez Severe made 'magic bullets', which he guaranteed would always kill their target. In 1992, the Port-de-Paix resident was killed with one of the bullets he had created – by a dissatisfied customer whose previous shooting victim had lived.

FAME GAME

Ever heard of indie band Bikini Black Special? No, well that's because they probably haven't achieved the heights of fame predicted by former bass guitarist Ben Smith. Ben, 18, was found hanged at home in Huddersfield, in August 2006, after being kicked off the band just before they were supposed to be landing a record deal from a major label. Two years later, Bikini Black Special still haven't made it big, so Ben probably shouldn't have bothered.

LAST ORDERS

Nobody wants to be known as the scrounger who never gets a round in, but surely it's all a matter of perspective and not worth killing yourself over. Apprentice stone mason Daniel Pickering, 17, from East Yorkshire, lost a £20 note he had borrowed for a pub crawl on his brother's stag night and stormed off before anyone could stop him. He was later found hanged on a building site where he used to work in 2003. The £20 note was discovered in his pocket.

EGGS MARKS THE SPOT

A notorious collector of rare birds' eggs fell to his death from a tree while examining a sparrowhawk nest. Colin Watson, 63, from Selby, North Yorkshire, was three-quarters of the way up a 40ft larch tree in woods near Doncaster, on 24 May 2006, when he lost his grip, plunging to the ground and suffering multiple rib fractures and a punctured heart. Colin had been convicted six times under wildlife protection laws, fined thousands of pounds and had virtually his entire collection confiscated after a raid on his home by the Royal Society for the Protection of Birds. His last attempt to feather his own nest proved fatal. Bet he didn't see the yolk.

FINALS FATALITY

Student Armandeep Bal was jubilant to have reached the end of his finals exams at De Montfort University, Leicester, in March 2005, and had a few drinks to celebrate. He then grabbed hold of railings on a wall outside the window of a fifth-floor flat and performed a handstand to show off in front of pals. Failing on the first attempt, and ignoring pleas to stop from his friends, the 21-year-old tried again, only to fall into a courtyard and die from multiple injuries.

HAIR TODAY, GONE TOMORROW

Fashion designer Nicola Faulkner was killed by a violent allergic reaction to the glue she used on her hair extensions in 2000. Nicola, 28, of Sydenham, south-east London, was allergic to nuts, but had previously used the American Super Hair bonding glue with no ill effects. But within an hour of fitting the extensions her face swelled up and a skin rash spread across her body. Her last words were: "Where's that damn ambulance?" Pretty hair-raising eh?

A LOT OF KNOWLEDGE CAN BE DEADLY

Eleanor Barry was a 70-year-old hoarder of old books, newspapers and magazines. She lived alone in a Long Island home that she had filled from floor to ceiling with towers of books and stacks of media clippings contained in scrapbooks.

Police, summoned by concerned neighbours who had not seen Eleanor for several weeks, broke down her bedroom door with an axe. They discovered she had been killed at least 10 days before when one of the mountains of books and magazines had crashed down on top of her. Coroners concluded the amount of paper had pinned her to floor and simultaneously muffled her attempts to call out for help. She had probably survived the first few days after the collapse before succumbing to the effects of dehydration.

MAKE SURE YOU'RE SURE

Don't change your mind about suicide, as it's often too late to do anything about it. Mind you, for engineer Russell Williams, 26, from Caerphilly, Wales, it was out of his hands when he swallowed 70 painkillers in July 2003. He went to the accident and emergency department of the local hospital, where he fell asleep on a trolley bed, only to be found dead there several hours later.

CLEARLY NUTS SQUIRREL KILLER

Malaysian man Harun Mamat climbed a tree near his village in the Kota Baharu territory to collect mangosteen fruit. However, his plucking came to a premature end when he was shot by a hunter who mistook him for a squirrel.

FIRST AND FINAL RIDE

A thrillseeking pensioner who had waited years for a motorbike was killed by the excitement of riding it. John Parsons, 71, suffered a heart attack on his 125cc Honda, falling under a car near his home in Barry, Glamorgan, in September 2006. His late wife Myra had refused to let him buy a bike, so when she died from cancer he bought the bike to comfort himself. Unfortunately the excitement proved too much for his heart.

BUTTON IT

Gran Laura Williams, 88, of Glamorgan, Wales, swallowed buttons she mistook for her tablets and choked to death in a hospital in Bridgend, in 2007.

FAREWELL PERFORMANCE

Top classical violinist Laurence Rowden-Martin, 48, tried to cut off his head with an electric circular saw. But Laurence, of Sheffield, only managed to sever every vein and artery in his neck. He bled to death in his bath in February 2006. He had become an alcoholic after a nerve condition ended his career.

IN THE FRAME

Boozed-up builder John Hallihan, 44, locked himself out of his flat in Bristol, in 2007. When he tried to break back in, he accidentally hung himself. He stood on an old fridge freezer so he could reach a broken window and hook open the ledge inside with a cable. But he slipped and wedged his neck in the frame, leading to a fatal heart attack.

THE INCREDIBLE BULK

The mother of 20-stone bulk Lorraine Robins, left to rot on a sofa, was more concerned about the embarrassment to the family than her daughter's welfare.

Mary Robins, 76, told a shocked nurse: "What a year it's been. I've broken my wrist, the rabbit has died and now this." She'd asked: "What will the neighbours think?" as five paramedics carried her unconscious daughter from her home in Bournemouth, Dorset, in 2005.

Lorraine, 39, died of a heart attack brought on by her immobility and obesity after refusing to leave the sofa for four months. She spent her time wolfing down eggs on toast provided by her mother, while watching US wrestling videos and daytime TV soaps. Her flesh rotted, she grew facial hair and talon-like fingernails, and didn't even get up to visit the toilet.

Mum Mary and son Stuart, 46, did nothing until Lorraine fell unconscious. At an inquest, they were both criticised for their complete failure to help her.

DO-IT-YOURSELF SUICIDE

This particular story prompts the question: how much research do you really need to undertake before topping yourself? Glen Hughes, 40, assembled a suicide kit from instructions on an internet website, building a device from a plastic bag, elastic bands and a £20 canister of helium gas in 2006. This doesn't in itself sound particularly complicated, but he then went to the further step of buying a video to show him how to use it. Maybe Glen, of Bridgend, Wales, wasn't the brightest tool in the box. His brother Tyrone seemed to agree, saying: "If it wasn't for the internet then my brother would still be alive."

FINAL RESTING PLACE

A bed turned into a coffin for two sisters, trapping them for four days when it fell on top of them. Alice Wardle, 68, and Mildred Bowman, 62, of Gateshead, were resting on a pull-down bed at the Levante Club holiday apartments in Benidorm, Spain, in 2005, when the heavy wooden frame it folded into fell off the wall. The thick wood prevented them from being heard and they eventually suffocated after several days buried alive in the makeshift tomb.

ILL WIND

In what was described as being like a scene from *The Matrix*, a freak wind swept a woman completely off her feet and she whacked her head as she landed in the road. Yung Kiu Wong, 60, was just walking along the road in Manchester, when she was caught in the bizarre gale. Passerby Ben Williams, 37, said it was like a scene from the sci-fi film "where characters fly through the air with apparent ease," and he had to grab hold of her when a second gust threatened to pick her up again. A retiree, Mrs Wong was one of 12 people who died when 80mph storms lashed Britain in January 2007.

DENTAL CALAMITY

Drunken cyclist Charles Lymer, 56, of Derby, died after swallowing his dentures. He was seen holding onto traffic lights, trying to stand up, after a Christmas drink, but had stopped breathing when he was later found in a lay-by with his bike. It is thought he may have panicked after swallowing the dental plate.

TROLLEYED!

Granny Vera Longfield, 86, died after being run down in a supermarket by a toddler pushing a shopping trolley. Vera was shopping at a store in Lancashire, on 4 January 2006, when a youngster steered a trolley into a 6ft high steel stock cage, ramming it into the pensioner and breaking her hip. She died in hospital two days later.

EYE OF THE BEHOLDER

Gardner Kevin Oldham, 30, looked perfectly normal, but suffered from a rare medical condition which made him think he was grotesquely ugly. Body dysmorphic disorder meant every time he looked in the mirror he thought his face was misshapen and hideous. Eventually Kevin, of Cardiff, couldn't take it anymore and hanged himself on 7 December 2004.

FROM TINY ACORNS...

A little scratch on the hand led to window cleaner James Murray, 36, dying from one of the worst cases of toxic shock syndrome doctors had ever seen. Nobody knows how James, of Marske, Cleveland, suffered the scratch in March 2005, but it became infected, and rapidly led to blood poisoning and organ failure.

MOWER MISHAPS

Some places in the globe seem to be hotspots for certain types of ridiculous death. It certainly appears as if Florida is the land of lawnmower accidents that lead to drownings. On average, at least eight gardeners and landscape workers per year die in Florida when mower mishaps end up with their users breathing their last underwater.

In just one fortnight in October 2006, two landscape workers were both found drowned, trapped underwater by their own mowers in separate, but uncannily similar, incidents. Professional lawnmower man Javier Rodriguez, 28, was discovered by a passer-by in Boca Raton who first saw his tractor-style mower partially submerged in a shallow pond. When the passer-by investigated he found that the tractor had pinned Rodriguez under the water. Less than two weeks later, 43-year-old Eugenio Cannuscio died when his mower went too fast down an embankment and flipped over into a pond. The mower fell on top of him, preventing him from moving just enough to mean he drowned in less than half a meter of water.

POLE-AXED!

Booze-fuelled Julian Brooks, 22, unwisely decided to hoist himself up a 22ft wooden flagpole as he walked to a party with friends in Pontypridd, South Wales, in 2005. Naturally the flagpole started bending and Julian fell off. He later died from internal and spinal injuries.

TRANSPLANT TRAUMA

After transplant surgery which should have given him at least 10 more years of life, unlucky Peter Dickinson contracted cancer from his new liver and died 11 months later. Peter, 41, from Morecombe, Lancashire, was jubilant to receive the organ in July 2002, but subsequently developed a rare, gastro-intestinal tumour that could not be treated. Another patient who received a pancreas from the same 26-year-old donor also developed a tumour.

MAD DOG AND ENGLISHMAN

A pit bull terrier savaged his epileptic owner after reacting to the adrenalin he pumped out while having a fit. Window cleaner George Dinham, 47, had collapsed on the floor of his home in Surrey, in May 2003, when Staffordshire Ben lunged at his throat. The dog crushed his windpipe and tore his carotid artery, causing torrential haemorrhaging. It also crushed his Adam's apple. Police dog expert PC Peter Tallack said the dog would have been frightened and confused by the adrenalin, and its natural reaction would have been to attack.

THE END IS NIGH

Committed and possibly committable Christian Jose Ricart was killed on 15 September 1998 while crossing the road in Burgos, Spain. He was carrying a banner proclaiming "The end of the world is nigh."

POO PAN POISON

Must have been a stinker! Fumes from a toilet killed grandfather Alan Wilson, 63, as he looked around a new house in Emerson Valley, Buckinghamshire, in 2002. He was overcome by a deadly vapour formed from cleaning fluid containing 91% sulphuric acid mixed with water in the toilet pan. Seconds after opening the loo door, he clutched his chest and collapsed, and was dead by the time he reached hospital.

BOILING POINT

On 11 March 1998, 45-year-old Marina Yarova was walking her dogs in a Moscow suburb when the ground beneath her collapsed. She was dropped into the underground heat exchanger system, where she was boiled to death.

TOP 10 RIDICULOUS
FOOD-RELATED DEATHS

10. In July 1993, a 23-year-old worker at a sweet factory in Marseilles was crushed to death when a bin containing more than 1,000 kilos of marshmallows accidentally emptied its contents over him.

9. Victor Villenti was a strict vegetarian from South Africa who had managed to avoid eating meat for 32 of his 50 years on the planet. While walking through Cape Town in 1991, a frozen leg of lamb fell from a third-story window ledge, where it had been defrosting, and hit Villenti on the head, killing him instantly.

8. If it is no use crying over spilt milk, it makes even less sense to die over burnt toast. However, that did not stop 68-year-old Francis Buhagiar from Malta shooting his sister Maria dead when she served him an incinerated bread breakfast in 1999.

7. Marlene Corrigan narrowly escaped jail for the death of her 13-year-old daughter Christina, who she had allowed to shoot up to a weight of more than 310 kilos. Christina died due to heart failure related to morbid obesity. When authorities discovered her body it was covered in sores and surrounded by fried chicken and burger boxes.

6. The Rev Claudio Mateo Medina, a 34-year-old Mexican monk from the Franciscan Order, was found dead in the Church of the Holy Sepulchre, Jerusalem. An autopsy revealed he had died from "ingesting excessive food and drink".

5. In 2003, Frenchman Jean-Louis Toubon choked to death after munching down on his girlfriend's edible underwear. Paramedics rushed to his home in Marseilles, but were unable to remove the saucy knickers from his throat.

4. Short-sighted 88-year-old Dennis Verity of Bridgend, Wales, died
    after frying up and eating some daffodil bulbs – which contain the
    poisonous substance narcissine. He thought he had been cooking
    onions.

3. In 1998, teenager Aaron J. Archibald was camping with a group
    of friends in Indianapolis. As they sat around a campfire toasting
    hotdogs and marshmallows, one of Aaron's mates tried to put out
    a burning marshmallow by swinging it around his head. The metal
    part of the toasting fork came loose, flew into Aaron's temple and
    killed him.

2. Food allergies can kill, but for one Californian woman who died from
    anaphylaxis in 1987, she did not even have to eat the shellfish she was
    allergic too. Kathleen Hunt merely smelled a crab and shrimp dish at
    a neighbouring table in a restaurant and suffered fatal anaphylactic
    shock.

1. BUGS BITE BACK
    Deep-fried and battered locusts are a popular snack in many parts
    of Asia and the Middle East, where they are often referred to as 'sky
    prawns'. In 2008, a plague of the bugs swarmed over the United
    Arab Emirates. One farmer, Mohamed Tayyar, feasted on the insects
    as they tried to feast on his crops. He consumed so many that he
    ingested a toxic dose of insecticide residue from the sprays that the
    locusts had been exposed to. Within a few hours of his gorging, he
    was blind, paralysed, raving and eventually dead.

SLIP SLIDING AWAY

A fisherman who tried to slide down a banister slipped over the rail and fell two storeys to the ground. Blair Robinson, 25, of Tauranga, New Zealand, had been drinking with pals at the Meetings Irish Ale House in Gisborne, in September 2006, when the freak accident occurred.

ROLLER SLAYED

Rolling backwards down a hill on rollerblades isn't recommended, even if you're one of Europe's top skaters. Richard Taylor, 23, and two friends were testing their nerve with the stunt near his home in Barry, Wales, in August 2004. They would often wait until the last second before turning round and skating across a junction in the middle of the road, but as Richard took drastic action to dodge a car, he clipped a boot on the kerb and crashed into a concrete lamppost, fracturing his skull and breaking both legs. He died later in hospital.

BOOM!

New boom box speakers in John Twaddell's car were too loud for him to hear a train coming on a railway crossing. The sound system had only been fitted a hour before John, 18, of Christchurch, New Zealand, drove to pick up a friend from the airport, on 8 October 2004. The crossing was controlled by a stop sign and had no alarms, but the stereo was found to have been set at a high volume following the crash.

WACKY WATER WALKERS

In October 1993, nine Tanzanian schoolboys and the priest in charge of them were travelling by canoe across Lake Victoria to a religious celebration.

As they came into view of the shore, witnesses saw them all get out of their craft and fall into the water. Tanzanian police spokesman Alfred Gewe said: "It appears they decided to test their faith by walking on the water like Jesus, but they all drowned."

According to an official spokesman of the Seventh Day Adventist movement: "Normal Adventists would never attempt to test their faith by walking on water." Shame no-one pointed that out to the abnormal ones.

SULPHUR, NOT SO GOOD

An artist died after being knocked out by fumes from a thermal pool. Joanna Paul, 57, from Wanganui, New Zealand, was found floating face down in the Polynesian spa at Rotorua, in May 2003. It is thought she may have collapsed from hydrogen sulphide fumes before drowning. The gas, which gives Rotorua its rotten eggs smell, has been blamed for 11 deaths in the city since 1946, including that of Austrian actress Ellen Umlauf-Rueprecht, who died in her motel room in February 2000.

SNAKES ALIVE, DRUNK DEAD

When workers at the Stravropol Circus mini-zoo in the southern Russian city of Stravropol turned up for work one Monday morning in January 2007, they had an extra reason for the start of the working week blues. Their colleague, 62-year-old Tatyana Mikhanovsky, was lying dead on the floor and a nine-foot python was missing from its cage.

Police who investigated the death discovered strangulation marks and multiple fragments of snakeskin on and around Tatyana's corpse. An official of the local branch of Interior Ministry said: "Autopsy showed the woman had gone into work inebriated. It is obvious this must have played a part in what happened and there is no doubt that the snake strangled her." The python was later found by police and circus workers, and safely returned to its cage.

LIFE EXTINGUISHED

A woman was killed after being hit in the head by a flying fire extinguisher in April 2005. The valve of the extinguisher had been damaged when it fell over in Uhlenberg Haulage in Eltham, New Zealand. The sudden discharge of high pressure gas sent it spinning round on the ground before taking off into the air. It hit 32-year-old Tracy Uhlenberg in the head, before smashing through a corrugated plastic window and coming to rest.

PITCHED AND PUTTED

Freakishly strong winds blew away a tent containing Joanne Davidson, 42, during a storm near Ngakuta Bay in New Zealand, on 9 January 2004. Gales reaching 120mph plucked up the tent, blowing it through the air and dashing her sleeping bag onto concrete before ending up 57 metres away from where it had been pitched. Joanne, from Christchurch, died from multiple high impact injuries.

FRUITY FATE

A New Zealand diplomat accidentally stabbed herself through the heart with a fruit knife she carried in her shoulder bag. Bridget Nichols, 50, the newly appointed deputy high commissioner to the Solomons Islands, tripped while carrying a box of office equipment in March 2002. As she fell, her open bag swung across her body, the small blade penetrating her chest as she hit the ground.

MIXED UP

A cheesemaker died after becoming trapped in a three-storey whey-mixing machine, after either falling or being sucked into a pipe leading to the device. Richard Kinloch, 23, of Matamata, New Zealand, died in March 2002 at the Lichfield factory near Tokoroa, in what was described as a one in a million mishap.

RAMMED

A pet ram charged a woman six times as she crossed a paddock to fetch mail. Doreen Lindsay, 72, was found badly injured at the farm near Levin, New Zealand, on 7 May 2003. The ram, which belonged to her niece, had run at her, knocked her to the ground and shoved her six times into a fence post, puncturing a blood vessel. The ram was destroyed after the attack.

BACKYARD BOTCH-JOB

A dream car became a death trap because the suspension was held together with coathanger wire. Benjamin Oswald, 19, of West Auckland, New Zealand, had carried up backyard modifications to his Honda Civic. This included cutting and rewiring the suspension to lower the vehicle. He lost control whilst driving and died in March 2000. The sub-par modifications were found to be a major contributor to the crash, as they made it both unroadworthy and lethal.

18 'TIL I DIE

Downing three pints of lager, five double whiskies and three double shots in just 40 minutes might have seemed like a good way to celebrate his 18th birthday, but Mark Shields, from Northumberland, couldn't handle the booze and died of acute alcohol poisoning that night, 7 April 2005.

GOING DOWN

Lift engineer James Raynor, 61, had that sinking feeling after losing his driving licence for drink driving in March 1998. He tied a noose to the top of an elevator shaft, stood on the top of the lift and waited in the dark for it to go down. James, of Netherhall, Leicester, was killed when someone called the lift to a lower floor.

MOLTEN MAN

Despite falling into a vat of molten zinc heated to 400°C, Alan Wardour, 52, managed to pull himself out of the liquid metal and only died after an eight hour fight for life. Alan, of Highham, Kent, suffered 100% burns after being completely submerged in the zinc at a galvanising factory in Witham, Essex, in August 1998.

KILLER KITE

A kite surfer was killed after being blown head-long into a sea wall by a freak gust of wind. Alasdair Porter, 38, of Oxford, lost control of his kite and was dragged along the beach at Calshot, near Southampton, in 2003, becoming the first kite surfer to be killed in the UK.

SKEWERED

Hosiery knitter Hardial Singh, 41, was impaled by a broom handle up into the gut after he slipped while resting on it as he tried to open a window in November 1992. The handle perforated his rectal wall and he died from blood clots two weeks later.

SNAKES ALIVE, IDIOT DEAD

When an acquaintance of 48-year-old Ted Dres called round to see him at his home in Hamilton County, Ohio, in December 2006 he got a nasty shock. Finding an open door and not get any response from calling Ted's name, he searched the house. He eventually found his friend's body lying inside the cage of his pet boa constrictor.

A spokesman for the Hamilton County Sheriff's office said: "When officers arrived, they found Dres' 13-foot boa constrictor still wrapped around his neck. We had to call in members of an animal protection group to get the snake off of him."

It later turned out Dres was in the habit of draping the snake around himself when posing for photos. Sometimes it is bloody hard to have sympathy for those who sow the seeds of their own destruction.

KNIGHTS OUT

A jousting tournament went tragically wrong for 54-year-old Paul Allen when a splinter from a wooden lance went through the eye slit of his medieval helmet and into his eye socket. Paul, from Heydon, Hertfordshire, who was taking part in a mock battle at Rockingham Castle, Northamptonshire, in October 2007, died a week later in hospital.

DREAMSCAPE TURNS TO NIGHTMARE

Two women were killed and 13 people injured when a giant inflatable artwork broke its moorings and flew into the air. The walk-in Dreamscape exhibition, which was half the size of a football pitch, was on display in a park in Chester-le-Street, County Durham, in July 2006. A gust of wind blew it into the air and tipped those inside onto the ground, flinging people out before flipping over. Locals Elizabeth Collings, 68, and Claire Furmedge, 38, died after falling out of the exhibit.

CLEAN LIVING

An obsession with personal hygiene proved the downfall of Jonathan Capewell, from Oldham. The 16-year-old was obsessed with smelling fresh and would spray his entire body with deodorant at least twice a day. He died from an internal build-up of propane and butane in October 1998.

SHEESH! KEBABED!

A 31-year-old woman was skewered after slipping onto kitchen knives lying upright in a dishwasher in Airdrie, Lanarkshire, in May 2003. She was taken to hospital, but died shortly after admission.

FEELING RUN DOWN

Allen Spencer, 64, managed to run himself over in a pub car park in August 2003. Allen, 64, from Tolleshunt D'arcy in Essex, was reversing his automatic Nissan Micra with the door open and looking out, but suffered a heart attack and fell from the vehicle under the wheels of the moving car, suffering fatal injuries in the process.

BITING IRONY

A reptile lover dedicated to educating the public about snakes and correcting schoolchildren's misconceptions died after being bitten by an Egyptian cobra. Larry Moor, 45, founder of the British Columbia Association of Reptile Owners, ran screaming into the street at his home in Langley, near Vancouver, but died in seconds in August 1992.

SPUN AND DRIED

Ray Washbrook, 26, foolishly climbed into a giant industrial tumble drier to remove some trapped linen in November 1996, only for it to start with him inside. For 20 minutes his body was thrown around the machine as it reached temperatures of 110°C.

GAGGING FOR SOME FISH

In an attempt to kill it, Harris Simbawa from Zambia bit the head off a fish he caught in the Chengu River. The head became stuck in his throat and Simbawa choked to death when he pushed a stick down his throat to try and dislodge it.

BLOWN AWAY

Winds of up to 90mph picked up pensioner William Taylor, 75, and flung him into the River Almond at Cramond, Edinburgh, in January 1999. William had been walking his dogs when the freakishly strong gales blew him to his death.

SHOCKING BLOW

A karate fanatic was killed by his own punching bag after accidentally wiring it up to the mains. Electrician Ian Norton, 25, from Weston-super-Mare, Somerset, used his know-how to rewire his gym room with new light fittings, but accidentally connected cables to the metal chains from which the bag hung. The rig-up pumped 240 volts through his body when he took a casual punch in August 1999.

PASSION KILLER

Malaysian man Lee Liang Soon escaped a murder charge for smothering his wife with a pillow in 1988. The judge believed his story that his wife suffocated while he was trying to stifle her screams of passion during sex.

THE SPIRIT OF FRIENDSHIP

Azam Ramili, a 37-year-old Malaysian man, beat his friend Koh Ah Wang to death with a metal pole when a magic ritual went wrong in May 2007. Ramili was convinced that Wang could conjure from an anthill a spirit that would provide them with the winning lottery numbers. Wang performed the occult rite, but when a drunken Ramili did not see a spirit rise from the mound, he became enraged and set upon his friend. When Ramili sobered up, he went into town to confess the killing to the police. When his case came to trial, Ramili received an 11-year jail sentence for manslaughter.

MONSTER FISH

A Scottish tourist was dragged out to sea after hooking a giant fish off a pier in Rockingham, Western Australia, in May 1998. The unnamed angler watched in amazement as his line screamed off his reel and jumped into the water after it was torn out of his hands, only to be pulled deep underwater and drowned.

BLADES OF DOOM

A DIY enthusiast was killed when the blade of his electric saw shattered and ricocheted pieces into his neck, severing the arteries. Leslie Pilling, 22, was using the handheld saw to help a friend cut stones in Lanarkshire when pieces of the blade exploded into his neck in June 1997.

DEADLY SLASH

Afghan asylum seeker Saliamin Akrami, 32, escaped persecution by the Taliban in his homeland, only to kill himself by urinating on a live rail, sending 600 volts shooting into the tip of his penis. Saliamin, who was living in Willesden, west London, convulsed and collapsed onto the rail on 23 October 1999.

BED DEAD

A blood transfusion worker died from the traumatic shock of severing the top of a finger after trapping his hand in the metal frame of a camp bed. Bernard O'Reilly, 44, from Lanarkshire, was last seen alive in the early hours of 2 January 2001.

ANOTHER REASON WHY SMOKING CAN KILL YOU

Moscow resident Zhenya Kasevich was smoking outside the doorway of an office block in the city's central business district in 1992 when a large icicle crashed down, piercing her skull and killing her instantly.

NOT STAYING ALIVE

A pub landlord killed himself after refusing to dress in flares and wig for a new seventies theme pub. Donald Cameron, 39, was told to wear the outfit by bosses who took over his former premises in June 1998. But he was adamant he wasn't going to wear the cheesy outfit and gassed himself in his car days after a dummy run for the re-branded venue.

NUPTIALS INFERNO

Church gardener Arthur Handy, 70, turned into a human fireball in front of wedding guests at a church in South Shields, Tyne and Wear, in July 1995. He had filled a lawn mower with petrol to prepare the churchyard for the wedding photographs, but was engulfed by flames after turning on a shed light.

SHORT ENGAGEMENT

Returning home after celebrating popping the question to his girlfriend, chef Pete Holland, 26, fell out of a cab as it pulled up outside their house in Cheltenham, Gloucestershire, in March 2002. He banged his head on the pavement. New fiancée Lisa King, 21, called an ambulance, but Pete died later in hospital.

DUST TO DUST

Welsh grandmother Ann Prydie, 60, wanted to help out while visiting her daughter's family in New Zealand, in December 2000. But she slipped and plunged 18ft to her death while doing the dusting at the luxury split-level home in Auckland. Anne, from Porthcawl, died nine days later from her head injuries.

GAGGING TO GET OUT

According to the US *Journal of Forensic Medicine*, suicide by choking is extremely rare. However, Japanese murder suspect Chika Mashimaro managed to stuff herself with toilet paper to the point where she choked her way out of any chance of a life sentence.

EYE EYE!

A physical education teacher taking an athletics session at Liverpool College, lost his footing and pierced his eye with the blunt end of a javelin. Jon Desborough, 41, fell into a coma following the accident in May 1999 and died several weeks later. Ouch.

WHOOPS!

Two Scots on a Blackpool stag weekend posed for a photo along the seafront, only to be swept to their deaths by a freak wave. Barry Bryce, 23, and Scott Hunter, 33, from West Lothian, stopped to take a picture on the famous promenade on the morning of 27 May 2006. But as they prepared to snap away, one of the men was suddenly caught by the stormy sea and, when his pal went to save him, both men were smashed against the sea wall. They should have had a lie-in...

LAST TANGO

Paramedics in Lisbon rushed to treat Alberto Fargo when he fell five storeys from a building and landed in the street bellow in 1998. Unfortunately, the dance teacher's injuries were too severe and he was dead before they had a chance to take him to hospital. Alberto had been teaching his students how to hold their heads up whilst dancing the tango and had inadvertently tangoed straight out of an open window.

AMONG FRIENDS

When Roman Catholic priest Father Liam Cosgrove died in a sauna in 1994, he received the last rites from two other priests who also frequented the establishment. Sauna staff said the late father was a regular visitor.

TOP 10 RIDICULOUS MOTORING-RELATED DEATHS

10. A female driver from Arapahoe County, Colorado, died whilst driving in Denver in February 1996. Fixing her makeup as she travelled along the highway, a car swerving in front of her forced her to brake sharply and the lipstick she was using flew into her mouth. It became lodged in her windpipe and she choked to death before anyone could come to her assistance.

9. Two South Korean lorry drivers died after crashing into each other on Route 1 – the main highway between Seoul and Pusan. Although unharmed, they got out of their cabs to argue with each other and were both run over by a city-to-city bus.

8. Hong Kong truck driver Ling Yi-hung spent so much time in gridlocked traffic in April 1997 that he was fatally overcome by carbon monoxide in the cab of his vehicle.

7. Retired lieutenant colonel Donna Jo Norder died as she drove into MacDill Air Force Base, Florida, in 2000. A malfunctioning security barrier came up under her Pontiac as she drove over it, causing her airbags to deploy and crush her.

6. If you thought being in your car at least made you safe from animal attack, think again. Two passengers died driving in a car near the Iranian town of Khaf in 2001 when an eagle flying overhead dropped a cobra into the vehicle. The snake promptly bit them.

5. Motorist Ray Langston was so determined not to be parted from his car keys that when they fell down a drain, in September 1996, he squeezed through the 48cm space to retrieve them. Unfortunately for

the 41-year-old from Detroit, he became pinned headfirst in the drain and drowned.

4. Skitch is a term used to describe the illegal act of being pulled along by a car while on roller-skates or a skateboard. Ian Henderson, a 19-year-old from California, decided to skitch a lift on a passing jeep in 2003. His grip on the vehicle was beaten off by its driver, causing Henderson to slam into the tarmac at high-speed.

3. Bobbi Jameson was driving in Ontario in 1986 when she discovered that she had an unwanted passenger in her back seat – an angry squirrel which leapt onto her back and became entangled in her hair. This bushy-tailed rodent distraction was too much for Jameson, who swerved off the road and into a highway sign. She was killed instantly.

2. Five motorists were killed in 2001 by rockslides on the roads between the Russian cities of Adler and Krasnaya Polyana. The rockslides were caused by Caucasian bears, which started killing cattle by rolling rocks down mountains, before moving on to cars. A local hunter said: "The bears are bad. They do it just for entertainment."

1. BLACK DOG
In folklore, a black dog is an omen of ill luck and a portent of death. It certainly turned out that way for 40-year-old Kelly Cordry when he motorcycled home along the highway outside of Commerce City, Colorado, in July 1993. As Kelly passed under a railway bridge, a 20-kilo stray black dog fell onto him, causing him to lose control of his bike, cross the central reservation and steer straight into oncoming traffic. He was hit by a truck and died instantly. The dog was injured, but lived to see another day.

FAST RESPONSE

Anthony Hall's bizarre obsession with ambulances and police cars led him to jump in front of emergency vehicles on their way to 999 calls. But the 45-year-old's cheap thrills came to an end when he was hit by a fast-response paramedic's car in Nottingham in 2008.

DIDN'T TAKE IT LION DOWN

A wildlife lover was mauled by lions while on safari in Zimbabwe, after failing to zip his tent door shut. David Pleydell-Bouverie, 19, fled from the tent after a lion stuck its head in. He ran away with the big cat in hot pursuit, following the attack in 1999. He was later found dead nearby. Tourists had been warned to zip up their tents and keep a whistle nearby to alert guides, neither of which David, from Bedfordshire, had remembered to do.

CHRISTIAN SPIRIT?

A fundamentalist Christian stabbed a fellow backpacker to death in a row about evolution versus creationism. Alexander York, 33, from Essex, attacked Rudi Boa, 28, a student from Inverness, while on a fruit-picking trip in New South Wales in Australia, in January 2006. The drunken row escalated to the point where York stabbed Boa with a kitchen knife, killing him instantly.

LOVE STRUCK

Adulterous pair Tomas Gormann and Maria Tlek snuck some time alone on Gormann's boat out on Steinhuder Meer, Lower Saxony's biggest lake. Their dead bodies were found fused together after by being struck by lightning. Almost romantic, really.

IN THE PINK

Alcoholic Rodney Jones, 30, was found with his hair cut into a Mohican and insults smeared over his body in bright pink lipstick. Rodney had passed out at a wild house party in Cwmbran, South Wales, in October 2000. He was then stripped, smeared with jam and given to a dog to lick off. Rodney was then dressed and dragged 20ft from the house to the door of a community centre. A post mortem revealed he had died from a cocktail of booze and heroin.

COPYCAT JUMPERS

The double death-plunge of two men from the eighth floor of a hotel bedroom in August 1999 was almost identical to a similar tragedy filmed in the building for hit TV crime series *Cracker*. Guests at the Renaissance Manchester Hotel heard a noise like two gunshots as the two 21-year-old men hit a concrete floor more than 100ft below. The hotel featured in *Cracker*, starring Robbie Coltrane, when rape charge detective Jimmy Beck leapt out of a window still handcuffed to a suspect. The men would have had to climb through a narrow waist-height window onto a narrow window sill to get out of their room.

ACCOUNT CLOSED

The advertising executive responsible for resurrecting the Ovalteenies in the 1970s ended his life naked in a dank underground water-chamber beneath his garden, his hands tied behind his back. Christopher Martin was found lying face-down in less than three inches of rainwater on 26 July 1995, with no obvious signs of injury. Police investigations failed to determine any motive for his death. Except, perhaps, revenge for the ad campaign.

LOO CRUSH

Student accommodation is never spacious, but a lack of room rarely proves fatal. Unfortunately for bio-chemistry student Lisa Nicholls, 18, the cramped bathroom in her room at James College, York University, was to be her undoing in September 2003. She fell whilst getting off the toilet in the 6.5ft by 3.5ft room, was knocked out when her head hit the sink, ended up bent double with her feet in the shower and her head under the sink, and suffocated as a result.

GOING OUT WITH A BANG

Vlad Cazacu was a 43-year-old fire-eater starring at the Big Top in Bucharest. On the matinee performance on 23 January 1998, Vlad accidentally swallowed some paraffin. When he belched while performing his act, his burp contained flammable vapours which his flaming stick ignited, leading to an explosion which blew him to bits from the inside.

Fellow circus troupe member Nicolae Antosu said: "It was the most terrible thing I have ever seen. He belched, then there was a flash of light. Some of the audience thought it was part of the act, but he was blown to bits. I pray to God for him." As a mark of respect, the evening performance of the circus was cancelled.

KILLED FOR A COCK

While we have had a great deal of empathy and sympathy for some of the tragedies brought about by the ridiculous deaths this book chronicles, it is impossible to shed a tear for Edwin Bangod. The 35-year-old resident of Makati City in the Philippines was engaged in cockfighting with his neighbour Ferdie But. However, when But's rooster rather sensibly ran away rather than fight an opponent with blades attached to its legs, Bangod became incensed. He attempted to strangle But, screaming that his victim was: "A coward just like his worthless cock." But defended himself by pulling out a machete and slicing Bangod to death – a fate that would have befallen on one of the fowls if But's cock had not been so chicken.

SHOCKING BEHAVIOUR

Whatever turns you on... Arthur Sharland, 77, from Shepherd's Bush, London, spent most of his life plugging himself into the mains for the thrill of it. He electrocuted himself to death in August 1989 and was found with two crocodile clips attaching bare electric wires to his chest, his body a mass of tiny scars from his years of abuse. Must have been the power...

POWERFUL PUNCH

Hard man Walter Hallas, 26, from Leeds, had a lifelong fear of dentists and asked pal Mark Waldron to cure his toothache by punching out a painful tooth. Unfortunately, the blow knocked him to the ground and he fractured his skull on the concrete floor. He died in hospital six days later, in November 1979.

THE LUCK OF THE IRISH

According to superstition, horseshoes are meant to be totems guaranteeing luck. However, for 84-year-old James 'Locky' Bryne of County Kilkenny in the Republic of Ireland, nothing could have been less providential.

As Byrne was driving along a lane near his home, he hit a piece of tape a farmer had stretched across the road. It was there to prevent the farmer's cattle straying when he was herding them from one field to another. One end of the tape was weighted with a horseshoe that was strung over the branch of a tree. When Bryne's car hit the tape and stretched it, the horseshoe was flung lose and came crashing through one of the car's side windows. It struck Locky on the temple, killing him instantly.

TIME TWISTED

A 21-year-old woman from the aptly-named Barking in Essex became convinced she was in a relationship with a businessman living in the 1600s. She lay down in front of a train in 1981, to reunite herself with her time-lost lover.

POT SHOT

Arvin Jah, a 48-year-old Indian businessman, was walking to work in New Delhi one morning in April 2000, when he was killed by a plant pot. It had been thrown from the sixth floor balcony of a block of flats – by a monkey.

SIGN OF THE TIMES

A 20-year-old man from Edinburgh hanged himself in July 1996 at Western Hailes railway station following a row with his girlfriend. Aptly, he chose the 'Way Out' sign to do it.

BRUSH OFF

It was an unpleasant end for 72-year-old Joan Davies, from Little Chalfont, Buckinghamshire. She slipped in her bathroom and impaled herself on the bog brush, sending it straight through her eye and into her brain.

DEATH'S A BEACH

Daniel Jones, a 21-year-old resident of Woodbridge, Virginia, died when his trip to the beach went awry in August 1997. Bothered by the wind at Outer Banks Beach in Buxton, North Carolina, Jones dug a 2.5 metre hole to protect him from the elements as he lounged on his beach chair.

Unfortunately, Jones was no architect or master builder. The hole collapsed. Fellow visitors to the beach were unable to dig him out and by the time the emergency services arrived with heavy earth-moving equipment, they found themselves exhuming a grave.

POSSESSED?

Something wasn't quite right about the death of Rear-Admiral Versturme at his home in Falmouth in January 1988. After enjoying dinner with his wife, he stirred up the fire with a poker before plunging it three or four times into his own bowels. As he lay dying, he blamed the whiskey.

MORAL HIGH GROUND

Religion drives people to do the strangest things. After learning a close friend was having an affair, a 41-year-old man from Norton, Yorkshire, tied a chainsaw between the branches of a tree, jammed it on and beheaded himself after walking directly into it.

LAWN BLOWER

Alabama resident Larry McAnally was exercising his dog whilst sitting on his lawnmower in 1999. A freak build-up of gasoline fumes caused the mower to explode. Both man and dog died, and debris was scattered into gardens up to 40 metres away.

THE BIG SLEEP

Irishman Thomas Brady was stabbed to death with a sharpened table knife while incarcerated at Dublin's Mountjoy Prison in 2000, because his constant, loud snoring drove his cellmate insane.

KEEP IT DOWN!

Noisy neighbours proved too much for John Vanderstam, 46, from Birmingham. Constant loud music and domestic disputes drove him to kill himself in November 1997. Coroner Dr Richard Whittington said he died from an assault on his eardrums.

DIGESTIVE DISTURBANCE

A post mortem examination of a 37-year-old machinist from Birmingham, revealed the cause of the abdominal pains which had led to her demise. Her missing false tooth and attached dental plate were found lodged in her inflamed lower colon. She thought she had lost it when it went missing three months earlier.

WHO'S THE DADDY NOW?

A 10-year-old boy from New Jersey killed his father in March 2000 by stabbing him with a kitchen knife. The lad's father had put the blade in his son's hands and goaded him to do it during an argument over a slice of cake missing from the refrigerator.

ELECTRIC SHOCK

Sanoon Thammakai was a 47-year-old farmer in the Thai province of Ayutthaya. He died from a heart attack caused when he opened his electricity bill in February 1997. Thammakai was so used to paying around 200 baht per month for his energy usage that seeing a bill for 19,249 baht triggered a coronary. Residents in his village said that they too had received ludicrous bills by mistake, but none of them had taken the power company seriously enough to drop dead.

LICKED!

After drinking twice the legal driving limit of booze, a cocky teenager in Littlehampton, West Sussex, boasted to pals that he could lick the live rail of a railway line But as the 16-year-old bent down a spark leapt from the 750-volt rail and he was fried.

TAMPON TRAGEDY

A DIY snoring cure killed 27-year-old Mark Gleeson, of Headley Down, Hampshire, in 1996. Obese Mark suffered from an incurable snoring problem, so he stuffed two tampons up his nostrils to try and stifle the noise. Unfortunately he suffocated in his sleep.

NOT VERY N-ICE

At her home in Dundee, Kareen Docherty was busy scraping ice off the windscreen of her car when it slipped down her driveway and dragged her underneath. Kareen, who was in her 40s, had left the engine running. Her head, abdomen and an arm were squashed under the wheels as it rolled down the sloping drive in January 2003.

BAD TOW

Birmingham man John Aldron, 63, was doing a friend a favour by towing his car to the garage on 25 September 1999. When the tow rope became detached, he stopped to fix it. Unfortunately he was directly under the front of the car when another vehicle careered into it, having failed to spot the stationery cars. He died from severe head injuries.

SHED DEAD

Retirement ended before it began for Noel Lumley in March 2008. He decided to spend the first day of the next phase of his life by pottering around in the garden shed at his home in Dublin. Unfortunately he sparked a freak fire which sent the wooden building up in flames.

DUNG IN

The life of K.J. Kanga, a student in Accra in Ghana, came to an end in 2007 when his urgent need to answer a call of nature led him into extreme action. Rather than wait in line at a public toilet, Kanga went behind the latrine and succeeded in prising the lid off its septic tank. However, while emptying his bowels, he overbalanced and toppled into the tank, which contained more than 400 litres of urine as well solid waste. One of Kanga's friends who had seen the unfortunate accident raised the alarm, but it was too late. Kanga was well and truly in the shit and all that was left for sanitation workers to do was retrieve his corpse.

BIN AND GONE

Rubbish collector John Moffat was killed after being crushed under his own garbage wagon. John, 51, had been collecting household waste in Morpeth and had walked round to the front of the truck when it rolled forwards over him. He died from his injuries following the accident in January 2006.

THE GAME OF DEATH

Lee Seung Seop has gone down in history as the first recorded fatality attributable to an addiction to internet gaming. The 28-year-old boiler repairman came from Daegu, South Korea. His acknowledged addiction to a game had already cost him his girlfriend and job. Instead of dealing with his problem by giving up internet gaming, Lee merely switched games.

In August 2005, Lee went to a local internet café and began a marathon stint playing a huge online sci-fi game. After playing for more than 50 hours straight, he went into cardiac arrest brought on by exhaustion and dehydration. A friend of Lee's commented: "He was a fool and an addict. Everyone knew about his problem, but he just could not stop himself."

SHALLOW GRAVE

A woman drowned in just 12 inches of water after tripping and falling head first into her ornamental pond. Rachel Greenaway, 32, was knocked unconscious when she hit her head in the accident, at her cottage in Bobbington, Staffordshire, in June 2000.

EMPTY KILLER

A runaway car ploughed into Leo Scurr, 56, as he made his way to work in Newcastle. The owner of the driverless car is believed to have left the handbrake off and it rolled away out of control before hitting Leo in November 2005.

JOB DONE IN

Self-employed builder Mark Jones, 39, was demolishing an outbuilding at his home near Dudley, Birmingham, in August 2004. Unfortunately when he went to check his work, the roof collapsed on top of him, burying him under concrete.

TOP 10 RIDICULOUS MARRIAGE-RELATED DEATHS

10. Ukrainian Alena Luchak from Alushta was so fed up with her husband's constant demands for sex that she began dosing his hot drinks with sleeping pills. Unfortunately for Mr Luchak, one night she misjudged the dosage and sent him into the big sleep itself.

9. New Delhi resident Raju Yadav was killed by his wife Tarucknisha in 1999 when she flew into a rage after he asked her for a second cup of tea before she was ready to serve it.

8. Vietnamese woman Siek Phan had been married to her husband for more than 40 years. However, when he crept up behind and tickled her as she chopped wood, she reacted instinctively and swung her axe at him, almost completely taking off his head.

7. Jackie Johnson from Kentucky argued with his wife about who should walk the dog. She lost the argument, but he was the bigger loser when he settled down on his sofa at the exact moment a boulder fell 300 metres down a cliff and crushed him in his mobile home.

6. The French have a reputation for strong expressions of emotion, so it is not surprising to learn that when Marguerite Girard from Alpes-Maritimes discovered her husband was having an affair, she did not take it calmly. Instead, she hit him over the head with her pet turtle, killing him instantly.

5. If marriage itself was not enough of a fatal prospect, some wedding day customs can lead to death. The Afghani tradition of celebrating nuptials by firing rifles into the sky took a deadly turn in July 2002, when the US military mistook celebratory rifle fire from a wedding party as an attack and bombed 48 party guests into oblivion.

4. Another wedding custom led to death when German-born Amy Weltz responded to the surprise of her new Australian husband smearing of wedding cake in her face by picking up a champagne bottle and hitting him over the head with it. The blow caused a rupture and her poor husband did not live to see the honeymoon.

3. In 2001, Iranian bridegroom Behrouz Rafi licked honey off the fingers of his bride Afsar, only to choke to death on one of her false nails. Afsar fainted from shock and was rushed to hospital. The ancient Persian tradition of newlyweds licking honey from each other's fingers is meant to ensure that married life starts together sweetly.

2. In February 1998, during a heated argument, Argentinian Juan Taphanel pushed his wife Celeste from the window of their eighth floor apartment in a Buenos Aires suburb. Celeste landed on some telephone wires and in an attempt to dislodge her, Juan fell to his death.

1. THE OLD BALL AND CHAIN
David Godin of Novia Scotia was returning from his stag party in 1992 when his car veered off the road and into a lake. Although his body contained a high level of alcohol, police blamed his failure to avoid drowning on the fact that his friends had attached an authentic 19th century ball and chain to his left leg.

STAIRWAY TO HEAVEN

A pensioner died after a man tried to clean his boots on the brushes of a moving escalator at Snow Hill Railway Station in Birmingham, in 2002. The laces of his boots jammed in the mechanism and triggered the emergency stop button, bringing the escalator to a sudden halt. Teresa Connolly, 77, from Leamington Spa, fell over and fractured her knee in three places. Despite an operation, she died four months later from an infection.

FUNERAL FATALITIES

Two men died in a freak accident at the funeral of a friend in County Limerick, Ireland, in November 2004. They were electrocuted trying to install temporary floodlights at the house of tragic car crash victim Billy Sheehan, 21. A nearby field was being used as a car park because of the large number of mourners expected and the men were hit by a massive shock as a tower light they were moving hit an overhead power cable.

FINAL OVER

Cricket veteran Jack Swain, 73, marked the last bowl of his retirement match by keeling over and dying at his club in Cuckfield, Sussex, in September 1995.

MIDSUMMER MADNESS

There is one time and place guaranteed to produce at least one ridiculous death every year – midsummer's eve in Finland. The celebrations surrounding the midnight sun see most of the country swept up in a drunken party mood which always ends up with dozens of idiotic, booze-related fatalities. According to Chief Inspector Seppo Mantyla of the Helsinki Police: "There's just something about the Finnish psyche that makes for this midsummer madness and the death that follows."

The most ridiculous midsummer death to come out of Finland in recent years was that of Jani Mikkonen. Having managed to set himself ablaze while drunkenly dancing around a bonfire, he ran straight into the nearest lake to try and put himself out, and quickly drowned. One of Mikkonen's drunken friends, Fredrik Lehtinen, rushed into the lake to retrieve the wallet from his body and also drowned.

A spokesman for the Finnish tourist board said: "Visitors should not stay away from Finland just because of the high number of accidents at midsummer. We do not like this phrase 'midsummer madness', and people should remember that although there can be many deaths, they are all stupid and related to drunkenness. People kill themselves accidentally at this time; they are not trying to kill tourists." Well, that's reassuring to hear, isn't it?

ATTACK OF THE KILLER SQUIRREL

A builder working at the top of a ladder in Quinton, Birmingham, fell to his death after being savaged by a squirrel. The pesky vermin had jumped out of the guttering and bitten the 61-year-old workman in the face, causing him to lose his footing and fall. According to a colleague, his last words were: "Get off! Get off!"

EAR TODAY, GONE TOMORROW

A successful operation in Bordeaux to cure deafness in one ear left solicitor Linda Harvey, 44, with an incurable tinnitus after cabin pressure on the flight home suddenly dropped and damaged her inner ear. It was so bad it drove her to jump to her death from a hotel room in Hastings in 1997.

FOR WHOM THE BELL TOLLS...

A bellringer used his own bell rope to hang himself in the village of Sheen, near Buxton, in England's Peak District, in April 1998. Geoff Birch, 52, Captain of Bells at St Luke's Church, also made sure to silence the bells first so nobody would hear his last peal.

MAD AS A BOX OF SNAKES

A Scottish computer expert found dead in a rental car in Little Rock, Arkhansas, had just collected a box of killer snakes. Garrick Wales, 48, from Renfrewshire, was found dead on 13 May 2004 in a rubbish strewn lane. A box of highly poisonous snakes with his name on top was later found on a roadside verge half a mile away. Strangely, no evidence of a snakebite was found on his body.

BUTT OUT

Farmer James McKenzie, 77, from Inverurie, Aberdeenshire, had his neck broken after being butted by a cow as he tried to get to her calf. Left paralysed, he died of pneumonia in hospital months later.

ISN'T IT IRONIC?

Susie Stephens' work on pedestrian and cycling issues had earned her the title of one of America's foremost experts on street safety. As the director of the Bicycle Alliance of Washington, the 36-year-old campaigner had helped bring the Bicycle and Pedestrian Safety Education Act into force and was the founder of the Thunderhead Alliance, a national campaign group on pedestrian and cyclist safety.

In March 2002, Stephens was attending a safety conference in St Louis, Missouri, when she crossed a road to photocopy some papers. However, a bus driver failed to yield to Stephens on a crosswalk, hitting her and dragging her under his vehicle where she was crushed to death. A fellow director of the Thunderhead Alliance commented: "It's gut-wrenching that someone who spent so much of her life fighting to reduce pointless tragedy on the streets of America is now a pedestrian death statistic."

FATAL STINK

Farmer Alex Millar, 63, and his assistant, Scott Herries, 23, fell unconscious after inhaling poisonous gases from a slurry pit on the outskirts of Dumfries, Scotland, as they tried to rescue a cow. They then fell into the pit and drowned.

FORKING PAINFUL!

Farmer William Salter, 68, was impaled on a tractor fork when its brakes failed near Slains, Aberdeenshire, in 2002. Yowsers!

HERMITS' HANGING HORROR

Reclusive twins Kevin and Paul Dane were just 20, but lived like hermits, only coming out at night when the rest of their family was in bed. So when their mum told them to go and sign on the dole, they hatched a double suicide bid in 2001. Unfortunately, although Paul helped Kevin successfully hang himself from the ceiling of their home in Carlisle, he failed in an attempt to strangle himself with his own belt, and was later found guilty of aiding and abetting his brother's suicide.

CLEAN SHOT

Bryan Borsa was cleaning his Chinese-made SKS rifle in a friend's apartment in Derry, New Hampshire, in 1994. Although he had failed to unload the gun for cleaning, Borsa was shocked when the gun discharged. It shot a bullet straight through the ceiling that then kept travelling all the way through the heart of Richard Brockway, who was watching TV on the sofa in the apartment above.

Although no criminal charges were brought against Bryan Borsa, the lawyers for Richard Brockway's widow Margaret managed to obtain $840,000 in an out-of-court settlement from the gun's manufacturers.

CHANCE MEETING

Neighbours Christina Owens, 44, and Douglas Hislop, 31, lived only eight doors apart in the quiet Scottish village of Aberfoyle, but were no more than casual acquaintances. They didn't know they were both going on holiday to Fort William in July 1999, but ended up colliding with each other on a notorious stretch of the A82. Christina died instantly, but Douglas survived with minor injuries. His uncle Robert Telfer said: "It is hard to believe that they crashed into each other when they were so far away from home."

METAL MUNCHER

When Charles Williams, 59, was found dead in his bedroom at his home in Kensington, Liverpool, in 2001, the fact that he was wearing a large dog chain and collar was bizarre enough. But pathologist Dr Alan Williams found he had ingested 26 5p coins, five 1p coins, 14 safety pins and 200 air rifle pellets. He had died from peritonitis caused by the perforation of the stomach by his unnatural meal.

WHAT'S COOKING?

Daniel McMillan dug himself a shallow grave in the outskirts of a derelict mansion in Granton, Scotland, before soaking himself in petrol and handcuffing himself. He then lay down, pulled a metal lid over his grave and set fire to himself, burning to death horribly in his self-made furnace. The 37-year-old's blazing body was discovered in the ditch by police officers on a routine patrol in July 2004.

EXORCIST EXIT

Self-styled 'Witch King' Teodoro Martinez and six members of his cult died in 2000 while performing an exorcism of a teenager in Mexico City. The mixture of coal and incense burnt during the ritual gave off carbon monoxide, poisoning them all.

'ELLO, 'ELLO, 'ELLO...

Police constable Andrew Rennie, 44, was found hanged wearing women's clothing. PC Rennie, from Aldridge, was discovered on 26 August 2001 after failing to show up on his beat. He was found suspended on a convoluted system of ropes and supports, clad in ladies' clothing and a wig as part of a sex game which obviously went wrong.

A ROD FOR HIS OWN BACK

A metal walking pole isn't the best option when you're rambling through open countryside, as hillwalker Derek Hunter, 40, found out when it became a makeshift lightning rod. The aluminium pole attracted a single bolt of lightning as Derek climbed Ben Oss mountain in Stirlingshire, in May 2004, killing him instantly.

KILLER WORKOUT

Exercise is supposed to be good for you. Try telling that to Christine Bromwich, 56, who died after tumbling off a cross-trainer during a workout at her local gym. She had been working out in Chelmsford, Essex, on 3 November 2005, when she keeled over, smashing her head on a radiator and dying in hospital the next day.

BULLET WITH HIS NAME ON

As the film franchise *Final Destination* illustrates, nobody escapes the Grim Reaper forever. Oregon student Richard Peek Jr, 19, survived a school massacre in America because a backpack of books stopped a fatal bullet. But it seemed he was always meant to die from a gunshot, as 18 months after the tragedy of 20 May 1998, Richard was accidentally shot by his brother Robert while hunting deer. As they crouched down to hide from a deer, the hammer on Robert's rifle either slipped or caught on his clothing, firing off a round and hitting his brother next to him. Destiny came calling.

SLAYING DRAGONS

Wealth, privilege and an impressive sounding title are no protection when the reaper comes calling, as Swiss baron Rudolf von Reding Biberegg discovered when he went hiking with friends on Komodo Island in Indonesia in 1974. As the name suggests, the island is home to the fearsome monitor lizard also known as the Komodo dragon – a giant reptile of up to three meters in length which can sprint after its prey at 25 kilometres per hour.

Feeling in need of a rest after a few miles of walking, the Baron sat down on a rock and waved his friends on, despite warnings from their guide about the danger posed by dragons if he stayed out alone. When his companions returned all they could find of the Baron was his broken camera, some torn clothing and a bloody shoe.

YELLOW PERIL

Sarah Hulphers, a 20-year-old volunteer at Yellowstone National Park, and two of her friends decided to take a moonlit dip in one of the park's many pools. Unfortunately, in the dark they picked a volcanic hot spring and Sarah was boiled alive.

DEADLY DRIP

The simple household chore of fixing a water leak proved a shocking experience for 22-year-old Emma Shaw of West Bromwich. The leak flooded a cupboard containing electrical contacts, giving her a fatal charge on 14 December 2007.

TRUNK TRIP

Sometimes people just ask for trouble. Daniel Paling, 17, of Solihull died from fatal head injuries after falling from the trunk of a moving car in July 2003. Driver Charmine Beedie, 19, had told him to get off the car and thought he'd done so until she saw him hit the ground in her rear view mirror, by which point she was going at almost 30mph. She was cleared of any responsibility for his stupidity.

THE LAST PICTURE SHOW

After a heavy day boozing, alcoholic Anthony Stubbs, 55, of Huddersfield returned home in a drunken daze on 4 November 2007. But as he stumbled down the stairs after going to the toilet, he knocked a picture off the wall as he fell, shattering it into pieces, with shards of glass embedding themselves in his neck. He was so drunk that he did not realize how serious his injuries were and he bled to death.

OVERBLOWN END

An apprentice tyre fitter was blown across a garage yard when a 5ft digger tyre he was working on exploded in his face. The 19-year-old, from Lanarkshire, suffered serious head and face injuries. One man at the scene of the accident in May 2005 said: "It was like a bomb going off."

SLIPPED DISC

A DIY enthusiast died after almost chopping his own leg off with an angle grinder. Claude Jones, 64, from Holywell, Flintshire, was working on dismantling a car on 26 April 2003, when part of the disc from the grinder flew off and tore through his thigh muscle and femoral artery. He tried to tie a makeshift tourniquet around his leg, but died in minutes. The disc had been designed for use on a fixed machine, not a portable grinder, so this was one case of the workman being right to blame his tools.

SHORT LOAN

Vicar Thomas Jones, 69, was hiring an automatic Vauxhall Cavalier from a garage in Llanelli. He was being shown the controls to the loan car when it slipped into reverse, hitting him in the head with the open driver's door in January 1998.

CRUSHED BY HER GROCERY

A supermarket travelator proved fatal for 73-year-old Betty Baucke, from Auckland, New Zealand. She was visiting her birthplace of Christchurch and had been grocery shopping with her husband at a shopping mall on 14 January 2005. They pushed the trolley onto the travelator and stood behind it to be carried up to the next floor, presuming it had been locked in place. But about half-way up it rolled backwards, toppled over and crashed into Betty, causing fatal head injuries when the trolley and contents fell on top of her. The locking mechanism was found to have failed.

MISER MISERY

Concerned neighbours of reclusive 81-year-old Amigdalia Balta broke into her home on the Greek Island of Euboea only to discover an emaciated corpse. She had starved to death despite good health and having more than $700,000 dollars in her bank account.

DIGGER DEATH

A 35-tonne digger went runaway after falling off a low-loader transporter, before crossing a trunk road and ploughing into a motorist making her way home. Christina Fraser, 24, from Arabella, near Tain, Ross-shire, died instantly in July 2006 after the digger appeared from nowhere and hit her car.

PISSING UP THE WRONG TREE

When Detective-Sergeant Daniel Edwards failed to return calls on his radio on the afternoon of 29 August 1997, colleagues from the Fish Hoek police station near Cape Town began to search for him. They eventually found the dead body of their fellow officer trapped between a tree and his patrol car. According to a senior office on the force, Captain Jaques Wiese, Sergeant Edwards had parked his car on an incline and got out to answer a call of nature. His vehicle then rolled down the slope, crushing him between his vehicle and the tree he was urinating against.

MIND THE DOORS, PLEASE!

A bus driver died when his head became trapped in the automatic doors of his bus. James McKay, 64, from Magherafelt, Ireland, had been driving to collect schoolchildren in September 2003, when he was found wedged in the pneumatic doors of his stationary bus by a passing construction worker. He had either fallen, tripped or collapsed as the doors closed, and was killed by the pressure on his neck.

DOWN THE DRAIN

New York City maintenance man Archie Tyler was standing in 60cm of water while clearing rubbish from a reservoir drain in the Bronx in 2001 when his unclogging caused a water vortex, dragging him down a 50cm-wide pipe, where he drowned.

HOUSEWORK HORROR

A house-proud pensioner set herself on fire as she dusted around her fireplace on 26 January 2004. The 80-year-old woman, from Kilgarven, Ireland, had just lit a fresh fire when she decided to tidy around the hearth, only to catch her clothes on the flames – perhaps when she tried to reach an awkward spot?

COLD END FOR CAVEMEN

Jake Shurnway and Robert Carr were two college students from Hopkington in New Hampshire who loved snowboarding. In March 2000, they travelled to the Stratton Mountain Ski Resort in Vermont to see the US Open Snowboarding competition. Unlike other students who travelled to the event and economised on motel costs by sleeping in cars and vans,

Jake and Robert decided to build a snow cave to sleep in at the edge of a parking lot.

Tragically for the boys, while they slept, a bucket loader was clearing snow to create more parking spaces. It dumped one of its loads of snow on their cave, collapsing it and smothering them. Their crushed and frozen bodies were found in the morning. The obvious lesson? Saving money can cost lives.

TV KILLS – FACT!

Student Nicola Cattle, 17, died in 2005 after being hit by a flying TV. She was a passenger in the back seat of a friend's car when he had a head-on smash. The 32in TV catapulted from the boot and straight into Nicola. She couldn't very well say there was nothing on.

MILK SHAKE

Milk delivery vans aren't exactly renowned for being vehicles of death. However, when one was shunted by a car in the Black Country on 30 April 2001, it mounted the pavement and fatally pinned a 24-year-old milkman's assistant to a wall. More than a case of just crying over spilt milk then...

SMOKED OUT

Passive smoking can kill and here's the proof. Jenna O'Keefe, 17, went to sit on a window ledge to avoid cigarette smoke at a party in Coatbridge, Lanarkshire. She lost her balance and fell more than 150ft to her death in 2003.

TOP 10 RIDICULOUS
PET-RELATED DEATHS

10. While the old story of Catherine the Great of Russia being fatally crushed while engaging in dubious activities with her favourite horse is pure myth, at least one royal ruler has suffered a ridiculous pet-related death. Alexander, King of Greece, died in 1920 as a result of a bite on the ankle from his pet monkey when he stepped in to break up a fight between his simian pal and his favourite dog.

9. Michigan woman Maxine Ann Keggerreis tried to save time by exercising her dog while riding her lawn mower. Unfortunately the dog's leash became caught up in the mower, sending machine, dog and owner into a pond, from which only the mower was retrieved in a working fashion.

8. In 1992, Venetian Giorgio Scrimin tried to silence a howling cat which was keeping him awake by shooing it away with a broom. As the cat leapt away from him it dislodged a roof tile, which fell and hit him on the head, killing him instantly.

7. Given that the official advice of America's Humane Society is not to own a python as they are aggressive, dangerous and do not make good pets, it is hard to feel sorry for Robert Paulerson from Florida. The body of the 32-year-old owner of five pythons was discovered in 1999 with fang marks on his forehead and one of his 3.4-metre pets wrapped around his suffocated form.

6. Vichai Thongto, a 30-year-old from the province of Ratchaburj in western Thailand, died in April 1997 while feeding his four pet peacocks. One of the male birds leapt up at him and clawed his head, causing a blood clot which killed him less than two hours later.

5. Harald Loosen, a 68-year-old resident of Bonn, Germany, collapsed from a heart attack in his home in 1995. His pet rottweiler Otto's aggressive behaviour kept paramedics at bay for long enough to ensure that it was too late for them to save its owner's life.

4. Police in Yekaterinburg in central Russia were called out late one night in 1998 to deal with the problem of a persistently barking dog. Deciding the best way to solve the problem was with guns, officers at the scene let loose nearly a dozen shots in the dark. However, they only managed to shoot the rope keeping the canine in his yard. With the dog free, the police gave chase, firing off more shots – one of which hit his elderly female owner in the heart.

3. Goro Ito, a 40-year-old from the Saitama Prefecture in Japan, died after his pet hamster called Aiko – whose name translates as 'little love' – bit him. A subsequent autopsy on Ita showed that he had died after an acute reaction to a protein in the homicidal hamster's saliva brought about a fatal case of pet-induced anaphylaxis.

2. When a family in Buenos Aries, Argentina, went away for a weekend they left their pet poodle, Cachi, alone in their 13th floor apartment. Cachi managed to get out onto the balcony and fell, landing on 75-year-old Marta Espina. Both dog and OAP died instantly. As a crowd gathered to study the carnage, pedestrian Edith Sola was forced to step out into the road and was fatally hit by a bus.

1. BAD GNUS
Klaus 'Dick' Radant had a penchant for keeping exotic animals as pets on his property at North Liberty, Indiana. Among his menagerie of peculiar pets were ostriches, emus, reindeers, llamas and a trio of blue wildebeest, also known as gnus. In August 2004, Radant made the mistake of getting into the gnu enclosure during mating season. The 225kg male gnu decided that Radant was a potential love rival, and proceeded to repeatedly ram, butt and trample his owner to death.

OF-FENCE-IVE FATE

A 480kg fence flew through the air and hit security guard Robert Street, 59, as he worked in high winds in the Wirral, in 2007, causing fatal head injuries. Ouch!

CHANNEL SURFING TRAUMA

Switching the TV channel should be one of the safest activities in the world, but as we have demonstrated over and over again, never be complacent about death's ability to find danger in the mundane. Welsh holidaymaker Karen Gibbs, 45, stood on a chair to reach a 6ft high wall-mounted TV at the luxury apartment where she was staying in Majorca. The chair's legs slipped on the polished marble floor, sending her careering onto a coffee table and puncturing a lung, in 2002. So who had the remote control?

PLAYING DEAD

Young James Wies was on a school trip to Central Cemetery in Ohio to see historic grave monuments. The nine-year-old's skull was crushed when a 1.5-metre tombstone he had been climbing and playing on a few minutes before fell on top of him.

ACHOO! WHOOPS!

You can become a menace to others when you sneeze. A motorist suffered a sneezing fit while driving along the M5 motorway in Gloucestershire, on 9 October 1998. She lost control of her vehicle, strayed from the inside lane, and hit Yasmin Zalam, 32, and her four-year-old son Kamran, from Birmingham, who were parked on the hard shoulder because Kamran was feeling unwell. Yasmin was killed instantly.

SIZE MATTERS

Why Donald MacKenzie, 65, didn't notice he was wearing his wife's lifejacket is a riddle he took to his grave. He was enjoying a summer cruise off Arisaig in Inverness-shire, in August 1999, when he tumbled into the sea. Instead of supporting him, the smaller jacket turned him upside down and pinned his face beneath the sea. As a former schoolteacher, he really should have spotted the error when his jacket seemed unnaturally tight.

TRAIN TWITS

How dumb would you have to be to get hit by a train in exactly the same spot that your father had been killed by one just eight months previously? As dumb as Mr V. Marathai of the northern Malaysian town of Ipoh. Mr. Marathai was run down and instantly killed at the precise place his father, N. Veerapan, had died when he tried to crawl between the wheels of a train he thought was stationary. Carriages had blocked N. Veerapan's way across the railway line and rather than walk to the back of the train, he tried to cross by going under one of the carriages. A member of the dead men's family claimed they had merely been unlucky in using a popular shortcut across the tracks.

MUSHED!

Dogs are stupid creatures, no matter what people say. How else do you explain why huskies pulling a dog sled in Calgary, Canada, suddenly decided to career off the trail, sending their sledge catapulting into a tree? Unfortunately for passenger Sheila Wisden, 48, of Hornchurch, Essex, the collision in December 2001 proved fatal. Canadian public safety official George Field said: "In my 19 years in this job, I've never heard of any other dog sled fatality."

MEDALLION MAN'S ELECTRIC PERSONALITY

Farmworker Paul Maroney, 20, of Barnard Castle, County Durham, died after lightning struck his gold necklace in 1996.

BUTT OUT, BUTT IN

When his son Ross Willetts, 17, from Walsall, died in 1997, his dad Robert said: "I always told him that one day smoking would kill him." Ross died after throwing a cigarette butt from the window of a Mini being driven by pal Edward Cooper. Edward lost control and crashed into a lamppost when Ross' butt blew straigh back in, landing on his lap.

PUKED HIS BRAINS OUT

A drunk teenager stuck his head out of a van window in Coulsden, Surrey, in September 2001, to be ill, only to whack his head on a metal bar holding up a fence by some roadworks. Shame he didn't have a sick bag...

TILLIKUM THE KILLER WHALE II

After being bullied by his female pool mates in Sealand Victoria, Tillikum – the killer whale with one human death already to his name – was moved to Seaworld in Orlando, Florida. Therefore it possibly should not have come as a huge surprise when, on the morning of 6 July 1999, workers discovered a dead body in Tillikum's pool.

Daniel O. Dukes, a 27-year-old whose registered address was a Hare Krishna temple, was found naked and draped across Tillikum's back. His lime green shorts were floating on the water and a post mortem showed he had received only one bite – in the region of his groin. While it became clear that Dukes had hidden in the theme park after closing time, it remains something of a mystery as to just what happened between him and the orca. Needless to say, given Tillikum's track record in fatal friendliness, we are not taking any bets.

PUT TO THE SWORD

Tang Xiaowan, a 25-year-old woman from Shanghai, was arrested and charged with the accidental killing of her husband with a sword after he refused to cook her a meal. Police said that Tang had practised swordsmanship since an early age and often forced her husband Li Weidong at sword point. On 3 March 2006, Li refused to cook her dinner because he was already late for work.

At this point Tang began to wield her sword, saying: "I'm hungry. How can you have the heart to leave?" When Li refused, she placed the sword against her husband's chest. According to Tang, she then slipped and accidentally stabbed Li, her sword puncturing his liver. She immediately called an ambulance, but Li died in the hospital from loss of blood. After a three-month investigation, the police have decided she was telling the truth, and it was a case of accidental death rather than murder.

A police spokesman said Li was an honest, hard-working and simple man who had come to accept his wife's aggressive outbursts during the three years of their marriage. They added that he would usually do anything he was told – hardly surprising if your wife was waving a sword in front of your face. The prosecutor in the case said: "It is really rare that a family tragedy is caused by a high-maintenance wife."

LAST RITES

Devout Catholic Nellie Doherty, 78, went to pray at the site of a neighbour's fatal crash in Donegal, Ireland, in June 2006. Her husband's car was hit by another car, ploughing into Nellie as she paid her respects at the crash barrier.

CURSE OF THE HOLY BANNER

A gang of thieves paid the price for stealing the icon of a Himalayan Saddhu holy man from Paisley Museum in Scotland when their pals were killed in a freak car crash just days later. Terrified of bad karma, the burglars replaced the image, leaving a note begging for forgiveness, in 2001. The thieves wrote: "The banner is back. It has brought us too much bad luck. Two of our friends have been killed in a car crash."

MEDICAL MADNESS!

A doctor couple killed their son by transplanting his blood into the body of his less intelligent brother. The bizarre transfusion, in Haryana, India, took place in October 2007 because Ashok Malik and his wife Promila wanted their less bright son to study to become a doctor. They had been told by their spiritual leader that they could transfer the lad's intelligence, but one of the boys bled to death. Apparently the less bright son took after his parents.

QUICK ROUTE TO THE BOTTOM

Trying to take a shortcut back to his hotel from 9,000ft up Italy's Piz Boe mountain was a bad move for skier David Mason, 49, from Birmingham. He had attached himself to a cord hanging from a disused ski lift cable and was making his way down the steel line using the cord as a brake. However, he was unable to control himself properly and slipped, hitting rocks on the way down before crashing into the cable's support pylon in September 2002.

PASSION KILLER

A taxi driver found the bodies of Brent Tyler and Chelsea Tumbleston naked in a street in the city of Columbia, South Carolina, in the early hours of the morning of 27 June 2007. The couple, both 21 years old, had fallen 15 metres from the pyramid-shaped roof of an office block. Although alive when found, they died from injuries sustained during their drop before arriving at hospital.

Police investigating the incident found their clothes in a vehicle at a parking garage adjacent to the office block. One witness, Naomi Mosely, reported: "A cute, young nude couple arrived at the garage in a car and climbed onto the roof. They were laughing and happy. He pulled her up onto the roof saying, 'Baby, I got you.'"

Detectives admitted they could only speculate about what had happened, but one admitted: "It looks as if they took a tumble during the height of passion."

POLE TO POLE

A motorist fell out of her moving car, which then drove into a pole which fell on top of her, in a bizarre accident in Melbourne, Australia, in January 2008. The 57-year-old hit a pole while reversing, knocking her out of the car. The vehicle then hit a second pole, which crushed the driver to death.

FAINTLY STUPID!

They're supposed to be the leaders of tomorrow's Britain, so the fact that pupils at elite public school Eton indulged in bizarre fainting games before evening prayers is worrying in the extreme. Groups of up to 10 boys would tie cords around each others necks and pull them tight until they fainted. It all went wrong when Nicholas Taylor, 15, tried to play the game on his own and accidentally hanged himself with his dressing gown cord in February 1999. The nation is in dangerous hands if this is the standard of intelligence coming out of one of the country's top schools.

CREAMED

A teenage athlete died after applying too much muscle cream. Arielle Newman, a 17-year-old cross country runner from New York, used excessive amounts of methyl salicylate, an anti-inflammatory drug used to sooth aching muscles, in June 2007. An abnormal amount was absorbed into her body, proving fatal.

DYING FOR HIS ART

Hungarian painter, poet and sculptor Mihaly Gubis was killed when his one and a half ton sculpture "Woman With Four Breasts" fell on him. Gubis and a Chinese sculptor had been loading the 24ft high artwork made from sand onto the back of a lorry in Mundelsheim, Germany, on 17 May 2006. At one point during their attempt to transport the sculpture to an exhibition, the huge piece of art lurched violently to one side, leading Mihaly to try and push it back with his body. However, the 58-year-old artist only succeeded in throwing it further off balance, causing it to fall onto him. He was crushed and died instantly.

Mihaly was somewhat accident-prone. He had been forced to give up his first career as a classical guitarist when an accident while making screen-prints resulted in him losing a finger.

FROM RUSSIA WITH DEATH

On 4 July 1989, a Russian MiG-23 fighter plane departed from a Soviet airbase near Kolobrzeg, Poland. Its pilot, Colonel Skurigin, decided to bail out shortly after take-off when the afterburner failed and the engine began to lose power. He safely ejected, but instead of the plane crashing, it remained airborne. The MiG continued to fly at a height of 150 metres in a westward direction on autopilot.

The now unmanned plane left Polish airspace, crossed into East Germany and then into West Germany. Despite being intercepted by two

American F-15s, it continued on into Dutch airspace before screeching across the farmland of Belgium. After flying 560 miles, the MiG finally ran out of fuel and crashed into an isolated, rural homestead, killing its single unlucky occupant – an 18-year-old farmworker called Hugo.

CHAIN OF COINCIDENCE

A motorist driving through the Bronx was shot in the back of the head in July 2005. He lost control of his car and ploughed into a street sign. He survived what should have been a fatal gunshot, but pedestrian Wellington Contreras, 43, was hit by the street sign and died later in hospital.

ALIEN INTERVENTION

Former basketball star Roderick W. Floyd, 41, was randomly murdered by Chicago truck driver David Teran, 39, in 1998. Teran thought the slaying would release an alien enzyme in his body, allowing him to board a spaceship coming to pluck him off Earth. Teran told ex-wife Tess Burke she couldn't come with him because she was a lower life form.

DIET OF DEATH

Four women starved themselves to death on a weird religious diet which they thought would give them perfect health. Twins Catherine and Ruth Mulrooney, 51, aunt Frances, 82, and their younger sister Josephine, 47, all from Leixlip, County Kildare, Ireland, didn't eat for six weeks, believing it would give them a better spiritual life. But they died one by one in their boarded-up home in 2000. You would have thought the first death would have been a clue...

MORONIC MOTORIST

When driving a car, what's wrong with just sitting behind the wheel and playing it safe? Ariel Figueroa, 24, from New Jersey, crashed his car in February 2002, after driving while leaning out of window and standing through the sunroof, all at speeds of up to 110mph. Idiot.

THE BIRDS

City-dweller Michael Nikonov was visiting a friend in the Russian village of Verkhovie when his decision to cool down by taking a swim in the River Shuya proved fatal. However, it was not the river's strong currents that led to his death. It was the Shuya's most deadly inhabitants – seagulls.

When Nikonov got too close to their nests on an island in the river, known locally as the 'Seagull Fortress', the birds became alarmed. The birds soared above the swimmer before dive-bombing him, engulfing him in a relentless onslaught of pecking and clawing. Shocked onlookers called out the emergency services, but Nikonov was dead before they arrived. A policeman said: "He fought hard, but was too injured by the birds to escape, or even keep himself afloat."

OVERCOOKED CHEF

The reign of Henry VIII of England saw numerous executions for treason. However, few were more gruesome or ironic than the death of Richard Roose. A cook to the Bishop of Rochester, Roose was sentenced to death by public boiling in 1531. His crime was undermining the King's government by attempting to poison the household of the Bishop with a sauce and successfully poisoning food given to the poor of the parish of Lambeth, which killed a man and a woman.

In front of a huge crowd gathered at Smithfield, Roose was fastened to a chain and repeatedly lowered into a vat of boiling water until he expired. It is said in some folk histories that one of his executioners was something of a wag and seasoned the water with bay leaves and other herbs.

AND FOR TONIGHT'S ENTERTAINMENT...

Cocaine-crazed Richard Wheeler, 33, of Lowell, Massachusetts, injected himself with the drug and stripped naked. He then ran through a restaurant stabbing himself with a pen and trying to electrocute himself by sticking his fingers into sockets during August 2004. He was taken, screaming and thrashing, to hospital, where he died. At least that saved him the embarrassment of going back to apologise.

VEIN HOPE

An animal lover bled to death after her pet cat scratched her leg. The 60-year-old, from Botley, Oxford, died when the animal clawed one of her varicose veins, starting a major bleed in July 2001. According to doctors, varicose veins contain so much blood that clotting rarely happens and therefore a sufferer can die of blood loss quite quickly.

STING OF DEATH

In March 2008, Judy Kay Zagorski travelled from her home in Pigeon, Michigan, to enjoy the pleasures of bounding around the Florida Keys on her father's motorboat. The 57-year-old was zooming around Vaca Key when a 75-pound stingray leapt out of the water and fatally hit her in the face. The initial autopsy of Zagorski was unable to discover whether she died from the impact or from a puncture wound, which had initially suggested that the ray's poisonous barb may have been the direct cause of death.

An expert from the Florida Fish and Wildlife Conservation Commission said: "Rays leap out of the water to escape predators. They do not attack people and pose no risk." Except, of course, when they accidentally manage to kill them.

EVERY DOG HAS HIS DAY

Although John M. Hwilka was shot to death in October 1998, the killer will never face charges, because he was a poodle named Benji. John, 37, a manager in a tyre store in Milwaukee, was demonstrating to his mother how to unload, load and use the safety on a .45 handgun he kept for their protection. But playful pooch Benji jumped on his chest, causing the gun to fire and kill him.

THE KISS OF DEATH

Xia Xinfeng, a 23-year-old woman from Maolou Village in the Henan Province in central China, was sentenced to death for killing her lover with a kiss. Xinfeng had been having a relationship with her lover and former childhood sweetheart Mao Ansheng for more than five years. They had proclaimed to each other that they would both rather die than be unfaithful. These turned out to fateful words for Mao when, on 8 January 2007, the jealous Xia saw him talking in what she though was a suspicious manner to another woman.

When Mao met Xia the next day, she filled a plastic capsule with rat poison, placed it under her tongue and then slipped it into his mouth while they were passionately kissing. Passion seems to have made Mao oblivious to the poison attack, as he swallowed the capsule and died within hours.

A KILLER APPLICATION

Computers have a lot to answer for. Besides having nearly started global nuclear war at least three times between 1960 and 1991, they are responsible for more than their fair share of bizarre and ridiculous deaths. It seems that if they are not driving pensioners in the UK to suicide by charging them £2172 for two-minute phone calls, they are constantly striving to wipe out their human masters by engineering disasters.

In 1983, huge floods along the Colorado River devastated hundreds of homes, caused more than $12 million worth of damage and killed seven people. An investigation into the cause of the floods followed. Their conclusion was that the seven died due to a computer cock-up. The machines decided they would rather assume their own averages of water coming from snow melt-off were accurate than take note of the actual amount of water behind the dams.

DEAD AS A DILDO

When we were both fresh-faced journalists, we worked with an older and wiser deputy editor called Phil Higgins who always used to say: "It is always the priests and ministers you need to watch." How right he was, as the tale of Baptist minister Gary Aldridge from Montgomery, Alabama, illustrates.

In June 2007, Aldridge's body was discovered in his home. He was found on the floor, hogtied, wearing two full wetsuits and a diving face mask. If that was not surprising enough, the full autopsy report revealed that underneath the wetsuit the minister had "a dildo in the anus, covered with a condom".

The report concluded that Aldridge had died of "accidental mechanical asphyxia" – what the average person usually thinks of as autoeroticism gone wrong. Very wrong. Ironically, the minister was renowned for being a vicious opponent of sex outside of marriage and of homosexuality, and had been a strong supporter of a law that banned the sale of sex aids in the state of Alabama.

PAYING THE PRICE FOR PIPER

In 2001, 28-year-old New Zealander Peter John Robinson slipped as he went to feed his cat Piper. He knocked himself unconscious and managed to fall face down into Piper's water bowl, where he drowned in less than 5cms of water.

TOP 10 RIDICULOUS POLITICALLY-RELATED DEATHS

10. General Sani Abacha was a military leader and politician who swept into power in Nigeria after a series of coups. His undemocratic, brutal and corrupt regime was so vastly unpopular that his death, on 8 June 1998 was met with widespread rejoicing. This redoubled when it emerged that Abacha had died in bed with two prostitutes, from an overdose of Viagra.

9. Eton-educated Crown Prince Dipendra of Nepal was always a trouble-maker. While at England's most famous public school, he was caned for selling alcohol and excused from going to chapel on the basis of claiming to be a living god. On 1 June 2001, he killed almost the entire Nepalese royal family at a banquet before putting a gun in his own mouth and firing. Dipendra survived three days on a life support machine, during which time, having killed his father, he was crowned king.

8. German politician Jürgen Möllemann had once served as his country's junior minister for foreign affairs. In 2002, while caught up in a scandal about election finances, he decided to keep up his tradition of parachuting into election rallies. Unfortunately it seems his mind was elsewhere when he made the jump as he forgot to check his equipment and his parachute failed, plunging him to his death.

7. The body of Ugandan Foreign Minister Michael Ondanga was found floating in a river in 1973 minus his liver. At the time of this gruesome discovery, his liver was sitting in the fridge of Uganda's then dictator, Idi Amin.

6. Robert 'Budd' Dwyer was a Republican congressman for Pennsylvania who was accused of accepting a $300,000 kickback. On 22 January 1987 he called a press conference. Assembled journalists expected him to declare he was resigning from office, but instead Dwyer took out a .357 magnum revolver, placed it in his mouth and shot himself.

5. Once well known for being the husband and singing partner of Cher, by the time of his death, Sonny Bono had gone on to become a congressman for California. In January 1998, Bono was skiing at the ironically named Heavenly Ski Resort when he became distracted, slammed headfirst into a tree and died. The epitaph on his tombstone takes its cue from one of his hit songs and reads "The beat goes on".

4. Monkeying around has caused the downfall of many a politician, but none more fatally or ridiculously than that of Deputy Mayor of Delhi, Surrinder Singh Bajwa. The Indian politician's fall from power came about one Sunday morning in October 2007. He was reading a newspaper on the terrace of his home when a group of three monkeys from the neighbouring Saj Baba temple attacked him. As he tried to ward off the simian menaces, he lost his balance and fell from the terrace to his death.

3. Félix François Faure was President of France during the height of the Dreyfus Affair political scandal. However, Faure was having another type of affair with 30-year-old Marguerite Steinheil. On the night of 16 February 1899, while she was giving him oral sex in the presidential office, Faure died of apoplexy mid-fellatio.

2. Japanese politician Nitaro Ito thought staging an attack on himself would boost his chances of election to the House of Representatives by generating a sympathy vote. He got an employee to punch him and stab his leg outside his home. Unfortunately, the injury to his thigh severed an artery, and Ito bled to death before he could crawl inside his house and get help.

1. ORANGE ALERT
   Stephen Milligan was a Conservative MP. On 7 February 1994, his cleaner entered the kitchen of his London home and found Milligan tied to the table by electrical flex that was also wound around his neck. He was naked apart from a pair of black stockings, suspenders and lace panties. A police investigation also revealed he had a piece of Satsuma orange in his mouth. His frankly ridiculous death was officially declared as resulting from 'auto-erotic asphyxiation'.

IMMORTAL IDIOT

There are idiots and then there are grand spanking idiots who help redefine the whole concept of idiocy. Dmitry Butakov from Lipetsk in Russia was one of those grand spanking idiots. Having survived an accident in 1994 when he came into contact with 10,000 volts of electricity, Butakov became convinced he was immortal. While most of us would have been happy to survive such a close brush with death and taken more care, the Russian decided that nothing could kill him. In 2004, to celebrate the tenth anniversary of his first accident, he called a press conference where he proceeded to drink a half-litre of antifreeze. Halfway through attempting to drink a second half-litre, Butakov collapsed, fell into a coma and died in hospital the next day. Butakov's only immortality was carving his name into the history books of stupidity.

BASTARD BADGER

In July 2007, people living around Basra in southern Iraq began to claim that the British armed forces had released man-eating badgers into the area. The local uproar became so huge that UK military spokesman Major Mike Shearer had to try and calm the situation by making a formal denial, saying: "We can categorically state that we have not released man-eating badgers in Iraq."

The British press enjoyed themselves, scoffing at the very idea of flesh-eating, man-attacking badgers and mocking the alleged stupidity of anyone who could countenance the idea of the British army deploying badger-based biological weapons. However, they might have been less sure of themselves if they had remembered the story of Serbian farmer Dragon Konjevic from 1995.

Konjevic was out hunting for small game in the woods around his home when he was attacked by a badger. The animal managed to knock him to the ground and then began to rip at his flesh with such severity that it severed a vein in his thigh and tore off two of his fingers. The injured man managed to stagger away, but died from blood loss within minutes of reaching home.

PROPHETS' LOSS

The end of the 20th century saw a lot of pre-millennial madness. Crazy cults proliferated more quickly than bacteria grow on a fast-food burger and led to some spectacularly ridiculous deaths. Bucking the trend of the believers of frankly insane things topping themselves was one tale of pre-millennial triple death from the east of Java.

Three cult leaders in the village of Sukmajaya were chased by an angry mob of fellow cultists after the world did not end at 9am on 9 September 1999 as they had prophesised. Their followers had sold or given away all their worldly goods and spent the last nine days locked in their homes in expectation of the imminent global destruction. When the specified date came and went without the four horsemen of the apocalypse putting in an appearance, feelings among the cultists were running high.

According to Saadi Arsam, village chief of Sukmajaya: "The members were really mad. When they caught the false prophets they lost control of their tempers. Nothing could make them see sense and they beat them to their deaths." Shame the self-styled seers had not seen that coming.

"BACK A BIT FURTHER..."

Anything for that perfect photo! A pub landlady stepped backwards into a volcanic pool of red-hot lava whilst trying to snap a photo of her husband during a trip to the Azores. Gillian Blann, 58, from Warwickshire, had asked her husband John, 64, to pose for a holiday picture and was trying to get him into shot when she fell into the boiling pool of liquid. She died a week later from her burns, in April 2005.

FLUSHED AWAY HIS FUTURE

Sometimes you really can be too old to party. Praying at the porcelain throne after a heavy night of celebrations on his 86th birthday cost Robert Talbot dearly. The retired accountant, from Devon, toppled over and hit his head on the toilet. He later died in hospital from his injury.

JOUST HAVING A LAUGH

Iranian student Mohamad Navab was larking around with friends in Tehran in 1998 by riding on his moped while holding a pole as if he was a medieval jousting knight. Unfortunately for Mohamad, instead of winning fair maiden's heart or slaying any dragons, he misjudged the distance between his makeshift lance and a wall and was catapulted off his bike with fatal results.

BURNING ISSUE

Surely there are better ways of proving a point? Michael Toye, 43, of Hampshire, died after dousing himself in white spirit and setting fire to himself. He had been having a drunken discussion with pal Paul Deacon, 18, over whether white spirit was flammable. Here's a clue Michael, yes, it is. He died from severe burns six days after turning himself into a human fireball in April 2007. The appliance of science.

HALLOWEEN HANGING

All Hallows Eve in some countries brings out the freaks. Instead of the undead, it can be the night for the soon-to-be-dead. A typical case in point is that of 41-year-old Milton Tyree of Boston, Massachusetts. In 1988, Tyree walked into the Cantab Lounge bar and asked if he could stage a mock hanging from one of the wooden beams in the bar's ceiling. The on-duty barman, Richard Fitzgerald, took one look at the drunken Tyree's safety harness and the six-inch thick rope noose around his neck and told him to beat it.

However, when Fitzgerald finished his shift and went home, Tyree seized an opportunity and hitched himself to a beam. He told people below: "Don't worry about me, I've done this stunt lots of times before." A crowd of 70 Cantab Lounge patrons then saw Tyree perform his mock hanging, not realising his harness had failed and his kicking, flailing and gurgling were not part of the act. By the time anyone cottoned on to the fact that something was wrong and he was cut down, it was too late for Tyree.

Seasoned death watchers might have been able to work out what the Cosmic Joker had planned for Tyree on Halloween by the costume he wore that fateful and fatal night. He went out wearing the garb of the grim reaper.

COUGHING INTO HIS COFFIN

When Alan Graham, 54, banged his head during a coughing fit from smoking at his local pub in Devon, he thought nothing of it and discharged himself before being seen by doctors at Torbay Hospital. But he was discovered dead at home a week later in January 2008 from an internal head injury, an unlit cigarette in his hand. So did the fags get him in the end after all?

THE LONG ARM OF THE GRAVE

Everything went wrong for thieves Wilbert Long Jr and Kenyal Scott when they set out to rob a motorcycle dealership in Tampa, Florida, in May 2003. Police on patrol discovered them attempting to break into Barney's Yamahas at 3:30am, forcing the would-be burglars to flee in a stolen truck. They then found it impossible to evade the pursuing police, despite a high-speed chase across several miles of the city.

In a last ditch desperate effort to evade the cops, the criminal duo turned into the Garden of Memories cemetery, disturbing the peaceful rest of the dead by crashing through the graveyard's gates and riding across the burial plots. Disaster struck when the truck hit a tombstone and Long lost control of the vehicle, veering into a clump of trees. The crash caused Long to be thrown from the truck, which then overturned and landed on him.

Surrounded by broken tombstones, Long breathed his last. While you can run from the long arm of the law for a while, no one can run forever from the long arm of the grave.

TIME UP

In a rather protracted means of bringing about his end, hairdresser Nigel French electrocuted himself by wiring his fingers up to the mains and setting a time switch for the power to turn on. Mr French, of Gloucester, lay on an insulated mat with a wet towel under his head, waiting for the timer to send the fatal shock coursing through his body in March 2007. Shocking behaviour.

TOTAL TUT

At nearly 190 metres, the 1960s-built Cairo Tower is among the tallest buildings in the Egyptian capital. With a café bar at the top, decorated in a kitsch mock- pharaonic style and offering a view of the distant Giza pyramids, it is a popular spot with tourists. It also seems to have certain appeal to suicidal nutters such as Adam Gotz.

The 34-year-old German was an amateur student of Egyptology and a self-styled 'spiritual psychologist'. He and a group of associated lunatics believed that ancient Egyptian ideas about the afterlife were correct in every detail, and the Great Pyramid was an energy accumulator that allowed those who died within its vicinity to transcend the bonds of humanity.

In 1998, to prove his beliefs to his girlfriend Sarah Kilmer, Gotz climbed over the railings at the top of the Cairo Tower. He then told her that, as they were so close to the Great Pyramid, he would be resurrected within minutes, and jumped to his death. Whether Gotz transcended humanity or not, the mess of bone and flesh at the bottom of the tower certainly did not return to life.

DIGGING HIS OWN GRAVE?

A cheery builder trapped his head in a mini-digger after accidentally nudging a lever while hanging out of the cab and waving at pals. Lance Taylor, 23, of Gloucester, jolted the machine's bucket arm, killing himself instantly when it swung back into his head. He had been working on a housing development at the time of the tragedy, in February 2005, but was not qualified to operate the machine. Teach him for showing off.

ZEN AND THE ART OF DROWNING

Mashario Oki played many roles in his life – smuggler, journalist, spy, founder of six orphanages and Zen monk. However, it was as the creator of Oki-do yoga that the Korean achieved the most renown. After roaming across much of Asia and the Indian sub-continent, Oki came to believe that his system of teaching, combining martial arts and yoga, not only brought huge health benefits, but endowed him with superhuman powers.

In 1985, Oki moved to Italy with a group of his students. To demonstrate the extent of his self-belief in his advanced yoga powers, he climbed into a tank of water, wearing traditional samurai armour weighted with additional lead ingots. Oki had told his pupils that by sitting in the pool in the lotus position and breathing through an acupuncture point at the top of his head, he could stay submerged for hours. Given this, none of his pupils worried when he did not surface after a few minutes. They only realized that Oki's alleged mystic powers had failed and that their teacher had drowned when after two hours he did not leave the pool for a swordfight he had scheduled.

NAILED!

Timothy Clews, 47, of Cheltenham, died suddenly as he was having his toenails clipped by a chiropodist in a care home. Timothy, who suffered from a rare complication of rheumatoid arthritis, had a fatal but silent heart attack when his nails were cut for the first time in six months in June 2007. The chiropodist had finished chopping his talons by the time she realized he was dead.

CROOK'S CHIMNEY DOWNFALL

When builders were renovating a historic building dating from the time of the American Civil War in Natchez, Mississippi, in 2001, they got something of a surprise. As local mason Duncan Morgan hammered on the wall backing a chimney on the second floor of the Riverboat Gift Shop Building, he unexpectedly exposed human foot and leg bones clad in blue jeans, socks and cowboy boots. Mason immediately called the police, who chiselled away at the chimney until a full, clothed human skeleton tumbled out of the stack.

A wallet found on the remains revealed the identity of the skeleton – Calvin Wilson, a 27-year-old who had gone missing some 15 years before. Trying to reconstruct the circumstance that led to Wilson's death, the police concluded that he had fallen headfirst down the chimney, knocking himself out so he was unable to call for help. They also believed that breezes from the river next to the building may have prevented anyone noticing the smell of decomposition.

According to local sheriff Tommy Ferrell: "Wilson had a criminal record as a burglar, so we believe he was crawling down the chimney to burglarise the business that was in the building at the time of his disappearance."

TIPPING POINT

Kevin Mackle was a 19-year-old student at Bishop's University in Lennoxville, Quebec. In 1998, a drunken Mackle attempted to get a free Coke from a vending machine on campus. With one arm buried deep in its workings, Mackle began to violently rock the dispenser back and forth. The 420-kilo machine tipped over, fatally crushing the already smashed student. Unsurprisingly, the minor facts that Mackle was drunk and was engaged in attempted theft did not deter his family from launching a law suit against the university, Coca-Cola Bottling Ltd., and the companies that made and operated the vending machine.

LUCKY ESCAPE?

A promising linguist who choked to death on a piece of roast beef escaped an agonising death from an incurable brain disease. Yumiko Boyle, 18, from Banbury, Oxfordshire, had developed an unusual brain condition which was only diagnosed after her death in December 2006. It would have resulted in severe and incurably deteriorating brain damage, so perhaps choking was a kinder way to go?

SNAKES ALIVE, PRINCE OF SNAKES DEAD

Boonruang Buachan was a 34-year-old former farmer from Prai Bung, Thailand, whose special relationship with snakes had earned him minor-celebrity status in his homeland and a place in the *Guinness Book of World Records*. In 1998 he had shot to fame by claiming the record for spending seven days in a Plexiglas box containing more than 100 highly poisonous snakes. Alongside the two king cobras, dozen spitting cobras and numerous monocled cobras, the box was also filled with 30 giant centipedes, 20 scorpions and more than 30 kilos of live frogs for the reptiles to eat.

When Boonruang emerged alive from the box, he and many others in Thailand took it as a sign that his claims to be the incarnation of the mythic Thai character the 'Prince of Snakes' were not completely hollow. According to Boonruang: "I communicate directly with reptiles. The snakes and I are friends. We understand each other and I have power over them."

In 2004, it turned out that Boonruang had less power over and less of a friendship with the snakes than he thought. While performing his daily snake show at a theme park, he was bitten by a cobra. As Boonruang was an epileptic, the watching crowd though that the convulsions he suffered after being bitten were a fit and no one tried to help him until it was far too late. The late Boonruang's father said: "I will give my son's 30 snakes to a zoo, because no else in the family can talk to them."

KILLER COFFIN

Jack Volkering was a 59-year-old Kentuckian undertaker. In February 1999, he was driving a hearse with along Highway 27 through Cold Spring, Kentucky. He was en route to a funeral when a car swung out from the other side of the road ahead of him.

Volkering swerved to avoid the head-on collision, but the rapid movement broke the coffin in the back of the hearse free of its restraining straps. The casket slammed forward, smashing into the unlucky undertaker and killing him instantly.

SLOW TRAIN TO THE GRAVE

A lesson in road safety here, even when the vehicle in question is moving at less than 10mph. Matthew Dear, 23, of Nottingham, was hit by a city centre tram which he somehow didn't see coming, despite its crawling speeds in October 2007. Matthew had been out celebrating with team-mates from his cricket club, and was running across the road when he became the first person to be killed by the trams since they were launched in the town three years earlier.

HER NUMBER'S UP

An American visitor to Malaysia, 35-year-old Carolyn Jamica Noraini Abdullah, went missing in November 1999. Extensive searches for her found no clues as to what had happened to the much-loved mother of four. By June 2001, Malaysian police had all but closed the case when one of her killers came forward.

The murderer led detectives to an oil palm estate at Sungai Siput in the northern state of Perek. After excavation, police found a body which was later identified as that of Carolyn. The murderer explained how he and a gang of other men had drugged and abducted her as a human sacrifice to the spirits of the forest in an attempt to obtain the winning number combinations for Malaysia's state lottery. According to the killer, their sacrifice had worked a lot better than the usual cockerels and goats, but he felt guilty and wanted no part in another murder being planned in an attempt to get another big win.

A CHARMING WAY TO GO

You would think that if anyone would stand a chance against a python in a fight for life, it would be a professional snake charmer. Hie Kerdchoochuay, a 53-year-old snake catcher from Thailand, was renowned in the northern province of Uttaradit for his charming skills. When a python was plaguing a village close to Kerdchoochuay's home in 1999, the charmer was called in, and he quickly subdued and caught the beast.

Walking home to his own village with the 4.5-metre long snake stowed safely in a sack, children gathered around him and asked to see the creature. Kerdchoochuay obliged and began to drape the python around his neck. He obviously was not charming enough, as the vengeful reptile was soon wrapped tightly around his throat and upper body. A choking and screaming Kerdchoochuay begged the children to get help, but by the time they had returned with their parents, the python had crushed him to death. It took half a dozen villagers and a local policeman to prize the snake off Kerdchoochuay's lifeless body.

STONE ME!

With dangerous hobbies and extreme sports claiming hundreds of lives every year, you would be forgiven for thinking keeping tropical fish is relatively safe. Not so for Daniel Davies, 30, of Tyne and Wear, whose search for stones for his new fish tank led to his untimely demise. Daniel was hunting for suitable rocks at the site of England's most powerful waterfall, High Force in County Durham, when he was swept over the edge of the 60ft falls in May 2007.

DIY SOS!

Labourer Gary Gardner, 42, was crushed to death beneath a weak wall he had built himself. Health and safety inspectors found the wall was not strong enough to hold the weight of the soil behind it, and Gary, of Nottingham, had also undermined it by digging into the foundations. It was a lesson too late for the popular builder, who died after firefighters spent two hours trying to free him from his fate in November 2006.

LARD ALMIGHTY!

It's not so much that Meryl Hawkins took the time to baste herself before setting herself on fire, but more of a question of who actually cooks with lard these days? Meryl, 57, rubbed the raw fat into her chest before setting herself alight at her home in Pontypridd, South Wales, in January 2008. Firefighters found her sitting in a chair in her living room smoking a cigarette, her charred clothes stuffed in the toilet. She died in hospital 12 days later, her goose well and truly cooked.

ASHES TO ASHES, WAVE GOODBYE

In February 1995, the daughter of San Diego Chargers' coach Dwayne Painter, Debbie Menta, and her brother Doug stood atop a rocky outcrop on the Mendocino shore in California. The siblings were at the wild but beautiful section of coastline to scatter the ashes of their mother who had committed suicide just a few weeks before. The area had been one of their mother's favourite places and she had regularly brought both Debbie and Doug to it when they were younger.

As they both stood on one of the rocks, holding an urn from which they were about to throw the last remnants of their mother into the ocean, a huge wave funnelled up between the rocks and swept them into the water below. Unable to get a grip on the razor-sharp cliffs, poor Debbie was pulled out to sea and drowned.

LIGHTS OUT

Stop, look, listen... A series of unfortunate events led to the death of pensioner Pamela Kirby, killed when a toppling traffic light column hit her on the head in 2006.

Mrs Kirby, 67, of York, was in the wrong place at the wrong time when 79-year-old Sheila Barron lost control of her car, hitting a traffic island safety fence, which in turn struck the traffic light column and knocked it over, straight onto Mrs Kirby's head.

Mrs Kirby, who had been waiting for the lights to change in her favour, died at the scene. Mrs Barron suffered a fatal stroke in hospital eight days later.

BUCKING TRAGIC!

Straddling a bucking bronco ride in a bar should have been a scream for new mum Nailah Ishaq, 28, on her first night out after giving birth to her daughter six months earlier. But nobody could have predicted that the 30 seconds she was on the ride would trigger an abnormality of the heart she had been born with. Nailah, of Wallsend, North Tyneside, collapsed half an hour later and died in hospital following the tragedy in July 2007.

HO, HO, WHOA!

2006 will not be remembered as one of the best Christmases for the Hughes family after 29-year-old James Hughes leapt head first out of a first-floor window while visiting his brother's flat in Bristol, for the holidays. James had been out drinking with his brother Andy earlier in the evening, but minutes after returning to the flat he ran to an open window and dived out, falling around 20ft to the ground. Londoner James died from severe head and chest injuries, taking the reason for his deadly leap with him to the grave.

NEVER SHIT ON A TIGER

Of all the bits of commonsense which are so blindingly obvious no-one would ever think of giving them as advice, the non-metaphorical 'never shit on a tiger' should probably make the top ten. However, 19-year-old Xu Xiaodong, a zoo keeper at the Jinam Animal Park in China, was so clearly lacking in commonsense that someone really needed to pass on the message about tigers and defecation. If they had, the unfortunate events of 21 February 2000 might never have happened.

On the morning of the day, Xu Xiaodong told colleagues he needed to take a toilet break and disappeared out of sight. The next time anyone saw him, he was lying at the bottom of a cage holding four Bengal tigers. His throat had been ripped open, his body showed the bloody signs of mauling and his trousers were down around his ankles.

Police investigating the death reported: 'Evidence found at the scene included a trouser belt, toilet paper and excrement. We believe Xu Xiaodong climbed onto a partially constructed building next to the tiger cage, to allow him to balance on the edge of the enclosure's railings, so he could attempt to relieve himself on one of the tigers. It appears he overbalanced and fell backwards into the animals' cage. It may have been the smell that enraged them and caused them to pounce on him."

DEATH PENIAL-TY I

In researching this book we have discovered that many popular tales of ridiculous death are nothing more than urban legends, fatal friend-of-a-friend stories. However, we have also found certain urban legends themselves can lead to death. In terms of these killer myths, it seems none is more deadly than that of 'penis snatching', which has been spreading throughout western and southern Africa since the 1980s.

The basic outline of the legend is that a sorcerer, simply by shaking hands with a man, can cause his penis to disappear, leaving him as smooth between the legs as a department store mannequin. The sorcerer will then extort money from his victim, offering to return his magically missing member only if he receives a cash payment.

Bizarrely, the fact that the very idea of penis snatching is nonsense has not stopped it causing outbreaks of mass hysteria and violence in certain parts of Africa. In 2003, 28-year-old Baba Jallow from Serekunda, Gambia, was accused by his fellow townspeople of being a witchdoctor and penis snatcher. According to a police spokesman: "So many men in the town believed that Baba Jallow had vanished their genitals that they formed a mob. They chased him with sticks and metal poles; when they caught him, they then beat him to death."

OFF THE RAILS

Here's a tip – checking to see what the underside of a train looks like is not only bloody pointless, but it's a recipe for disaster too. But that's what Oxford student Yasha Mozaffari, 21, decided to do after celebrating his degree success with a pal.

Yasha was killed instantly when he touched a live rail and his friend Peter Coventry, 21, of Braintree, Essex, suffered bad burns as he pulled him off the 750-volt line at Winchester railway station. The brainless pair had decided to crawl beneath a stationary train to see what it looked like underneath after a night's drinking to celebrate finishing their courses.

KAYAKED!

It's all very well acting all gung-ho on a mock night-time military raid, but surely even the toughest member of the SAS would bring along a life jacket if they couldn't swim? To make matters worse, Jacob Elliot, 18, of West Ham, London, wore thick, water-absorbent woollen army garb as he crossed a river at Beltring Hop Farm Festival, Kent, in an old kayak in July 1999. His aim was to throw a fake thunderflash at a pill box on the other side, but the canoe capsized and he sunk beneath the water. Bet he didn't feel so hard then.

TOP 10 RIDICULOUS
CELEBRITY DEATHS

10. American-born dancer Isadora Duncan achieved global fame in the 1910s as the epitome of bohemian glamour and the mother of modern dance. Known in later years for public drunkenness and a scandalous love life, Duncan was in Nice in 1932 when she climbed into a friend's car while wearing one her trademark flowing scarves. As the car pulled away, the scarf became entangled in one of its wheels, yanking her from the vehicle and breaking her neck.

9. Owen Hart, a professional WWF wrestler, died during a May 1999 pay-per-view event called *Over The Edge*, which was filmed at the Kemper Arena in Kansas City, Missouri. As part of a grand stunt entrance it was planned to lower Owen down from the rafters, but the safety harness broke and he dropped 24 metres to his death.

8. American writer Sherwood Anderson died in Panama at the age of 64 from peritonits caused by swallowing a piece of a toothpick embedded in a martini olive he had eaten at a party.

7. Award winning American playwright Tennessee Williams died in 1983 at the age of 71 when he swallowed an eye drop bottle cap in his room at the Hotel Elysee, New York. He would routinely place the cap in his mouth, lean back, and place his eyedrops in each eye, but alcohol and narcotics may have contributed to the choking.

5. French pop star and songwriter Claude François was the man who penned "Comme d'habitude", the original version of "My Way". A megastar in his homeland, he died in 1978 trying to change a light bulb while standing in a bath full of water. François was known to have an OCD-like need for both cleanliness and order.

4. Terry Kath was a guitarist and founding member of the huge pop-rock band Chicago. At a band party in 1978, Kath began to play a game of mock Russian roulette with an empty .38 revolver. He next moved on the playing with a 9mm automatic pistol. Showing an empty magazine case to his friends, Kath then put the gun to his temple and pulled the trigger, saying: "Don't worry, it's not loaded." However, one bullet remained in the chamber of the gun, and he was killed instantly.

3. Australian Steve 'the Crocodile Hunter' Irwin was an internationally renowned naturalist who was world famous for his very genuine love of nature and his larger than life personality. Known for taking ridiculous risks in pursuit of making great TV, he died in a freak accident in 2006, when his heart was impaled by a short-tail stingray barb while filming a documentary entitled *Ocean's Deadliest* in Queensland's Great Barrier Reef. The stingray was regarded as one of the safer animals that Steve had intended to film.

2. Randy Rhoads was a celebrated heavy metal guitarist for Ozzy Osbourne. He died in 1982 when he was a passenger in a small plane that tried to buzz Osbourne's tour bus, but ended up clipping it with one of its wings and smashing to the ground.

1. IN-ELEGANTLY WASTED
In 1997, the body of global rock icon Michael Hutchence, lead singer with Aussie rock band INXS, was found dead in his room at the Ritz-Carlton hotel in Double Bay, Sydney. A belt found at the scene suggested he had died by hanging, but it later emerged that the cause of death was autoerotic asphyxiation, when Hutchence's attempts to strangle himself during a sex act had gone wrong.

FOR HEAVEN'S SAKE

Makakichi Kindaichi was a master sake brewer from Fukoshima in Japan who had more than 40 years experience of making the potent alcoholic drink. However, in January, 1997, his spotless safety record became fatally blemished when he fell into a two-metre deep and two-metre wide metal vat while pouring fermented rice into it.

Several hours later, when his colleagues were ready to finish their shift, they realized that Kindaichi was missing. By the time they found him it was already too late. The 58-year-old brewer had become overcome with fumes from his potent brew and had suffocated. A Fukushima police spokesman commented: "There is no place to grip in a slippery metal vat. It is like being in a wet bath. The fermentation fumes of sake are always potent; once in he was doomed to die."

L'IDIOT SOUS LE TRAIN

There are easier ways of crossing to an opposite railway platform then choosing to crawl under a railway carriage. But Frenchman Guillaume Rebours, 22, decided to do just that when travelling from Uckfield Station, East Sussex, in January 2002. He jumped off the platform to try and catch a southbound service, only to be decapitated while scrabbling underneath an initially stationary train when it began pulling away.

HOLY FOOL

On 19 December 1999, 45-year-old Chalil Chathothu Ravindran from the Kanur District of Kerala, India, announced to his parents that he was going to his room. This would not have been too unusual if he had not also told his mother that she was not to disturb him or come into the room for 41 days. It was Ravindran's intention to stay isolated, completely abstain from food and water, and say prayers until he obtained 'siddhi' – a Sanskrit word for 'attainment' or 'divine gift'.

When Ravindran failed to come out after the specified time, neighbours tried to gain entry into his room, but his mother, father and other members of the family physically prevented them. After a further nine days, neighbours persuaded the police to investigate. When they broke down the door to Ravindran's room they discovered his body in a highly advance state of decomposition. Autopsy reports suggest he died within three days of beginning his fast.

Ravindran had told friends that when he obtained siddhi he would manifest incredible powers such as a flight, teleportation and the ability to become as small as an atom. Unfortunately for the holy fool, instead of turning into a one-man version of the Justice League of America, he just turned into a corpse.

KILLER KARAOKE

Anyone who has been exposed to the horrors of a karaoke night will have probably felt the urge to grab a gun and relieve the pain between their ears by either shooting themselves or the so-called performer in front of them. However, it was not the singer that ended up getting shot when policeman Lieutenant Corporal Jirawat Sangworn got up to perform at a downtown Bangkok karaoke bar one night in June 2000.

The policeman was enraged when his attempt to sing the same sentimental Thai ballad for a fourth time that evening was met with jeers. When one karaoke bar patron called out, "Get this limp prick off, we are sick of his shit," Corporal Jirawat pulled out his service revolver and fired six shots into the crowd, instantly providing the ultimate heckler putdown.

COWARD'S WAY OUT

Running away from the field of battle is a tried and tested way of living to see another day. However, for Louis II of Hungary and Bohemia, it was running away from the Battle of Mohács of 1526 that actually proved his downfall. Fleeing across a stream, the weight of his own armour caused him to sink into the mud and drown.

FIRING LINE

Hundreds of rounds were fired by members of the Rotherfield Rifle Club, based in East Sussex, towards the end of the 19th century. So it's remarkably unfortunate that the only shot which went astray in all this time ended up killing a volunteer marker. The cartridge exploded out of the gun, deflected off the ground and ended up in the groin of EHM Wood, 30, who subsequently died from peritonitis a few days later.

WHAT A PRICK

Americans and guns is a combination that seems to generate a never-ending stream of tragic deaths. However, the cocktail of American idiot and gun at least produces some highly entertaining ridiculous deaths. Amongst these is the tale of Phoenix resident David Grundman, who went out into the Arizona dessert to practice his marksmanship by firing at one of the state's protected saguaro cacti.

However, Grundman's continuous firing at one particular seven-metre cactus caused its base to crumble. As he reloaded his gun, the cactus collapsed, falling forward. Grundman was impaled by the tumbling plant and so badly crushed and speared by spines that he died before his friends could get him to hospital.

HEDGING YOUR BETS

Death by hedge is hardly a noble way to shuffle off this mortal coil. But for Miguel Fernandes, 31, of Paddock Wood in Kent, 15 April 2004 was his time to go. Miguel had been helping to cut a 6.6.m tall hedge at the factory where he worked, using a long-arm grabber to clear cuttings to the ground. He didn't bank on the overhead power lines carrying 33,000 volts. They killed him stone dead when he caught them with the grabber. A coroner at his inquest described it as "an accident waiting to happen".

AGAINST THE ODDS

Ohio teenager Milika Stone made extra money selling magazines door-to-door. The 18-year-old was so good at it she had earned a place at a sales conference and training program held at a Maryland hotel in 1995. It was her first ever out-of-town trip and she was brimming with excitement.

Unfortunately, she arrived at her hotel soaking wet. Drip drying as she walked up to her room, she took off her shoes and padded along the corridor in her bare feet. Arriving at room 573, Milika ran her electronic key card through the steel lock at the exact moment a faulty air conditioner unit caused a huge power surge. The combination of electrical fault, wetness and being barefoot while opening the door caused what a medical examiner described as a "million-to-one accident". Unfortunately for Milika, 1,000,001 was not her lucky number and she was electrocuted.

DON'T SPICE UP YOUR LIFE

A dash of nutmeg gives that lovely Christmassy taste, but too much can prove fatal. Childminder Raheela Hussain, 32, from Walthamstow, London, died after accidentally overdosing on the common spice. Apparently she suffered from feeling cold and was told that taking a little nutmeg warms up the body. Unfortunately, she began taking powdered nutmeg by the teaspoonful, which led to her becoming dehydrated and needing to drink glass after glass of water in April 1998. Nutty.

FANTASY FATALITY

Anthony Houghton, 42, fell into the waterway in the Seaquarium ride at Fantasy Island amusement park, in the English seaside resort of Skegness, and died surrounded by magical fish and mystical sea creatures in July 2002. His body was discovered by staff, but attempts at resuscitation proved unsuccessful. It was thought he died of natural causes.

SLEIGHED!

When researching this book, there have been a fair few newspaper headlines that have stopped us in our tracks or made us splutter over tea, but none more so than: 'Giant Bavarian Beer Garden Sled Kills One, Injures 14'.

The story behind this classic of journalism is just as ridiculous as the headline would suggest. In March 2000, more than 5,000 people gathered in the Spitzingsee region south of Munich to watch the annual sleigh race. While some compete on speed, other contestants aim to win the prize for having the most elaborately decorated sled that manages to get safely to the bottom of the ski run.

One entrant in the 2000 race was a giant sled built in the shape of a Bavarian beer garden. Attention to detail on the sophisticated vehicle saw it fitted with benches and beer barrels full of lager. The alcohol onboard may have played a part in the tragedy that unfurled as the sled left the top of the ski run. Its driver lost control of the Bavarian behemoth and it left the designated course, hurtling down at an accelerating speed until it crashed into a hut used by race officials.

According to Horst Hornfeck, head of the local mountain police patrol: "There were 14 people on the sleigh, but 17 were injured in total when it demolished the hut. The one man killed on the spot was a sleigh rider." As a mark of respect, the event organisers stopped any other giant beer gardens coming down the mountain for the rest of the day.

BY GUM!

A pensioner tortured by the pain of his swollen gums shot himself in the head because it became too much to bear. Kenneth MacKay, 66, of Berwick, Northumberland, suffered from a malignant swelling in his mouth, but doctors had assured him this could be treated. Unfortunately it all got too much for Ken and rather than wait for treatment he decided to blow his brains out on 11 November 2003. We guess that's one solution.

SNAPPY JUSTICE

Oswaldo Martinez, a 28-year-old criminal from Panama City, had a reputation as a tough guy, someone even other members of Panama's underworld feared. In 2002, a warrant was issued for his arrest for murdering Judge Harmodio Mariscal during a failed robbery, after Martinez boasted to other criminals: "I took out that bastard judge. I spat on the body."

With the Panamanian police searching for him, Martinez fled across the border to neighbouring Costa Rica, where he was soon picked up by the local authorities. However, Martinez had no plans to be tried for murder. After a week in a high security jail in Puerto Limón, Costa Rica, he broke out of prison and decided to make his way back to Panama.

Martinez tried to re-enter his home country via the dense jungle which surrounded the Terraba River. His bid to sneak across the border was going fine until he actually began to swim across the Terraba. Eyewitnesses who had been guiding him through the Costa Rican mangrove swamps saw him make the midpoint of the river when he was snapped up by a crocodile. Panamanian police eventually recovered enough body parts from the scene of the attack to ascertain Martinez had met karmic justice in the jaws of the killer croc.

RAT TRAP

Maybe hell hath no fury like a woman scorned, but it all got too much for serial love rat Jamie Mountain, 27, when three of his lovers gathered to confront him about who he wanted. Whether he stumbled or jumped is uncertain, but he ended up falling into the River Haven in East Sussex as he tried to escape the feuding trio.

The three women had ambushed Jamie as he left the pub just after midnight on 12 December 2005. They demanded that he choose between them, but a row broke out and Jamie tried to make his getaway, ending up in the river and being washed away to his death. Police Det Sgt Paul O'Connor said: "Mr Mountain led a complicated domestic life in which a number of females were involved."

THE WAGES OF SIN

While it is very clear that for many crooks, crime not only pays, but pays exceptionally well, it does appear the maxim about the wages of sin being death sometimes does hold true. A good case in point is that of 21-year-old lowlife Obadiah Videau from Fremont, California. In May 2003, Videau went on a misguided crime spree which saw him bungle one crime after another until he paid the ultimate price for his lawbreaking.

Videau's first botched crime was stealing a charity collection plate from a store. When a shopper saw what was happening and tried to prevent his escape from the store's parking lot, Videau dropped the plate. He then snatched a purse from a woman on the street, only to be forced to drop that when he was chased by the victim's boyfriend. In his next desperate effort to find a crime that paid, Videau then tried to break into Park Villa apartment complex in central Fremont.

Unfortunately for him, he cut the brachial artery in his arm while smashing a window. He then fell down onto the balcony of one of the apartments and could not get up. Despite being quickly found by police officers alerted to his earlier crimes, Videau bled to death before he could be taken to hospital.

OFF HIS HEAD I

Religious faith can often take people to strange, ridiculous and fatal places. A prime example of this happened on 20 July 1999 at the Siddhanath Shiv temple in Junagadh, India. Naranbhai Babubhai, a 60-year-old farmer from the village of Visavadar, went to the temple to seek forgiveness for his sins.

For Babubhai, achieving forgiveness meant committing the act of 'kamal puja' – ritual beheading. In some forms of kamal puja, through the act of losing one's head, a person can be cleansed of any deeds that are currently keeping them from being liberated from the cycle of death and rebirth. When none of his friends or family would volunteer to lop off his noggin, Babubhai decided to take matters into his own hands – despite the fact that self-decapitation is said to be the most difficult form of suicide to undertake successfully.

With the aid a sharp farm scythe, Babubhai somehow managed to perform the ultimate sacrifice. He neatly decapitated himself, leaving his head by the temple's shivalingam – an altar representing the supreme deity of Hinduism. Now that really is an act of faith.

HAMMER TIME

It's bordering on cliché, but farmer Ewen Fowler died after removing his loaded shotgun from his Land Rover, snagging the hammer and shooting himself in the head in March 2000. Ewen, 58, used the gun for shooting birds on his land at Bernwood Farm, Botolph Claydon, Buckingham, but often forgot to unload it.

BASE-IC MISTAKE I

BASE (Building Antenna Span Earth) jumping is a somewhat mad sport in which idiots use a parachute or a wingsuit to jump off the fixed objects in the acronym. As you can imagine, leaping off skyscrapers, broadcasting antenana, bridges and rock formations provides numerous entries in the annals of ridiculous deaths. However, possibly the most ridiculous BASE-related death of all time happened on 9 June 1999.

Frank Gambalie III, an experienced 28-year-old BASE jumper, successfully managed to throw himself off the 910-metre rock formation in Yosemite National Park known as El Capitan. His jump had been illegal – as most are – and as soon as he hit the ground, Gambalie found himself running from park rangers. In his attempts to evade them, he plunged into the Merced River. Weighed down by all of his jumping kit, the fast currents quickly pulled him under. His body was eventually recovered nearly a month later. According to Gambalie, the only scary thing in life was "the prospect of working in a 9-5 job".

IT'S ALL DONE WITH MIRRORS

Grandmother Melek Mehmet, 71, fell to her death after being disorientated by mirrors in a shop. Mrs Mehmet, from Battersea, London, fractured her neck and died instantly after falling down stairs in the store in nearby Lavender Hill, on 15 January 2007. A jury at Westminster Coroners Court said she had probably been confused by the arrangement of a mirrored wall at the top of the stairs. That aside, what exactly was she doing in a lingerie shop at her age? Mirror, mirror on the wall...

HAY HO!

Victor Bradshaw, 82, was killed by unexplained bales of hay he was carrying in his car. Victor, from Winslow in Buckingham, crashed his car into a people carrier on 13 January 2003. The force of the collision meant the hay shunted him into his steering wheel, causing fatal injuries to his chest and upper abdomen. His daughter told an inquest no one could understand why her father had hay bales in his car.

DEATH DIVE

Some tragic deaths seem ridiculous because they appear to be recreating the type of unlikely events usually only seen as slapstick gags in classic *Looney Tune* cartoons. Sergei Chalibashvili was a diver taking part in the World University Games in 1983. Attempting to perform a three-and-half reverse somersault, he knocked his head on the diving board and plummeted unconscious into the pool below. Chalibashvili remained in a coma for a week before finally succumbing to the head injuries he had sustained.

KILLED BY QUITTING

Smoker Alan Ridley, 46, decided to quit the evil weed with the help of an anti-smoking drug. He dropped dead at his home in Monkwearmouth, Sunderland, shortly afterwards, in August 2000. Coroner Martin Shaw refused to rule out a connection to the drug, which begs the question of whether the fags were so bad after all.

HOLY SMOKE!

In November 1998, the Buddhist Phra Pathom Jedi temple in Thailand achieved a brief moment of national news coverage when it unveiled it had secured the world record for having the tallest joss sticks. A towering 27 metres tall, the three joss sticks were made by bundling together thousands of smaller joss sticks onto giant wire frames. The news attracted hundreds of pilgrims who flocked to see the burning of the skyscrapers of incense.

Although being burnt to celebrate the 84th anniversary of the construction of a Buddha statue and designed to bring blessings, the joss sticks did not bring good luck to some of the visitors who had come to see them. Weakened by overnight rain, the joss sticks crumbled under their own weight, collapsing onto five of the pilgrims and killing them.

JUST POPPING OUTSIDE FOR SOME AIR...

Plane passenger Charles Bruce, 45, fell to his death after making the unusual decision to step out of the door at 5,000ft. Charles, from Brackley, Northamptonshire, quietly undid his seatbelt, slid back his seat and jumped out of the single-engined Cessna 172 as it hit speeds of 120mph. Pilot Judith Haig said he told her she was doing fine before climbing out of the door in January 2002.

DIED LAUGHING I

On the night of 24 March 1975, the BBC aired an episode of their hit TV comedy *The Goodies* called "Kung Fu Capers". In the show, one scene showed star Tim Brooke-Taylor dressed as a Scotsman using a set of bagpipes and the Scottish martial art of 'Hoots-Toots-ochaye' to defend himself against black pudding-wielding co-star Bill Oddie, demonstrating the Lancastrian martial art of 'Ecky Thump'.

The slapstick comedy fight certainly seems to have tickled the funny bone of many viewers. None more so than Alex Mitchell, a 50-year-old bricklayer from King's Lynn. According to his wife, the sight of seeing a man in tartan being beaten with a sausage caused him to begin laughing uncontrollably. After 25 minutes of out of control guffawing, he gave one final belly laugh and collapsed onto his couch. A subsequent autopsy showed he had died from heart failure brought on by the extreme fit of laughter. His widow wrote to the Goodies to thank them for making her husband's last minutes of life so happy.

DYING FOR A PEE

The ironic machinations of the Cosmic Joker combined with the inherent perils of alcohol seem to have played a part in the freakish demise of 33-year-old Anaïs Gloreaux. The woman from the northern Belgian town of Pulle had spent a Saturday night in 2005 out drinking at a variety of bars. On her way home she decided to take a short cut through the town's cemetery.

Needing to answer an urgent call of nature, Gloreaux crouched down between the gravestones to relieve herself. As she tried to stand up, she lost her balance and seized hold of one of the tombs to try and stop herself from falling. Unfortunately the tombstone she grabbed came loose and fell on top of her. According to the public prosecutors office, which originally investigated the discovery of Gloreaux's body as a possible murder, she died of suffocation when she was unable to lift the stone.

CAT SLIP

A cat burglar snatched a video recorder from a neighbour's flat and tried to edge around the outside of a tower block with his loot, only to fall to his death. Known crook Anthony George, 28, climbed out of a communal hallway window at the block in Wandsworth, London, on September 19 1998, tiptoed around the narrow ledge and clambered into the flat of Milica Radic. But he slipped as he made his return journey and fell nine floors to his death, his fingerprints on the outside of the windows the only evidence of his daring raid.

TIGHT SQUEEZE

Arthur P. King Sr, a 41-year-old from Wisconsin, had a long history of arrests for burglary. It was this life of crime that eventually led to his death when the notably unsuccessful crook tried to burgle a business in the town of Racine. King managed to squeeze his 76 kilo frame into the 40cm by 40 cm chimney opening on the roof of the Magna Tool Corp. However, once dropping passed the roofline, the chimney suddenly narrowed and King found himself stuck.

Some three months later, a maintenance worker investigated reported problems with the chimney and discovered King's decomposing corpse. According to Thomas Cloyd, the medical examiner for the area, "The chimney was so smooth there was nothing to grab. Once he became wedged there was no way he was going to get out. We think he died from starvation rather than suffocation, so it would have been a long and lonely death."

ITCH YOU CANT SCRATCH

Titus Flavius Sabinus Vespasianus – more commonly known as Titus – was Roman Emperor between 79-81 ACE. According to the Babylonian Talmud, he died when a mosquito flew up his nose and became embedded in his brain.

TOP 10 RIDICULOUS DEATHS
FROM AUSTRALIA

10. Francis Tovey, an 81-year-old from the Gold Coast, did not take the news well that his family wanted him to move into sheltered housing. Tovey scoured the internet in an attempt to find information to help him commit suicide, settling on plans for a gun-firing robot built from power tools. He built the machine and was found dead in the driveway of his million-dollar home. His suicide-assisting robot had shot him three times with a .22 semi-automatic pistol.

9. Wayne Condo, a 45-year-old mime artist from Melbourne, died of a heart attack midway through a performance on 13 July 1998. The 300 members of the audience initially thought that his collapsing to the floor and remaining motionless were part of the act.

8. Richard Wells was a 19-year-old deckhand on the trawler Arrow Sea working off the Queensland coast near Fraser Island. He was electrocuted in November 2001 when a wave crashed over the boat's wheelhouse while he was playing on his Playstation 2.

7. A 51-year-old man from Perth was cleaning a truck-mounted cement mixer in Carnarvon, Western Australia, in 2002 when the bowl moved and he became caught up in the agitator. He received an extreme mangling and died from internal injuries.

6. A 77-year-old woman from the Sydney suburb of Punchbowl fell into her top-opening freezer after overbalancing while attempting to retrieve some food in 1994. Her body was found frozen in the freezer, but an autopsy was unable to determine whether she had died from the cold or a blow to the head sustained when she tumbled in.

5. BASE jumper Torben Petersen leapt from the top of Bungonia Gorge, NSW, on 4 August 1997. Unfortunately for Petersen, his canopy became entangled on the limestone rocks and he was trapped, hanging on the cliff for hours until night fell and brought his death from exposure.

4. A 26-year-old bulimic woman from Adelaide died when she wolfed down four meals in quick succession, causing her stomach to swell to the point where she looked pregnant. The coroner said: "She consumed the food at such an abnormal rate her intestines went into paralysis, causing internal bleeding and cardiac arrest."

3. A 25-year-old woman drowned while performing fellatio on 34-year-old Christopher Sean Payne off Pee Wee Camp beach in Darwin. The couple had consumed 11 bottles of beer before getting kinky in the surf. Payne was charged with manslaughter when he admitted putting his hands on the woman's head during the sex, but was cleared when the court accepted his pleas that she had passed out from alcohol and he had no idea she was drowning.

2. In 1994, Sydney resident Cory Quinn took an overdose of sleeping tablets and climbed into his estranged wife's freezer while she was on holiday. He attached a note to himself for his 120-kilo ex-partner to read when she eventually found his body that read: "Gorge on this, you fat pig."

1. BUBBLE BLUNDER
Australian motorist Abner Kriller was driving back to his home in Albany in January 1995 when his harmless habit of gum-chewing took a deadly turn. Police investigating the crash that claimed his life concluded that Abner's last moments on this planet had seen him blow a large bubble that burst, leaving gum stuck to his glasses. This obscured his view which, rather inevitably, led him to swerve off the road. The car plunged down a hillside to Abner's fiery and twisted metal death below.

MURDER HE WROTE

A city high-flyer wrote a 2,000 word thesis about his doomed relationship before battering his girlfriend to death with a coal chisel and hanging himself. Banker Adam Beaumont, 33, of Putney, London, had endured a very intense relationship with colleague Kate Cole, 31, and penned a detailed account of their ups and downs which ended with a final chapter entitled "So why should I live?" He obviously came to a definitive answer, lured Kate round to his flat and took matters into his own hands on 7 June 1999.

But attempts to cover his tracks by mopping up blood on his kitchen floor, cutting Kate's wrists with a Stanley knife, and moving her car four miles away proved insufficient. It was thought he killed himself because the evidence against him was too strong.

CABLE GUY

A teacher on a school skiing trip died when the cable from a broken lift hit him on the head. Graham Lee, 34, from Hornsey in London, was supervising a trip to Risoul in the French Alps in April 2001 when the cable came off the pulley on the ski-lift, crashing down on the ski party and whacking Graham on the head. He died in hospital from his head injuries later that night.

LIKE MOTHER LIKE SON

Loving son Floyd Hightshoe from Bemidji, Minnesota, wanted to dig his own mother's grave as a final tribute and expression of filial duty. As he laboured away, the 39-self-employed logger chatted to family and friends who stopped by the cemetery to keep him company as he worked. Suddenly, he clasped his chest and collapsed into the freshly dug grave.

By the time those around the graveside had pulled Hightshoe from the hole he had just dug, he was dead. A week later, on 27 April 2001, he was buried next to his mother in a grave dug by his family and friends as their own form of tribute. According to the Reverend Bruce Peterson who conducted the burial: "It was hard on everyone there as you could see where the fresh grave was right next to his. Floyd loved his mom very much and was broken-hearted when she died. We all think that, as well as the grave digging, killed him."

WATER CALAMITY!

Shocking electrical wiring in pensioner Sheila Russell's garden led to her being found dead in her fish pond, next to an urn containing her late husband's ashes, in May 2006. Sheila, 72, from London, suffered electric shocks after the current leaked into the water from an old and outdated system which included unearthed wires and outdoor cables which were not waterproof. She came into contact with the electrified water when she used a metal-ended net to fish out a frog which used the pond. Daughter Christina Russell said: "That frog was a constant source of annoyance to her."

TOO LONG IN THE TOOTH

Sigurd, the first Earl of Orkney, was a fearsome warlord whose bloody ways, military might and tactical flair saw him conquer most of northern Scotland. After a fever-pitched battle against Maelbrigte of Moray, Sigurd decapitated Maelbrigte and placed his head on his saddle as a gory trophy. However, Maelbrigte had revenge from beyond the grave when his teeth opened a cut on Sigurd's leg, which became infected and led to a fatal case of blood poisoning.

THE ULTIMATE SACRIFICE

Our political leaders have it easy these days. Back in the ninth century, High Prince Álmos, the first Grand Prince of the Magyars, was killed as a ritual sacrifice – alongside several white stallions – after he led his men to a defeat in battle. According to historians, Álmos accepted his fate with total equanimity believing that was the only honourable thing to do. We just wish our current leaders would do the same when they screw up.

PLANE UNLUCKY

Australia is huge. As a European, the first time you fly over it, seeing the miles and miles of earth unscarred by man is a novel and wondrous sight. It can also lead to morbid thoughts that, if the plane crashed, you would be an awfully long way from anyone or anything representing help.

This makes it seem all the more ridiculous that poor Joe MacLeod died when a block of ice fell from a plane passing over his outback homestead in Western Australia in 1987. The freak accident was discovered when neighbour Bob Roberts called round to borrow some equipment from MacLeod and noticed a huge hole in the roof of the home. Getting no response from MacLeod, Bob entered the property and found the partly pulverised body of his friend still in bed.

A subsequent investigation by police suggested that Joe MacLeod had been killed when a large icicle, formed by a leaking plane toilet, had broken off the plane and plummeted like a frozen dagger of death down towards MacLeod's remote home more than 200km away from Broome, the nearest town. The ice made a 60-centimetre tear through the plywood and metal roof before smashing into MacLeod's noggin. A police spokesman said: "A faulty O-ring probably caused toilet fluids to leak until it all froze into an icicle which then just popped off. As we don't know exactly what time this happened we cannot tell yet which plane was responsible. It is a one in a million thing. Mr MacLeod was just very unlucky." No shit, Sherlock.

CRIME DOESN'T PAY

Divorcee Kathleen Yeoman, 46, plotted to win back the affections of her lover and neighbour Paul Cockerhill by staging an elaborate fake burglary on 30 October 1998.

She ransacked her house in Brixworth, Northamptonshire, tipping out drawers, throwing jewellery on her bed and piling electrical goods in the front room. Then she taped her mouth, put a plastic bag over her head and tied her hands together with self-tightening plastic ties, before leaving her front door open and laying across the doorstep of her former lover. But as she waited for his return, she vomited and choked to death because she was unable to remove the tape from her mouth. Police dismissed the incident as suspicious after realising nothing had been taken and she still had £918 in her handbag.

WRONG WAY ON THE M-WAY

Quite how someone manages to end up driving in the wrong direction along a major motorway is baffling, but that's what happened to Georgia Philippou, 65, when she became lost and confused on the M11. Despite asking numerous other drivers for directions on the evening of 8 January 1998, she couldn't find her way back to her home in Ilford and ended up driving into a motorway works unit, doing a U-turn and driving north on the southbound carriageway. Other motorists were forced to take evasive action as she ploughed relentlessly towards them, but she eventually crashed her Vauxhall Cavalier into another vehicle and died at the scene from multiple injuries.

ILL FORTUNE

A fortune teller advised Thai businessman Boonchai Lotharakphong to put a flag on the factory roof to ward off bad luck. As Boonchai climbed onto the roof to raise the flag, he slipped and fell to his death.

GONE IN A PUFF OF SMOKE

A chronic smoker who was dependent on oxygen to breathe died after using her oxygen mask while puffing on a cigarette. Wheelchair-bound Marion Greig, 83, who had a 60 cigarettes-a-day habit and suffered from chronic obstructive pulmonary disease, used her oxygen mask to assist her breathing when she smoked at her Worcester home. But on 11 March 2007 she inadvertently ignited the tubes and pumped her room full of smoke, choking to death as a result.

DEATH METAL

Frederick I was Holy Roman Emperor during the 12th century. In 1190, he organized an army of 15,000 men – including 3,000 knights – to go on the Third Crusade. Leading them across the overland route to the Holy Land, as he Frederick crossed the Saleph River in Anatolia, the shock of the cold water caused him to have a heart attack. The heavy weight of his armour then caused him to topple into the water, where he drowned

FOR MY NEXT TRICK...

Pub chef and ex-Para Mark Hunt, 40, accidentally stabbed himself in the chest with a 12-inch blade after a trick went horribly wrong, in 2005. He was showing off in front of a teenage kitchen porter at a pub in Leckhampstead, Berkshire, by plunging the knife towards his stomach and then reversing it at the last second, making it appear he had stabbed himself. But he mistimed his switch and ended up thrusting the blade in so deeply it severed his spinal cord. Mark, from Coventry, West Midlands, had only been at the pub for two weeks and hadn't even been drinking.

PUMMELLED BY PANEL

Severe gales blew James McEwan off his feet as he tried to fix a loose fence panel, fracturing his ribs and leading to a fatal inflammation of the lungs. Heavy smoker James, 59, from Padgate, Cheshire, was unable to get to hospital because the roads were so jammed with traffic and it was too late to avoid infection by the time he made it the following day. He went downhill fast and died on 22 January 2007, four days after the gale. Coroner Nicholas Rheinberg said: "The fence panel must have acted almost like a sail and caught the wind."

FOR WHOM THE BELL TOLLS...

A man broke into a derelict church to drink cider, but plunged to his death when the bell tower staircase collapsed beneath him. Christopher Davies had spent all day drinking and smoking cannabis with pals Dean Roach and Thomas Riley, and after buying a bottle of cider they decided to seek refuge from the rain in Oxton Congregational Church, Birkenhead. Christopher jumped over gaps in flooring to reach the bell tower, but fell 50ft when the staircase collapsed beneath him, dying from major head and chest injuries in May 2006.

WHEN CATTLE GO BAD I

Cows are not known for being particularly violent, but these bovine bastards can turn on you quicker than milk curdles and inflict all manner of fatal injuries. A total of 27 people in the UK were killed or seriously injured by cattle while using footpaths between 1991 and 2001. Dogs featured on 20 occasions and cattle with calves were involved in every case. These stories prove that cattle can be killers and show why we're much better off when they're on a plate covered in peppercorn sauce.

HAIR RAISING RIDE

Doug McKay, the 40-year-old co-owner of an amusement park on Whidbey Island, Washington, was working on the Super Loop 2 rollercoaster in 2003 when his hair got caught in the ride. It pulled him 12 metres into the air and scalped him before he fell to earth to be impaled on a fence.

DISCOUNT SUICIDE

If you're going to hang yourself, you really don't worry about saving a few quid in the process. But penny-pincher David Wackett, 25, used a 20 percent discount from the DIY store where he worked to buy the rope he used to kill himself in 2003. David, from Bridgend, South Wales, had fallen for a girl from work, but his feelings were unrequited so he tore off his own head by tying the rope from his car to a lamp-post and driving off. Life is cheap and so is the means to end it.

THE COSMIC JOKER STRIKES AGAIN I

Despite her 76 years, Nanette 'Nucy' Meech was a keen outdoor woman and canoeist. On 15 July 1993 she was canoeing down the Brule River in Wisconsin with her daughter Laurie. Nanette's canoe hit a rough patch of water and overturned, but she managed to swim safely to one of the banks.

As she hauled herself out of the water she might have thought she had escaped a narrow brush with death. However, the cosmic joker had other plans. At that moment she called out to her daughter she was safe, a 13-metre tall popular tree crashed to the ground, crushing Meech beneath it and killing her. Subsequent investigation showed that the tree fell because it had been gnawed by beavers.

WHEN CATTLE GO BAD II

Walker Bernard Hanrahan died when a crazed herd of cows chased him across a field and trampled him to death. The 65-year-old retired builder from Wigan had been strolling across farmland with his two dogs when the crazy cows started chasing after him. He suffered injuries so severe it was as if he had been in a car crash.

ALL GLOVED UP

Gary Harmon, a 47-year-old from Pontiac, Michigan, was admitted to hospital suffering with asthma and emphysema. He then spent nine days being treated by doctors and nurses for the conditions before returning home. Although his breathing seemed better, Gary had a persistent cough and was convinced there was something stuck in his throat.

According to his wife Karen: "He just kept coughing and coughing, so we had to take him back to St Joseph. He said there was something there." When he arrived back at St Joseph Mercy-Oakland Hospital, doctors were unable to prevent Harmon from choking to death. When medical examiners later examined his body, they found a latex surgical glove had been left inside his throat.

WATER WAY TO GO

They say it's good to drink lots of water. Within reason. But thirsty Matthew Davies, 32, drank so many pints each day it flushed away his body's vital chemicals and he died from the rare condition of water intoxication in 2002. Matthew, 32, of Llandudno, North Wales, drank water in preference to tea or coffee, but it washed away essential salts from his body and he sank into a coma from which he never emerged.

RINGTONE RAGE

Otto Berndt, a 42-year-old German businessman, spent the night of 8 August 1999 drinking in a Hamburg beer garden. While others patrons tried to enjoy themselves, show-off Berndt was constantly making and taking calls on his mobile phone. He consistently refused requests to speak more quietly, turn down his ringer volume, switch off the phone or take calls somewhere else.

It all became too much for some of his fellow patrons. Infuriated both by Berndt's constant pointless jabbering and his annoying ring tone, one of them picked up a beer bottle and began to beat Otto with it. Berndt tried to make a run for it, but fell and smashed his head on a bench. Later, a witness told police investigating the death of Berndt that, "The problem was not only that his phone was loud, but it had one of those terrible melodies, too."

The German press claimed it was the first example in the country of 'fatal mobile rage'. You just know it is not going to be the last.

WHEN CATTLE GO BAD III

A half-ton bullock was catapulted onto the roof of 28-year-old Piers Williams' car after wandering out into his path. The animal had escaped from a field outside Milton Keynes when local man Piers collided straight into it, bouncing it onto the bonnet and roof of his Renault Clio. He was knocked unconscious and lost control of his car, crashing off the road on 15 January 2002. He later died in hospital from his injuries. The bullock didn't make it, either.

STRIKE!

Margaret Weir was "bowled over like a nine-pin" as she helped test the rear lights of her husband's car. An inquest heard how retired headmaster David Weir, 74, put his Honda Accord into reverse, but hit the accelerator instead of the brake, whacking into 78-year-old Margaret and eventually coming to a halt 60ft away from their house in Alphington, Devon, in November 2004.

SHOULD HAVE SEEN IT COMING

French fortune teller Patrick Depalle was so supremely confident in his alleged mystic powers that to impress a customer he pulled out a revolver and began to play Russian roulette. His horrified client was too stunned to intervene as Depalle claimed, "I have been to Haiti, so this is nothing for me. I am never wrong. My spirit contacts on the other side are strong. They will protect me."

At this point he pulled the trigger and the gun fired, smearing his brains onto the wall. Obviously, the fact that Depalle's spirit contacts did not protect him is something his death will allow him to take up with them in person.

HORA-IBLE WAY TO GO

No Jewish wedding is complete without the hora – the chair dance where the groom and bride are hoisted on chairs by guests and danced around. It is a custom that is thought to have its origins in the time of ancient Jewish royalty and shows no signs of dying out. These days the dance is usually performed to a medley of popular Jewish songs including "Hava Nagila" – 'Come let us be glad' – and "Siman Tov U Mazleltov" – 'May good luck come to us'.

Unfortunately for Adam Macho, who got married in the Tel Aviv suburb of Brak in 1994, it was one wedding custom that brought neither gladness nor luck. While aloft at his wedding party, one of the family members holding Adam's chair took a tumble, tipping the hapless groom to the floor, where he broke his neck.

DIED LAUGHING II

A Fish Called Wanda is not a film that would top our list of comedy classics. However, it certainly amused renowned Danish audiologist Ole Bentzen. In 1989, the specialist in low-cost hearing aids for developing countries went to his local cinema to see the smash hit movie. While watching a scene in which John Cleese dances in his underwear, Bentzen began to roar with laughter. His heart rate soared and he went into cardiac arrest. In the spasms of the attack, Bentzen continued to laugh, masking the seriousness of what was happening with him. By the time anyone realized what was wrong, it was too late. Bentzen had stopped laughing forever.

WHEN CATTLE GO BAD IV

A man was killed and two others badly injured when a bull ran amok at a farm near Leominster, West Midlands. Mike Dawe, who was in his 60s, sustained fatal injuries when the bull went out of control and attacked workers at a farm in Stoke Prior on 1 March 2007. Farmer Graham Beaumont, 54, was hospitalised with head and facial injuries, and another man in his 60s suffered chest injuries and leg fractures. Mike had been to feed the bull in its pen when the animal charged – maybe it had a beef with him?

STICK TO THE BARBIE DOLLS

Keen readers of this book will have noticed it is short on reporting any ridiculous deaths relating to young children. There are few things more tragic than parents outliving their offspring and we found nothing humorous in the numerous accounts we came across. Except possibly, that is, for the death of seven-year-old Jessica Whitney Dubroff, where it is hard not to smile at the thought that any parent could ever think it was a good idea to let a child attempt to fly a plane across the United States.

However, that is exactly what the parents of Jessica thought when the pint-size trainee pilot began her 'Sea to Shining Sea Flight' in April 1996, in an attempt to become the youngest person to have piloted a plane coast-to-coast in America. Maybe they thought their daughter becoming an instant media celebrity was a better for her than playing with Barbies. They certainly thought their daughter was special in spectacularly ridiculous way. Two days before seven-year-old Jessica Dubroff took off, her mother, Lisa Blair Hathaway, was asked if the bad weather might delay her flight. Hathaway replied: "The weather will move for her. It is not luck. Jessica knows that. It is the power of her being. There is something about Jessica that things move for her. She is just a wonderful person."

Unfortunately, the power of Jessica's being was not enough to clear up the weather on 11 April. Her plane took off in exceptionally heavy rain and within minutes returned to ground with a crash, making it less 'Sea to Shining Sea Flight' and more 'Air to Land in Fatal Smash'. Even after the crash which claimed her daughter's life, Lisa Blair Hathaway was unrepentant and unable to see how indulging your children is sometimes a really dumb idea. Hathaway said, "I still beg people to let children fly if they want to." While you are at it, why not let your children play on train tracks and busy highways...?

KILLED BY THEIR OWN INVENTIONS I

William Bullock's invention of the web rotary printing press in 1863 helped revolutionise the printing industry, thanks to its great speed and efficiency. Unfortunately, it also proved the death of him. On 3 April 1867 he was adjusting one of the new presses that was being installed for the *Philadelphia Public Ledger* newspaper. He tried to kick a driving belt onto a pulley, but his leg became caught in the machine, and was crushed and broken. Gangrene set in and he died on 12 April during an operation to amputate the leg.

TOP 10 RIDICULOUS SUICIDES

10. When Filipino Enrique Quinanola's attempts to commit suicide through hanging and overdosing failed, he ran into a café and threatened customers before trying to slash his wrists. When police intervened, he tried to stab them and they reacted by shooting him dead. Given Quinanola's obvious suicidal bent, it seems wrong that his family successfully sued the officers who had inadvertently given him his death wish.

9. Robert Williams, a chief psychologist with the Kansas prison service, lost his job in 1974 after announcing he was a "witch with vast occult powers". Unfortunately for Williams his powers did not extend to conjuring up another job and he shot himself.

8. Herbert Pickey was a prisoner at a jail in South Carolina in 1992 when he decided to take the ultimate way out. He died after eating eight bars of soap and five cans of shaving foam. His suicide noted claimed that, "The Lord Almighty told me to take my life."

7. Guillaume Tanoh was so upset by the death of Félix Houphouët-Boigny – who had been president of Côte d'Ivoire for 33 years – that he committed suicide by jumping into the crocodile-filled moat around the presidential palace.

6. Japanese heavy metal rock star Hideto 'Hide' Matsumoto hanged himself by attaching a towel to a doorknob in his Tokyo apartment. His suicide so upset legions of his female fans that two of them copied his odd exit from the world of the living.

5. Manic depressive mother of three Emily Shreaves from Devon managed to commit suicide by drinking more than 20 litres of water

in less than an hour. Her H2O binge led to water intoxication and eventual death due to the swelling of her brain.

4. As you might expect of one of the scientists involved in the creation of the explosive Semtex, Bohumil Sole went out with a bang. He travelled to the Priessnitz spa in his hometown Jesenik, Czech Republic, strapped with a homemade belt of Semtex, and blasted himself and the building to oblivion.

3. Former British war hero Lieutenant-Commander Ian Cobold converted his vacuum cleaner into an air pump to deploy homemade nerve gas derived from rat poison. His suicide led to the evacuation of the entire village in Devon in which he killed himself.

2. Petty criminal Franco Brun was found dead in his police cell at the Metro East Detention Centre in Toronto in 1987, after having committed suicide by choking on the miniature Gideon bible that was provided in every cell. Police psychiatrists said that he had shown incredible will to force the book down his throat and that he may have chosen this particular way to end his life as an attempt to purge himself of demonic forces.

1. HOLLYWOOD OR BUST
Peg Entwhistle was a Welsh-born actress who achieved fame on Broadway. In 1932, she was lured to Hollywood with a one-picture film deal, but after poor reviews in RKO's *Thirteen Women*, she found it impossible to get work and was reduced to topless modelling. Depressed by this state of affairs, Entwhistle climbed to the top of the H in the famous Hollywood sign (which at the time still read Hollywoodland) and jumped off. It looks like the Cosmic Joker played a hand in her suicide, the ridiculous irony being that her post, delivered the next day, included an offer for a role in which she was to play a character who killed herself.

LEST WE FORGET...

Maybe Richard Swindles should have shown a bit more respect before climbing up a war memorial in West Kirby, in the Wirral. The 30-year-old Birkenhead man had spent Valentine's Day 2007 drinking with two friends, who climbed up the memorial to drink booze. But when they decided to get down, Richard lost his balance and plunged 10ft onto metal railings, rupturing internal organs in the process. His pals thought he was fooling around about the extent of his injuries and left him lying in undergrowth, where he was found dead the next morning. With friends like these...

UP, UP AND AWAY!

Every boy who dresses in a Superman costume as a child wishes he could fly, but even the youngest of children generally realize that wearing a cape does not convey on you the ability to defy gravity. Therefore it is a shame that Texan student Dave Millar – studying for his masters in mathematics – did not have the common sense of a four-year-old.

After a night of heavy drinking while on a student bar crawl in Houston in 1994, Miller went attired as Superman to a fancy dress party. However, alcohol rather than kryptonite proved Miller's undoing as a superhero. He stood on a table, shouted: "I'm Supes! Look up in the sky, I can fly!" and then leapt into the air. Unable to fly or even leap tall buildings in a single bound, Millar crashed to the floor, smashing his skull and ending his life.

CUPBOARD OF DOOM

Ronald McClagish died after trapping himself in a bedroom cupboard for a week. For reasons unknown he had been in the cupboard at his home in Murrow, Cambridgeshire, when a nearby wardrobe fell across the door, trapping him inside. His neighbour reported repeated digging sounds coming from his home, which were later revealed to have been made as

Ronald, 51, banged desperately on the inside of the cupboard with a copper pipe he had dislodged, sending water gushing over him.

Police found his body on February 15, 2004, and a post mortem examination revealed his body and skin was so badly water logged it was as if he had been immersed in water, possibly leading to bronchitis. They ruled out foul play, and blamed his death on a bizarre accident. Coroner William Morris said: "I don't know why the wardrobe fell over... but sometimes there are questions that are just never answered."

HOMEMADE HIJACKER GOES TO GROUND WITH A BANG

In May 2000, a hijacker wearing a ski mask and swimming goggles broke into the cabin of Philippines Airlines flight PR812, en route from Davao City in the southern Philippines to the capital Manila. Armed with a revolver and a hand grenade, he ordered the captain to return to Davao.

According to the Captain Emmanuel 'Butch' Generoso, the hijacker – Reginald Chua – was upset because his wife was having an affair with a policeman. Chua thought that robbing the 289 passengers of their money and valuables would help him to win his wayward partner back.

Having successfully relieved all passengers and crew of cash, credit cards and jewellery, Chua forced a flight attendant to open one of the plane's doors. He then pulled on a homemade parachute and still clutching the hand grenade asked the pilots if any of them knew "how to jump". Even though they could not offer him any advice, Chua still leapt 1,800 metres from the Airbus 330.

Miraculously managing to escape being sucked into the jet's engines, Chua might have thought his chances of making a getaway were looking good. However, his homemade chute proved difficult to steer and he slammed into a remote piece of ground. Chua might even have survived this difficult landing if he had thought to let go of the hand grenade, which exploded upon impact.

KILLED BY THEIR OWN INVENTIONS II

Known as the German "Glider King", Otto Lilienthal was a pioneer of human aviation who became the first person to make repeated successful gliding flights. He was an inspiration to the Wright Brothers. On 9 August 1896 he fell from a height of 56ft after crashing one of his hang gliders. He broke his spine and died the next day from his injuries. His final words were: "Kleine Opfer müssen gebracht werden!" ('Small sacrifices must be made!')

DIED LAUGHING III

Damnoen Saen-um was a 52-year-old ice-cream salesman from the Muang District in the Trat Province of eastern Thailand. One night in August 2003, he woke his wife by laughing out loud. She was surprised to see that he was asleep, apparently finding something in a dream so amusing that he kept guffawing even when she tried to wake him. After more than two minutes of continuous, hysterical laughter, he suddenly stopped breathing.

According to Dr Somchai Chakrabhand, one of the medical experts who investigated the death: "I have never seen a case like this. It is possible that a person could have heart seizure while laughing or crying too hard in their sleep. However, in this case it seems he died from asphyxiation due to laughter causing problems with his thoracic diaphragm. We cannot know what he was dreaming, but it must have been very funny."

WHEN CATTLE GO BAD V

A bull pawed the ground and rolled its eyes in anger before charging 75-year-old farmer Robert Crothers, headbutting him into the air like a stuffed doll and trampling his body to death. The animal became agitated at the farm near Gilford, County Down, and attacked Mr Crothers as he went to take his cows to be milked on 25 September 2006.

BORN AGAIN DEAD

In 1985, Pastor Michael Davis of the Christian Fellowship Church in Laros, Louisiana exalted his flock to "cast off the burden of sin and prepare for rebirth". He then stripped down to his bathing shorts and climbed into a pool of water in which he intended to rebaptise all those who wanted to be born again.

Once in the holy pool, one of the pastor's faithful assistants passed him a microphone so he could keep spreading the word. Unfortunately, the microphone had a fault and as soon as it connected with the wet man of God, there was an almighty electrical explosion. However much Davis may have wanted others to be born again, when the smoke cleared there was no escaping the fact he was dead for good.

OFF HIS HEAD II

Sometimes certain ridiculous forms of exiting the world of the living seem to become popular in one geographical area. It can almost appear as if an outlandish way of dying is made viral. An example of this may be seen in a 1999 outbreak of deliberate self-decapitation in the Indian state of Gujarat.

All of the suicides were related to the concept of 'kamal puji' – a form of sacrifice involving ritual beheading. The first fatality in the death meme seems to have occurred at a temple in Gadhula, a village in the Bhavnagar district of Gujarat. Amarsinh Mavji, a 40-year-old farm labourer, went to the temple along with other villagers to seek forgiveness for sins committed across the previous year.

Unable to find anyone who would fulfil his plea to behead him as a sacrifice to appease the main goddess worshipped by the village, Amarsinh decided to come back to the temple later. When no one was looking, he attached a sword to a rope and managed to swing it in such a way that it cleaved his head from his body in one clean strike.

In the following months of 1999, at least six other people in Gujarat managed to successfully perform the same self-administered ritual.

PROPOSAL PLUNGE

Dramatic declarations of love are all very well, but they're no good if you're not around to enjoy the consequences afterwards. Romantic Paul McGregor, 31, was determined to win the hand of new girlfriend Emma Priestley, 19, after just two weeks of being together. While walking along the River Trent in Nottinghamshire, in 2000, he asked: "If I swim across to the other side will you marry me?" before diving in. But after she crossed a bridge to the other side he was nowhere to be found, having been sucked beneath the surface by strong currents underneath the self-same bridge. Ironically, she said afterwards she had already decided she wanted to marry him.

BEDS ARE BURNING

Poor Lionel Buckley, an 86-year-old deaf and diabetic pensioner, had been in the wars. After collapsing in the street while shopping in Salford, he was admitted to Burton House, a special unit at the Withington Hospital, leading him to joke with staff: "My luck's so bad this place will probably be the death of me." Ironically, it was. To ease his pain and help his recovery, Mr Buckley was put on a special air mattress. However, the very piece of equipment meant to help him ended up killing him.

In December 1998, nurses at the hospital heard an enormous bang and rushed into Mr. Buckley's room. They found the OAP thrown out of bed, suffering from severe burns as the smouldering remains of his exploded mattress set off the fire alarms. All Buckley could tell the nurses was: "The bed got warm, then hot, then there was a flash, a bang and it burst into flames."

A subsequent investigation showed that the airbed's compressor had overheated, causing the explosion in what fire investigators called a "million-to-one freak accident". However, this was no comfort to poor Mr Buckley. He died within a week after contracting septicaemia and broncho-pneumonia as a result of the burns.

WHEN CATTLE GO BAD VI

Dog owners were warned not to walk their pets on land where cattle are grazing following the death of Wendy Tustin, 55, from Pembrokeshire, in September 2005. She was found dead in a field of around 40 suckler cows with calves, having suffered horrendous injuries consistent with trampling, crushing and butting by cattle.

She was last seen walking her dog nearby and had told a neighbour she was going to take a shortcut through farmland to get home. Coroner Michael Howells said the presence of suckler cattle and a dog had been extremely dangerous, as their reactions could be unpredictable and aggressive.

WHEN SEX GAMES GO WRONG II

Life must be pretty dull in the Welsh valleys if this is the best they can do for entertainment... Damian Batley, of Kidwelly, Wales, accidentally hanged himself while taking part in a bizarre sex act, filming it all on his mobile phone in February 2008. A family member found Damian hanging naked from his bedroom door, with footage of his last moments captured on his mobile for posterity.

NO JAM TOMORROW

A top scientist overdid it with his marmalade preparations and gassed himself with deadly carbon monoxide fumes. Keith Turnball, 61, was stirring a large cauldron of the preserve on the stove at his house in Wark, Northumberland, just before Christmas 2003. But he had used six pounds of oranges and the stove simply could not cope, eventually pumping out excessive levels of odourless and invisible carbon monoxide. Biochemist Keith collapsed and died alongside his dog Cleugh in the kitchen of his isolated home.

THE COSMIC JOKER STRIKES AGAIN II

Mari Collier was an Australian operatic star who first came to widespread international fame in the role of Floria Tosca in the 1963 Covent Garden production of *Tosca*. She became even more synonymous with the role in 1965 when Maria Callas cancelled her appearance in a revival of Franco Zeffirelli's production and Collier stepped in at the last minute to huge critical acclaim. According to some critics, Collier was, "The ultimate Tosca" and had, "become forever more Floria."

Anyone familiar with the story of Puccini's opera will know that in its last moments the character of Floria Tosca falls to her death. It certainly seems as if the Cosmic Joker is a fan of Puccini, because there was a grim irony when the fates called for the final curtain in Collier's life. In 1971, at the age of 44, Collier was in her London home discussing an upcoming tour of the United States, when she leaned against a balcony window that unexpectedly opened, plunging her more than 10 metres to her death in the street below.

WHEN SEX GAMES GO WRONG III

A church organist found dead in a huge plastic bag attached to a vacuum cleaner was killed when a bizarre sex act went tragically wrong – not exactly the sort of behaviour you would expect from a church-going man. In 2006 bachelor Ian Kemp, 48, of Teesside, was found naked, lying in the bag in a foetal position, his legs bound at the shins with brown parcel tape and his wrists tied together by a silver chain.

The coroner said there was no indication Mr Kemp had intended to die, but the vacuum had sucked all the air out of the bag. It was not known exactly what his intentions were prior to his death, but the pathologist said it was unlikely he had been forced into this position. "He was a self-taught amateur," said his minister Philip Tait, referring to Mr Kemp's organ playing, not his sexual deviancy.

THE ART OF DEATH

Award-winning British wildlife artist Simon Combes earned a reputation for getting close to the animals he painted. His canvases featuring a parade of African animals proved highly popular, with both his original paintings and prints in constant demand – partly because they featured such a wealth of detail gleamed from firsthand observation. When asked by newspaper interviewers if his artistic approach involved any risk, he would regale them with an assortment of anecdotes about having survived being chased up trees by rhinos and elephants or being bitten by a Bengal tiger. He was often quoted as saying: "The only animal I fear is man."

In December 2004, Combes was walking with his wife and a friend in the Great Rift Valley in Kenya, scouting for subjects to paint. Suddenly a water buffalo appeared and charged at him, knocking him to the ground. As his wife and friend tried frantically to scare the beast off, it trampled him and gored him in the chest. Well Simon, you should have feared the buffalo as well, mate.

BUNGEE BODGE

William Brotherton thought his luck was in when he was offered the chance to make a free bungee jump from a balloon in exchange for providing his services to check hot air balloon inflation equipment. It is a shame that the bungee equipment itself had not been checked by Brotherton on the fateful day he made his jump in July 1993. If it had been, a ridiculous, but tragic accident may have been avoided.

Unfortunately for Brotherton, the bungee rope attached to his feet was 80 metres long, but when he was told to jump, the balloon was hovering at just 60 metres above the field it was tethered in. People on the ground realized the danger and shouted warnings, but Brotherton and the bungee crew in the balloon could not hear over the roar of the burner, mishearing the cries of "Don't jump!" as "Jump!" Brotherton jumped and the 20 metres of excess cord made his death grimly inevitable as he crashed head-first into the ground.

RUBBISH MORTIS

Homer and Langley Collyer were reclusive brothers who lived in their home at 2078 Fifth Avenue in New York. Despite persistent rumours in their Harlem neighbourhood and in New York newspapers that they lived in 'oriental splendour' or 'were sitting around on stacks of cash too afraid to deposit it in a bank', the truth was altogether stranger and sadder.

In earlier days, Homer had obtained a degree in engineering and Langley was an Admiralty lawyer, but the increasingly eccentric behaviour of both men saw them retreat into their brownstone building and live as reclusive hermits. After several attempted burglaries by criminals attracted to the property by rumours of the brothers' non-existent fabulous wealth, they began to booby trap their home. They also began to collect and hoard absolutely everything. When police tried to force their way into the brothers' home in 1942 to talk to Langley about an unpaid bill, they could get no further than the front door thanks to the sheer wall of junk piled from the floor to the ceiling.

In 1947, acting on an anonymous tip-off that there was a dead body in 2078 Fifth Avenue, police smashed down the front door. After removing more than four tones of junk, including thousands of newspapers, parts of a wine press, more than a dozen broken pianos and half-assembled engines, officers found the dead body of Homer caught in one of his own booby traps, where he had died from starvation and dehydration. Police continued to empty the house of more than 84 tones of junk, eventually discovering the body of Langley who had been trapped under a fallen pile of newspapers. It seems Homer had been on the way to free the trapped Langley when he had been caught in one of his own traps, leaving his pinned brother to starve to death as well.

DEATH SPOON

Unloading the dishwasher in her new fitted kitchen was the last act of housewife Mary Wherry, 34, at her home in Hampton Hill, south-west London, in July 2004. Botched building work meant a metal, wall-mounted utensil rack gave out a tiny electric shock whenever a metal object was placed inside it. But as Mary put away a metal spoon, her ankle touched the metal-fronted open door of the dishwasher, completing a circuit and fatally electrocuting her. A later investigation found the building firm had broken a string of safety guidelines.

WHEN SEX GAMES GO WRONG IV

Electrical engineer Brian Smith, 45, made himself a special harness which he attached to the ceiling of his bedroom. He carefully recorded his efforts setting it up, taking a load of photos, then stripped naked and climbed on board. But his efforts to achieve auto-erotic asphyxiation went sadly wrong, as a problem with the ligature around his neck caused it to strangle him. Barry's trussed-up body wasn't discovered for more than a week. A coroner ruled out suicide because he didn't make arrangements for his dog, which was found hungry and thirsty when police eventually raided his home, near Eastbourne.

BEAM ME UP, NUTTY

Alleged space aliens played a role in the death of 48-year-old registered nurse Laverne Landis. In November 1982, under the orders of UFOnauts who Landis believed were beaming messages directly into her brain, she and companion Gerald Flachs headed out into the frozen wilderness of north-eastern Minnesota. They locked themselves in their car and began to fast while they waited for further messages from the aliens they expected to land shortly. Local police felt unable to do anything to intervene until a week after their vigil began, when a motorist reported seeing two unconscious bodies in a car on the highway. When they broke into the vehicle, they found a hypothermic, dehydrated and starved Flachs, and a very stiff, entirely dead Landis.

DRAINING EXPERIENCE

A pair of trainers protruding from a manhole was all that could be seen of Kevin McKeon when he fell down a drain and drowned in May 2003. Kevin, 25, of Taunton, Somerset, was on his way home from a night out when he dropped his mobile phone and it skidded down a drain. He lifted the grate, knelt down and leaned over, but lost his footing and fell head first into 6ft of water. Glug!

WEEDED OUT

Who keeps deadly weedkiller Paraquat in an unmarked bottle in the fridge? Council gardener Gary Knight poured 250ml of the poisonous liquid into a dark plastic drinks bottle at the city council depot where he worked in Sheffield, intending to use it on a friend's patio. Confusion ensued as it was subsequently passed between four different people before turning up at the home of Mark Langton, 35, after his mother put it in the fridge thinking it was a fizzy drink. Mark wet his lips with the liquid before spitting it out, but it was already too late to save him. Internal damage caused by the weedkiller is inevitable and irreparable, and he was slowly poisoned, dying three weeks later in 2005.

KEYRING KILLER

Wannabe gangster Fabian Flowers, 19, accidentally killed himself with a keyring. A member of the Longsight Crew of Manchester, he was playing with a miniature designer gun disguised as a key fob in a local lap-dancing club. The tiny gun, just over 4ins long, was one of several that had been smuggled into the UK from Bulgaria and modified to fire twin .25 bullets, used by gang members as fashion accessories. On 23 February 2004 Flowers was showing off in front of friends and demonstrating how the gun worked. Undoubtedly believing the safety catch was on, he put it to his head and fired, killing himself instantly.

WHEN SEX GAMES GO WRONG V

It was no laughing matter when Gary Ashbrook, 31, of Newhaven, Sussex, was found dead in bed with a condom over his head after experimenting with nitrous oxide, known as laughing gas. Nine empty canisters of the gas, which is used for sexual gratification as it creates feelings of euphoria, were found next to his body on the evening of 13 May 2007. It wasn't the gas that killed him; that was suffocation from wearing the condom. Still, at least he went out with a smile on his face.

NOTHING TO WINE ABOUT

George Plantagenet, Duke of Clarence, was the brother of kings Edward IV and Richard III of England. In 1478 he was imprisoned in the Tower of London for plotting against his brother Edward. Due to his Royal status he was granted a private execution which, at Clarence's own request, took the form of being drowned in two hogsheads – equivalent to 477.3 litres – of malmsey wine.

LEAVE IT TO SANTA

Inquisitive kids can be a nightmare at Christmas, hunting for presents and peeling back the wrapping paper to peek inside. Mum-of-five Karen Russon, 24, decided to hide her presents in the loft of her home in West Bromwich, West Midlands, in December 2005. But she lost her footing and banged her head, causing fatal injuries. Her body lay wedged in the loft hatch for more than 24 hours. She was discovered by neighbours the next day, who found that her two youngest children had been cared for by their six-year-old sister, while the other two brothers were away with their grandparents.

TOP 10 RIDICULOUS SEXUALLY RELATED DEATHS

10. American tourist Robert Giles died in a Philippines hotel room in 2001 while taking pornographic pictures of a local 21-year-old woman. The 53-year-old Californian became so overly excited while taking photos that he suffered fatal cardiac arrest.

9. Sandra Orellana died after she fell from an eighth floor hotel balcony in Los Angeles while having sex with her boss, Robert Salazar. According to Salazar, they had been changing positions when she lost her balance, toppled over the railing and plunged onto the concrete below.

8. In 1999, Romanian soccer star Mario Bugeanu and his girlfriend were so desperate to express their passion that they made love in Bugeanu's Mercedes as soon as it was parked in his garage after a night out. Unfortunately, in their rush they did not switch the engine off and both died during sex from carbon monoxide poisoning.

7. Pennsylvanian couple Toby and Kirsten Taylor regularly used electricity as part of their sex play, but it all went wrong in January 2008 when Mr Taylor accidentally administered a lethal shock to his wife with the power cord from her hairdryer.

6. A pair of 34-year-old Japanese virgins who had waited more than a dozen years to physically consummate their relationship died on their wedding night. Sachi Hidaka and his wife Tomio died from heart attacks during the act as they made love for the first time.

5. Rosa Vela, a 22-year-old Peruvian woman, died from septicaemia caused by the rusty padlock on a homemade leather chastity belt that her husband made her wear when he was away on business.

4. In 2002, the wife and mistress of Hagibis Jungao ran screaming into the lobby of the Dragon Hotel in Manila to get help. Both women had been making love to Jungao in Room 106 when it all became too much for the 45-year-old. An investigation conducted by the Western District Police Homicide section revealed: "Viagra and the kinkiness of sex were his killers."

3. Circus animal trainer Hannibal Cantori strangled his wife and then committed suicide in May 1993. According to Bucharest police, the note he left explaining his reasons mentioned his horror when, the night before, he walked into a stable and saw his wife pleasuring a horse.

2. After a wild night of drinking in August 2002, a group of male friends from Antipolo City in the Philippines challenged each other to show their manhood to determine who had the biggest penis. When Eduardo Cristomar laughed at the size of his pal Arnel Orbeta's penis, Orteba took out a gun and shot him six times in the head and groin.

1. THE WRONG TYPE OF CRUSH
The Condor Bar in San Francisco earned a place in American history as the first officially sanctioned topless dancing bar in the United States. It also has another claim to notoriety: as the venue where one of the most ridiculous deaths in the annals of sex occurred.

The club featured a white baby grand piano that was lowered from the ceiling every night. A dancer would climb onto it through a trap door in the ceiling to make a grand entrance. After the bar had closed one night in November 1983, bouncer Jimmy Ferrozzo and dancer Theresa Hill decided to make love atop the piano. During their sex session, they managed to accidentally start the hydraulics that raised the piano. Ferrozzo was crushed to death between the piano and the ceiling while the deeply traumatised Hill was trapped for several hours below her lover's body until the janitor found her in the morning.

WHO'S A NAUGHTY POPE THEN?

It seems that being God's vicar is no guarantee of protection if you are caught in the wrong place at the wrong time. Pope John XII held office from 16 December 955 to 14 May 964. He died after being violently beaten by a merchant who returned home to find the Pope in the act of making love to his wife.

JIM'S FIXXED

Jim Fixx came to prominence in the 1970s with his best-selling book *The Complete Book of Running*. Widely credited with helping to kick-start the keep-fit movement and popularizing jogging, the book established Fixx as a health guru. He was an impassioned preacher on the physical and psychological benefits of running, including how it gave a legal 'high' and helped you live longer by making you better able to cope with pressure and tension.

In 1982, while taking his daily run on Route 15 in Hardwick, Vermont, Fixx died of a massive heart attack. An autopsy revealed he had atherosclerosis which had blocked one coronary artery by 95%, a second by 85% and a third by 50%. Among certain sections of the community of health claim debunkers, Fixx's death was met with jubilation. Dr Scott Garrett said: "It's one in the eye for every smug jogger pontificating about running helping to make them healthier and live longer."

BUSH-WHACKED

Walking her pug dog Ming on moorland in Exmouth, Devon, was something 74-year-old Erica Cranmer did every single day. But in March 2006 she scratched her arm on a gorse bush, contracting the rare flesh-eating bacterium necrotising fasciitis and dying two weeks later. She was the second person to die in less than two years after being scratched by gorse on the moors.

DELAYED JUSTICE

The Cosmic Joker may have taken a hand in dealing out some deadly delayed justice to Henry Ziegland of Honey Grove, Texas. In 1893, Ziegland jilted his lover after having had his wicked way with her. The girl committed suicide and her aggrieved brother tried to ensure she was revenged. Waiting at Ziegland's farm, he ambushed the cad, letting off a shot that grazed his victim's head and left the bullet embedded in a tree. Believing Ziegland to be dead, the brother then turned the gun on himself and committed suicide.

However, Ziegland survived and thrived. More than 20 years later he attempted to cut down the tree with the bullet in it. When it proved stubborn, he resorted to trying to blast it out of the ground with dynamite. Some reports claim that the subsequent explosion dislodged the bullet from the tree which then killed Ziegland. The truth is a degree less strange, but still ridiculous. Ziegland stood too close to the tree when blasting it and it – and the bullet – toppled onto to him, crushing him to death.

WHEN SEX GAMES GO WRONG VI

Milkman Christopher Harris, 47, died after a kinky sex experiment involving a Russian biological warfare mask. The divorcee, from Newport, Wales, died in 2008 after running tubes from the hooded mask to a bottle of chloroform. Unfortunately he inhaled too much and died.

PHOTO FINISH

Capturing that perfect photograph is every snapper's objective, but for British backpacker Mark Thomas, 28, it cost him his life. He was taking a picture at 80ft Stewart Falls, in Wanaka, South Island, New Zealand, in May 2004, when he slipped off the edge and fell to his death on rocks below. The body of Mark, of Barnsley, South Yorkshire, wasn't discovered until a year later.

TOSSED OFF

To some people, dwarf tossing, a 'sport' that seems to have originated in Australian pubs during the early 1980s, is barbaric, brutal and demeaning to those of restricted height. To others it is a grand laugh or a way of making a living. Through the actions of the group Little People of America it has been outlawed in Florida and, in Ontario, the Dwarf Tossing Ban Act was brought into law in 2003. Despite this, bars across the world still continue to hold regular dwarf tossing contests and tournaments.

Australian dwarf Big Bob was one of the early pioneers of the sport, who made a successful living out of wearing a special padded costume and being thrown at walls lined with mattresses. After one contest in rural Australia in 1985, despite wearing a crash helmet, Big Bob began to feel dizzy. Shrugging it off, he allowed himself to be thrown eight more times before the night ended. As he made his way back to his hotel, Bob's dizziness became worse and he slipped on the pavement. The fall broke Big Bob's neck and he died instantly.

PREMATURE POST-MORTEM

Washington Irving Bishop was an infamous mentalist – a stage magician with an act using apparent psychic powers – in 19th century America. Prone to go into apparent cataleptic fits while on stage, he often claimed his great fear was being buried alive. In 1889, at the age of just 33, Bishop collapsed unconscious and apparently dead into the gutter of a New York street.

Given his notorious reputation for alcohol and narcotic abuse, Bishop's sudden death would possibly not have surprised the medical examiner called to look at the body. In a strange echo of his worries about being mistaken for dead and interred alive, an autopsy was performed whose main discovery was that Bishop was not dead. Well, not dead, that is, until the premature post-mortem broke open the bones in his chest and slit his cataleptic form open from the thorax to the pelvis.

WHEN SEX GAMES GO WRONG VII

If you're going to push the boundaries of sexual experimentation, it's always worth checking that your equipment is working properly. Bondage lover Simon Burley, 38, of Lincolnshire, put a noose around his neck while lover Elizabeth Hallam pretended to be a neo-Nazi hangman. Unfortunately, he gave her a blunt knife which couldn't cut him down before he was strangled to death in April 2007.

FORMULA 1 SCOOTER KILLS OAP

A mobility scooter painted like racing driver Michael Schumacher's Formula 1 Ferrari ran down and killed an 88-year-old man. Witnesses said disabled pensioner Peter Jenkinson, 66, was driving too fast, even though the red battery-powered buggy only had a top speed of 8mph. It ploughed into the Zimmer frame of Ernest "Jim" Carpenter, along Brighton seafront, and knocked him off his feet in October 2004. He later died in hospital from his head injuries. Triple-heart bypass patient Peter, who was wearing a Ferrari hat at the time, said he thought Jim would move out of the way.

POCKET ROCKET

Putting stuff in your back pocket, forgetting you put it in there and then sitting on it can be a real pain – especially if you break your glasses or bend your credit card in two. However, if what you put in your back pocket is blasting caps the definition of pain can be a lot more literal. That was certainly the case for American Barry Walles in 1976. He put three blasting caps into his back pocket and then sat on them on a bar after finishing his day's work in a quarry outside of Austin, Texas. The resulting explosion led to so much soft tissue damage that surgeons were unable to save Walles' life.

YOU COULDN'T MAKE IT UP

Through a bizarre set of mechanical faults, motorist Alison Taylor actually managed to drive over herself with her own car on 28 September 2004. Alison, 36, of North Tyneside, had lifted the bonnet of her Peugeot 405 to try and start the engine. The keys were in the ignition but switched off, and she tried to free the starter motor by banging it with a hammer. But the car, which had a broken handbrake and was in first gear, lurched forward. Alison reached out to steady herself, grabbed hold of the throttle cable, and caused the car to accelerate over her, dragging her body down an embankment and leaving her trapped underneath. She died from multiple injuries.

ATTACK OF THE KILLER HAIRDRIERS

For years, hair salons across the world were packed with women drying their locks under hood-style driers, an apparently harmless image popularised in movies and on TV. But these innocuous items contained a layer of asbestos inside the hood which prevented customers from getting burned. As these linings crumbled, asbestos dust blew around the salon of hairdresser Janet Watson, and she eventually died after contracting the cancerous condition mesothelioma. Janet, 59, of Keighley, West Yorkshire, had worked in salons for 30 years before she died in August 2004.

WHAT A SUCKER

Eating live baby octopus – known as sannakji – in South Korea is seen as something of a health kick. However, it was not healthy for Seoul resident Hyong Hee Chun in 2001, when the still living tentacles stuck to his throat and he choked to death.

HOW TO MAKE YOURSELF EXTINCT

With prize fossils fetching large sums of money, competition among both amateur and professional fossil hunters is keen in the extreme. One UK collector, Richard Neagle of Derbyshire, was so determined to get first dibs on anything found at a quarry that he snuck over a fence and decided that signs warning him of the danger of being caught in a blast did not apply to him. He might have regretted his decision as his life flashed before his eyes when he was caught in a fatal rock fall following a planned explosion at the quarry.

WHEN SEX GAMES GO WRONG VIII

Are you ever too old for a bit of perversion? Widower Frank Burton, 85, of Horndean, Hampshire, was found dead in 2004, two months after indulging in an auto-erotic sex game. He choked to death by gagging himself with a rubber bathing cap and was found with a length of string tied around his genitals.

BODY MOVING

Tadeusz Rogala travelled for more than two miles body-surfing on the roof of a car – but unfortunately he was dead at the time. Motorist Craig Gant, 28, hit 74-year-old former hospital porter Tadeusz as he crossed the road outside his home in Wakefield, West Yorkshire, in December 2000, severing his leg in the process. But Gant was so traumatised by what had happened that he carried on driving for two and a half miles with the pensioner's body on top of his car and an arm hanging through the sun roof, ignoring people who signalled him to stop.

KILLER COFFEE

Joseph Stoyer, a 51-year-old from Seaford, Long Island, stepped out of his front door in 2002, holding his coffee mug. He tripped and fell onto one of the broken mug's ceramic shards, which entered his carotid artery, and he bled to death.

HOUSE HICCUP

A drunken mistake cost Michael Robinson dearly in 2005. After celebrating his 36th birthday in local pubs he went to the house in Cardiff, Wales, which he had moved out of nine years earlier, after 27 years. But he was mistaken for a burglar by new occupier David Gentles, 30, an amateur boxer. David confronted him in the garden and punched him. Michael fell over and banged his head on a pathway, dying in hospital eight days later from brain damage and a fractured skull.

LOOK WHAT THE CAT DRAGGED IN

A thief in Port Elizabeth, South Africa, climbed under a Range Rover to steal its catalytic converter in April 2008. Unfortunately for the crook, the vehicle left the car park as he was still working on it, reversing over him and dragging him along for more than 200 metres before his death.

WHEN SEX GAMES GO WRONG IX

Teenager Stuart Hutchinson, 19, of Stanley, County Durham, was found dangling naked from a banister after his own solo sex thrill went wrong. Girlfriend Kay Stanyer discovered him with a duvet cover around his neck after he failed to meet her for a date in 2004.

SAUNA OF DEATH

Biological warfare suits were required to recover the body of shipping magnate Sir Derek Bibby from his sauna after he poured rat poison onto the coals. Sir Derek, 80, mixed the poison with water and used a wooden ladle to pour the mixture over the sauna coals at his home in Neston, Merseyside, on 9 October 2002. This produced the deadly gas aluminium phosphide, which killed him. Sir Derek, president of the Bibby Group, left a note warning his daughter not to approach the sauna, but to call 999. When he was brought into Arrowe Park Hospital, the accident and emergency department had to be evacuated because his body was still toxic. Sir Derek had taken his own life after learning he had prostate cancer and leukaemia, but – like many leading business tycoons – didn't really contemplate the consequences of his actions for everyone else.

LOUSY LUMBERJACKS

Two loggers working in the American state of Maine in 1906 –Andrew Alsop and Daniel Brougton – began an argument while rolling a log up an incline. Going from exchanging words to exchanging fists, the pair let go of the log which rolled down and crushed three colleagues to death at the bottom of the hill.

DYED AND DIED

Covering her grey proved fatal for chemist's wife Narinder Devi, 39 on 25 August 2000. She had switched from her usual product to a different dye to hide her first grey hairs, but within minutes suffered irritation to her scalp and was dead in an hour from a severe anaphylactic shock. Narinder, from Birmingham, had suffered an allergic reaction from the dye.

DEATH GOD TOURS

In 1933, sensitive soul Kiyoko Matsumoto confided in her friends that she was "perplexed at becoming a woman and wanted to commit suicide". Her helpful circle of pals suggested she throw herself off a department store – at the time such stores were amongst the highest buildings in Japan. Unfortunately for the 21-year-old student, Tokyo had recently seen such a rush of suicides committed in this manner that all department stores were hiring extra security guards to patrol their upper floors and roofs to prevent any jumping.

One of Kiyoko's friends, Masako Tomito, offered her the alternative suggestion of throwing herself into a volcano and even offered to guide her to one she thought would be "perfect for your needs". Masako then took Kiyoko to Mount Mihara, a volcano on the island of Izu Oshima, where her chum duly leapt to her death in the sulphurous fires below. Tomito's tales of her friend's suicide created a craze and over the next few years more than 950 men, women and children took the death plunge at Mount Mihara. At one point, the Tokyo Bay Steamship Company even ran trips advertised as "Tours to Meet the God of Death" to ferry curious tourists and eager jumpers to the volcano.

WHEN SEX GAMES GO WRONG X

Sado-masochist Macmillan Von Albrecht, 59, accidentally caught his death on video while using a bizarre noose and pulley system for auto-erotic sex. He took 12 agonising hours to die at his home in Battersea, south London, in 2004. He was found in a specially equipped dungeon, surrounded by whips, chains, rubber wear and gas masks, and videos with titles including *Rubber Nuns*, *Bondage Selection* and – strangely – one named after *The Good Life* TV star Felicity Kendall. A video tape showed him pulling a noose around his neck, with the cord suspended from pulleys and a urine-filled sweet jar acting as a counterweight.

BARBECUE TIME I

Accused pervert Terrance Keane gassed himself using disposable barbecue trays rather than face court on child porn charges. Terrance, 45, of Beaconsfield, Buckinghamshire, had been charged with 24 counts of downloading internet child porn. He was found in his bedroom surrounded by several cheap burnt-out BBQ kits, having sealed doors and windows to kill himself with deadly carbon monoxide fumes in 2005.

DUMB DETECTOR

Austrian metal detector enthusiast Manfred Bosch was delighted when he got a new detector for his 56th birthday and went out straight out into the countryside to test it. When he got a ping, he took out his spade and began digging, hitting an old landmine which exploded, causing fatal injuries.

SHRED HEAD

Factory worker George Kenyon, 25, died after being dragged headfirst into a shredding machine in Haslingden, Lancashire, in 1988. He was diced and sliced after his overalls became caught in the cutter, and was dead before anyone could turn it off.

SECOND TIME AROUND

The death of a 33-year-old horse rider in Abinger Hammer, near Dorking, in March 1987 came about when her horse bolted and threw her headfirst into a stone monument. The monument was in memory of outspoken Bishop of Oxford, Samuel Wilberforce, killed at that very spot when his horse threw him onto his head in 1873.

BULLET CATCHING CALAMITY I

Unlike almost every other magician who has performed a bullet catching trick, German Ralf Bialla was the real deal. Instead of presenting the audience with an illusion, he actually did catch bullets. In fact, many magicians looked down on Bialla, accusing him of cheapening the idea of bullet catching by turning a clever trick into "nothing more than a ridiculous stunt".

The 'stunt' involved the bullet being fired through three panes of glass, while Bialla wore bullet proof gloves which he held over most of his face. Finally, he would catch the bullet in his front teeth, which were made of steel. Footage filmed for the TV show *The Wild World of Sports* and slowed down actually caught the process frame by frame. Given the dangerous nature of his routine, it is no surprise to learn that Bialla had lost both earlobes, been hit in the cheek and even taken a bullet in the throat during his career.

However, when Bialla's bullet catching-related death occurred in 1975, no gun was actually fired. For several months Bialla had complained of suffering extreme periods of dizziness. His doctors linked these spells to the impact of his act on his brain and urged him to take a long break. Bialla went on holiday and was taking a clifftop walk when he was overcome by a bout of dizziness and tumbled over the edge of the cliff to his death.

DOWN AND OUT

George Allen was a NFL football coach whose decades in the game saw him earn a reputation as one of the hardest working men in sport. He had the third best winning percentage in NFL history and the achievement of never having coached a team to a losing season. Allen was also highly paranoid, believing that his coaching methods and practices were being spied upon, and that his offices were bugged, leading him to become the first coach to employ a full-time security man.

After his glory years of coaching the LA Rams and Washington Redskins, Allen put no less passion into coaching the Long Beach State college team, which would eventually end up helping to kill him. On 17 November 1990, Allen led his Long Beach team to a season-ending victory over the University of Las Vegas. To celebrate this, his team soaked him by dumping a whole bucket of Gatorade over their beloved coach, before hoisting him on their shoulders.

Allen then spent more than an hour in a biting wind giving media interviews and signing autographs. Within days of his Gatorade shower, Allen began to feel ill, dying shortly afterwards from ventricular fibrillation brought on by pneumonia resulting from the celebratory but fatal soaking.

BARBECUE TIME II

It's nothing short of idiocy to take a lit barbecue into a tent – if the fumes don't get you, there's every chance you'll set the thing on fire! But Bristol campers Deborah Alker, 45, and Daryl Porter, 40, decided to cook under canvas at a holiday park in Somerset, in April 2003, taking their disposable barbecue inside their tent. Unfortunately they were then poisoned by carbon monoxide fumes released by the barbecue and were found dead two days later, having not even managed to finish their food.

BACKSEAT BONK ENDS IN RIVER

An amorous couple having sex in the back of their car were so engrossed in their passion that they failed to escape when the vehicle rolled into a river. Anita Harold, 34, and boyfriend Richard Lang, 30, died when their car plunged into Beverly Beck in East Yorkshire, in November 2002. They had previously told friends they enjoyed going to remote places for alfresco sex. Police did not rule out the possibility that they may have been murdered, but had no proof. So did the bouncing of their car during their heated lovemaking lead to their deaths or was it pushed by an unknown killer? We may never know.

JUST LIKE THAT

Ron Watson styled himself "Uncle Ron the Magnificent Magician" when performing charity magic shows in the Waikato region of North Island in New Zealand. The 69-year-old entertainer originally hailed from England, where he had been a member of the Magic Circle. Watson also had an abiding interest in comic magician Tommy Cooper, who had died on stage whilst muttering his famous catchphrase: "Just like that!"

On 12 March 2000, Uncle Ron was performing to recovering stroke victims – including his own wife Sheila – at the Tokoroa Hospital. A few minutes into the act, he clutched at his chest, screamed: "My heart! My heart!" and collapsed onto the floor. Patients and staff applauded wildly, thinking it was part of the act. Only Sheila Watson knew something was wrong and the paralysis from her stroke prevented her from raising the alarm. By the time Uncle Ron had remained motionless for more than a minute, it was too late for the doctors who were watching to revive him.

'TIL DEATH DO US PART

The stress of getting married is always a lot for a bride-to-be to deal with, but for Penny Taylor, 27, it brought on an acute migraine which killed her. Penny, of Newton Aycliffe, County Durham, collapsed as she went through a wedding rehearsal in Hurworth, near Darlington, in September 2001.

NOT THE SHARPEST KNIFE IN THE DRAWER

One thing researching this book has shown us is that stupidity related to alcohol is nothing new. A ridiculous alcohol-related death is recorded in a newspaper from 1822. It tells of how American sailor John Cummings saw a sideshow act, which involved swallowing knives, and when he returned drunk to his ship he bragged to his mates that he could duplicate the feat.

Challenged to prove it, Cummings took his own switchblade knife, used his tongue to close the blade and then swallowed it down, earning himself cheers and several extra drinks. Encouraged by his shipmates, he performed the same trick again on the following night, swallowing another two knives. By the time his ship crossed the Atlantic and docked in Boston, he had swallowed 35 knives. People at a tavern in the city heard about his exploits and bought him several drinks, egging him on to give a demonstration. Cummings then swallowed a further three knives.

However, this seems to have been a drunken stunt too far. The next day Cummings began to vomit constantly and reported incredible stabbing pains in first his stomach and then his bowels. A doctor was called, but could do nothing for the sailor who died in screaming agony. When his stomach was opened up, more than 14 knives were discovered in it.

DRILLER KILLER

As several entries in this book have shown, owning snakes can be a dangerous hobby. However, as the death of Thomas Giacometti from Brooklyn, New York, attests, even when the reptilian menaces are not crushing, constricting or biting you, they can still prove a deadly risk.

Giacometti, a 36-year-old sculptor, was known to his friends as 'Anaconda Tom'. He had built up a collection of a dozen snakes, including several pythons and anacondas, some of which weighed more than 50 kilos. On 16 October 1999, Giacometti was building new shelves and cages for his reptilian menagerie at his loft apartment. He had climbed up a ladder to drill a hole when he fell. According to police spokesman Detective John Giammarino. "As he fell, Giacometti struck his head on a power drill. It penetrated the right side of his skull, killing him instantly." Proof, if it was needed, that owning exotic pets can be a real headache.

TOP 10 RIDICULOUS
SPORT-RELATED DEATHS

10. Olympic gold medallist Vladimir Viktorovich Smirnov was the Soviet Union's top fencer. At the 1982 World Fencing Championships in Rome, his opponent's foil snapped and a splinter pierced the metal mesh of Smirnov's mask, entering his eye and piercing his brain. Smirnov was then kept alive on life support for nine days, until one minute after the Championship had officially ended.

9. J.G. Parry-Thomas was a Welsh car designer and racing driver obsessed with the world land speed record. In 1927 he was racing his car, Babs, at Pendine Sands in Carmarthenshire. Whilst approaching the then-record speed of 170 mph, the car's external drive chain broke. It whipped up and partially decaptitated Parry-Thomas. However, Babs hit 171mph and it was officially declared to have broken the record.

8. Chris Bowie, a 29-year-old from Palm Beach, Florida, died while taking part in a fishing contest at Morehead, North Carolina, in 1994. He managed to hook a giant blue marlin, but unfortunately his line became entwined around his hand and the fish dragged him off the boat and down to Davey Jones' locker.

7. Emil Kijek, a 79-year-old golfing fanatic from Massachusets, was delighted to get the first hole-in-one of his life at his club Rehoboth where he had been playing for more than 30 years. However, the shock of the perfect shot proved too much for him and Kijek collapsed from a fatal heart attack.

6. Jeff Reese, a 21-year student and Olympic wrestling hopeful, died in 1997 as he trained in a specially-heated gym while wearing a rubber

suit in an effort to drop his weight. That same year, two other young American wrestling hopefuls – Joe LaRosa and Billy Jack Saylor – died in similar circumstances.

5. Kite fighting is a serious sport in India, Pakistan and Afghanistan. Contestants often add glass to the string of their duelling kites. This helps explain why R.C. Senal of Orissa, India, died of a slashed throat in 1994 when he lost control of his flyer.

4. Japanese golfer Masashi Moromizato got so annoyed when his golf buddy Jiro Yamada laughed when he sliced a shot that Moromizato charged Yamada to the ground and beat him to death with his 5-wood.

3. Ray Chapman played shortstop for Cleveland Indians Major League baseball team. On 6 August 1920, during a game against the New York Yankees, he achieved the distinction of becoming the first man to be killed by a baseball pitch when a ball thrown by Carl Mays hit Chapman's skull so hard that it killed him.

2. Indonesian soccer star Mistar was warming up with his team for a forthcoming cup match in 1995 when the training pitch was invaded by a herd of pigs. Mistar was known for being swift on the ball, but he was not quick enough to avoid being trampled to death by the marauding swine. His funeral was attended by more than 5,000 fans.

1. PUCKING HELL
Hockey fan Brittanie Nicole Cecil was attending a game between Columbus Blue and the Calgary Flames at the National Arena in Columbus, Ohio, in March 2002 as part of her 13th birthday celebrations. She was cheering on the home team when she was struck in the head by a puck. A shot by the Jackets' Espen Knutsen was deflected by the Flames' Derek Morris and went over the glass behind the net, striking her in the left temple.

LAST VERSE

The final work by poet Roy Blackman was far from his best: "Don't go upstairs. Phone the police. Please feed the cat," read a note headed "Poem", left in his home in Little Glemham, Suffolk, in 2002. Roy, 59, who co-edited a poetry magazine and had his collection *As Lords Expected* published in 1996, planned to hang himself from a noose attached to his loft hatch. As he climbed the ladder to do so, he slipped and fell to the landing floor, dying from fatal head injuries. How poetic.

FATAL FRANCS

In March 1993, police discovered the body of Daniel Pitoret in woods near his home at Bourg-en-Bresses, France. His head had almost been decapitated by a shotgun blast fired from behind him. Pitoret was described by his local paper as "Machiavellian, smart and hideously cynical". Their words seem pretty fair given that when the 43-year-old jobless petty criminal decided to end his life, he also ruined the life of another.

Detectives did not have a hard job finding Pitoret's killer as his pockets held the stub of a cheque made out to his friend Thierry Dieryckx for 50,000 francs. In the margins he had written: "For relieving me of my suffering by having the courage to pull the trigger". Pitoret had persuaded his mentally sub-normal pal to kill him in return for a cheque that would have bounced even if Dieryckx had ever been able to make it to the bank. At the time of his death, Pitoret did not have a single cent to his name.

BOULDERED OVER

A British businessman died on an Austrian skiing holiday after a boulder smashed through the roof of the taxi taking him to his hotel in March 2008. The 48-year-old man was being driven along a mountainous road from Salzburg airport to a resort near Tyrol when he was caught in 140mph winds which blew the huge rock down onto his vehicle. A friend sitting next to him was unharmed.

OWN GOOOOOOOOOAL!

English soccer manager Bill Shankley once said: "Some people think football is a matter of life and death. I don't like that attitude. I can assure them it is much more serious than that." He might have a point.

Andrés Escobar Saldarriaga was a Colombian international football player who had to suffer the shame of scoring an own goal in a crucial match in the soccer World Cup in 1994. In a match against the United States on 22 June, Escobar managed to deflect a ball from American midfielder John Harkes into his own net. It was a piece of pure bad luck, but as a result the USA won the game 2–1 and Colombia was eliminated from the tournament in the first round.

Less than a month later, on 2 July 1994, Escobar was shot outside El Indio bar, located in a suburb of the Columbian city of Medellin. According to Escobar's girlfriend, the killer shouted "Gooooooooooooooal!" – mimicking South American sporting commentators – for each of the 16 bullets fired. Whether murdered by an aggrieved Columbian fan or shot because his bit of bad luck on the pitch brought terrible gambling losses to several drug lords, there is no denying being murdered over a goal is a bloody ridiculous way to die.

BOWING OUT

Archery is a dangerous sport, but it's usually the arrow you have to worry about rather than the bow. However, ace archer Douglas Mitchell, 58, managed to kill himself while adjusting his bow in his workshop near Crieff, Perthshire, on 13 December 2002. Part of the equipment flew off and hit him on the head, but although he was able to walk into his house to ask his wife for help, he died five days later.

AIN'T THAT A KICK IN THE HEAD?

Pensioner Florence Ledwidge, 87, only went to see her doctor about recurring nosebleeds, but as the doctor swung his chair round after the examination, he accidentally kicked her in the leg. Although Florence, from Roehampton, south west London, initially seemed fine, her leg soon became bruised and she underwent an operation to drain it. But following a series of complications she suffered heart failure and died on 21 June 2007.

BULLET CATCHING CALAMITY II

One magician who achieved great fame in the 19th century as a daring bullet catcher was Dante, the Mormon Magician. In fact, Dante's act became so popular that in 1899 he became one of the first big American magicians to tour Australia. Taking time off from his sell-out tour, Dante and his theatrical entourage of promoters, glamorous assistants and musicians decided to go hunting in the bush, determined to massacre some kangaroos and wallabies just outside of Dubbo. Dante shouted out to his companions that he could see some kangaroos, causing his pianist to turn to look at him while holding a loaded gun. The gun accidentally discharged and Dante caught a bullet straight to the groin. His grave in Sydney's Waverley Cemetery is still visited by tourists coming from Salt Lake City.

A LITTLE TOO PLAYFUL

Most people have heard the folk maxim: "All work and no play makes Jack a dull boy". However, for Teddy Realo, a 27-year-old janitor from Makati City in the Philippines, too much play at work made him a dead man. According to Realo's colleagues, one of his workday pleasures at the multi-storey garage where he was employed was to be chased around by incoming cars. If they pursued him all the way to the edge of the garage's roof on the sixth floor, he would fool around and threaten to jump off. One afternoon in 2005, Realo's hijinks took a deadly turn. As he did his usual 'I will jump' pantomime, he lost his footing and smashed into the sidewalk below. A colleague commented: "If he had been less playful he would still be breathing."

WARTIME ROAD SAFETY LESSON

War is hell and with death being dealt from every quarter you have to be prepared for any eventuality. But training to dodge the bullets wasn't enough for Scottish soldier Craig Rae, 18, who was run over by an armoured vehicle. The guardsman was on an exercise on 21 September 2007 while preparing for deployment in Iraq. He dismounted from his vehicle to provide ground support, only to be struck by a Warrior armoured transport which couldn't see him.

FROZEN OUT

The body of a Stockholm woman stayed frozen on her porch for months during the Swedish winter without her neighbours realising she was dead. Margaretha Marsellas had died on New Year's Eve while watching fireworks, but her death was not noticed until the middle of March.

WE HAVE LIFT OFF

A photo opportunity turned sour when health club manager Brian Stevenson was carried off by a hot air balloon. Brian, 33, from Coatbridge, Lanarkshire, found himself clinging to the outside of the basket after it unexpectedly took off from a site in California in February 2003. He finally lost his grip at 300ft and plunged to his death on a tarmac car park.

BED HEAD

A pensioner was crushed beneath her hospital bed after accidentally triggering a release mechanism when she fell out, causing it to collapse on top of her and causing fatal head injuries. The 95-year-old woman was in Edinburgh Royal Infirmary when the tragedy occurred in November 2003.

ALL HAIL THE WITCH DOCTOR

Canadian poet and writer Anthony Tripi recorded a ridiculous tale of death from the Ugandan village of Rewnyangi in 1987. According to Tripi, a travelling witch doctor called Kazaalwa came to a village and threatened to cause their crops to fail by bringing about windstorms and falls of hail if they did not provide him with hospitality. When, after a couple days of his arrival, high winds and ferocious hailstorms swept across Rewnyangi, the villagers forced him out of the house where he was staying. They then severely beat him and left him outside to face the full force of the hail that was pelting down. A combination of the villagers' blows and being pelted by golf ball-sized hailstones ended both Kazaalwa's life and the unseasonable weather.

THE COSMIC JOKER STRIKES AGAIN III

When 70-year-old Evelyn Houser emerged from a crash that saw her car overturn on a snowy state highway outside Pittsburgh in March 1992, she must have thought she was the luckiest woman alive. Despite the fact her car had been totalled when it struck an embankment, overturned and skidded for several metres, Houser emerged without a scratch on her. Other motorists saw the accident and reported it to the police who arrived at the scene within minutes.

As Houser stood at the highway's guardrail talking the police highway patrolman through what had happened to her, the fire brigade arrived. However, it seems no-one had told the firemen about the ice on the road that had caused Houser's crash. As they sped to the location of the crash, they lost control of their vehicle on the slippery road, spun and smashed straight into Houser. Ironically, in a typical Cosmic Joker twist, the ambulance that had first been summoned to the original crash, and sent away when it was established Houser was uninjured, was recalled to take the fatally wounded woman to hospital.

LAST POST

Postman Dennis Nunn, 54, drowned in a village pond after falling off his bike in October 2005. Dennis, from Leatherhead, Surrey, was found hidden in undergrowth by a passer-by with his bicycle and postbag nearby. It is thought he lost control of his bike.

BOTTLE JOB

Wine producer George Musgrave, 66, was crushed by hundreds of bottles in a freak accident at Polmassick Vineyard in Cornwall. George, 66, was helping to guide a lorry making a delivery when a pallet containing half a tonne of empty bottles shot off the back and landed on top of him.

"DON'T TOUCH THAT BUTTON!"

Being ejected from a plane at 1,400mph is bad enough, but it can only get worse if you are upside down at the time. An engineer was shot out of an RAF Tornado jet while testing the fighter plane at RAF Marham in Norfolk, on 14 November 2007. It is thought the plane was flying upside down when the civilian was blasted out, his body ending up 30 miles from the base.

WHEN WINDOWS CRASH

Gary Hoy was a 38-year-old lawyer for the firm Holden Day Wilson. His company worked out of the 24th floor of the Toronto Dominion Centre – a gleaming, glass-walled skyscraper in the city's financial district. On 9 July 1993, Hoy was at a party in the building with a group of visiting law students when he decided to shock them with an unusual party piece.

This involved demonstrating his knowledge of the tensile strength of glass and proving his claim that the windows were 'unbreakable' by running hard at the windows. According to colleagues, he had done this before and had merely bounced off. However, this time he crashed straight through the middle of glass and ended up as street pizza 24 stories below in the Dominion Centre's courtyard.

BULLET CATCHING CALAMITY III

Anyone who takes a cursory interest in the history of stage magic will know that the world's deadliest trick is the bullet catching act. Although a relatively simple illusion in which blanks are swapped for live bullets, it has killed more magicians and their assistants over the years than any other trick, including escaping from tanks of water

There is always something frankly absurd about dying on stage while performing a trick meant to demonstrate alleged magical powers. However, most of the fatal bullet calamities result from the simple cock-up of not replacing live bullets – used to show that the gun is working – with the blanks needed for the actual illusion. Yet among the dozen or more recorded deaths due to bullet catching, some really stand out as ridiculous.

One of these is the death of magician Adam Epstein in 1869. As part of his spin on the bullet catching illusion, he used to ram the bullets into the barrel of the gun with his magic wand. However, during his last performance, the wand broke and when the gun fired, it shot out shards of wood that pierced his chest and throat, killing him.

TANKS FOR THE MEMORY

A merchant seaman was killed by fish, but he was on dry land at the time. Former sailor Clive Brolls, 58, from Cardiff, had bought a fish tank to remind him of his days at sea, but fell and smashed his head on the glass in 2006. He was found slumped next to the tank, which had two large cracks and was drained of water. He died from a severe blood clot three days later.

WEATHER VAIN

William Henry Harrison was the ninth president of the United States. He also holds the distinction of being the first president to die in office, as well as being the shortest serving president, managing only 31 days of his term before breathing his last. At his inauguration in 1841, Harrison was determined to show his virility despite his 68 years. Despite the cold and wet weather, he took the oath of office without wearing his overcoat. To make matters worse, he delivered the longest inaugural address in American history. At 8,444 words, it took nearly two hours to read.

Within days of this ridiculous display of bravado, Harrison became ill with a cold. His doctors tried various methods to cure him, including opium, castor oil, Virginia snakeweed and even actual snakes. However, the treatments only made Harrison worse, and he went into delirium and died. The moral of the story? Listen to your mother when she tells you do not go outside without a coat.

FOOTBALL VIOLENCE

When dad David Martin, 40, asked a neighbour to return his 10-year-old son's football after it accidentally ended up in his back garden in January 2008, he was beaten with cricket bats, golf clubs and metal poles, and then stabbed to death with a sword. It is believed there was an ongoing dispute between the two families.

SIZE COUNTS

A tiny 2mm cut was enough to finish off welfare officer Robert Chrimes, 45. He nicked his hand on chicken wire while building a patio at his home in Cricklade, Wiltshire, in April 2004. Eight days later he succumbed to the flesh-eating bug necrotising fasciitis. His wife Caroline said: "I can't believe he died so quickly from something so silly. The cut didn't even go septic."

BOLTED

Pals Sunee Whitworth, 39, and Anuban Bell, 24, both from London, were killed instantly after being struck by a massive bolt of lightning while seeking shelter from a storm in Hyde Park. The pair were left lying under the tree for more than 15 hours, because passers-by thought they were either tramps or drug addicts and were too frightened to approach them. The two women, originally from Thailand, were killed on the night of 22 September 1999 by a bolt so powerful it even melted the metal inside their bras.

PAYBACK

Sometimes making amends for the sins of the past can have a detrimental effect on the future. A 72-year-old man from Somerset took up nine paper-rounds a week to make it up to his wife for all the money he spent on whores when he was younger. But the exhaustion of these jobs drove him to kill himself with a mix of whiskey and painkillers.

BASE-IC MISTAKE II

As we have already seen, the madcap 'sport' of BASE jumping takes a special kind of idiot. However, Paul Belik was an idiot's idiot. Not satisfied with the ridiculous risk of leaping off tall objects, Belik decided that gravity was not the only law of nature he thought he could get round, deciding to have a crack at the one about water turning to ice at 0°C.

On 7 March 1983 in Sweden, Belik made a jump into very deep snow. Once safely down on the ground, he ignored basic commonsense about brushing off the snow on his canopy prior to repacking it for the next jump. Before Belik and friends drove to another site for another jump, his equipment was then stowed in a warm room where the snow turned to water. During the drive in the trunk of an unheated Saab, the water on his canopy turned back to ice.

When Belik made his next jump of the day from a radio antenna in Stockholm, the moment he pulled the cord to inflate his canopy he discovered that it had become a solid block of ice. There are some laws you just cannot break, unlike bones – most of which Belik's autopsy showed had been smashed when he hit the ground.

A VERY BAD FRIDAY

Method acting without limits can have deadly consequences, as 22-year-old Italian Renato Di Paulo discovered on Good Friday 2000. Di Paulo was playing the part of Judas Iscariot in a traditional Easter play undertaken by villagers from Camerata Nuova, 50km east of Rome. When re-enacting the part in the story where Judas hangs himself from a tree, the young actor leapt from a rock with a rope around his neck, the other end of which was attached to the branch of an olive tree.

However, Realo's safety harness failed and the noose tightened around his neck. His fellow actors and audience thought his desperate choking was just part of his performance and it was only after he had remained motionless for several minutes that it occurred to anyone that something might be wrong. By the time he was cut down it was too late and there was no chance of resuscitating him.

BASE-IC MISTAKE III

The names of Brian Lee Schubert and Michael Pelkey have become legendary to all those mad fools involved in the ridiculous sport of BASE jumping. On 24 July 1966, Schubert and Pelkey kick-started the sport by leaping off the 910-metre vertical rock formation El Capitan in Yosemite National Park. Both jumpers broke ankles and leg bones during their jump, but lived to tell the tale and inspire others.

Feted as pioneers by the growing community of BASE jumpers, in 1995 both Schubert and Pelkey attended the 26th annual Bridge Day festival, where more than 450 BASE jumpers gather to throw themselves off the New River Gorge Bridge into the water 263 metres below. Watched by a crowd of 144,000, Schubert announced that he and Pelkey would recreate their infamous inaugural jump from El Capitan on the 40th anniversary next year and that he was going to make his first jump in years from the bridge. However, as Schubert plummeted, the hordes below gasped as he did not open his shoot. With thousands screaming for him to deploy his parachute, Schubert left it until he was just 10 metres above the water. Too little, far too late: Schubert hit the water with a velocity that was terminal.

According to one BASE jumper watching Schubert's death dive: "It was the most basic mistake. There was no reason for it. Either he was too old and out of practice for it, or he just thought he could do something ridiculous for all the people watching and shouting him on."

WHEN HIPPOS ATTACK IV

Although the often-circulated story of a hippo swallowing a trampolining circus dwarf in Thailand is nothing more than an urban legend, there is no getting away from the fact that hippos are killers. Each year in Africa, more people meet their makers because of hippos than from attacks by lions, crocodiles or any other large animal. The vicious beasts so easily trample and chomp their way to the top of the wild beast killer league that most of the fatalities they are responsible for are commonplace rather than ridiculous.

However, the story of James Ngobeni's death from 2008 has more than a touch of the bizarre about it. It seems that the ring tone of Ngobeni's cell phone so enraged a hippo as he walked beside the Limpopo River that it charged him. Once it had brought him to the ground, it bit his right leg with such ferocity that it severed it below the knee. As Ngobeni struggled to remain conscious, he used his phone to dial for help. By the time a rescue party arrived there was nothing to find but a crushed phone, a piece of leg, and marks in the mud suggesting his hippo nemesis had dragged his body into the river.

THE COSMIC JOKER STRIKES AGAIN IV

Welsh novelist George Alexander Graber achieved literary fame and success writing under the pen name of Alexander Cordell. His evocative books such as *The Rape of the Fair Country* and *The Hosts of Rebecca* capture the landscape, people and turbulent history of early industrial Wales.

On 9 July 1997 at the age of 83, Graber began to climb up to the Horseshoe Pass in the mountains of Denbighshire. With a bottle of brandy in one jacket pocket and a huge stash of barbituates in the other, it was clear he had one thing on his mind – suicide. However, he sat down, propped up photos of his two beloved late wives and promptly dropped dead before he had the chance to touch either the drink or the drugs. The exertion of climbing had brought on a fatal heart attack.

SQUEEZY DOES IT

A city broker was squeezed to death by her commodities dealer boyfriend when she told him their relationship was over. Police believed the 32-year-old was initially only returning a show of affection, but resorted to crushing the life out of his 30-year-old girlfriend at their flat in Fulham, London, in October 1992. He then laid her body in the bed, placed a wreath of flowers around her head, and slashed open his chest, wrists and throat before hanging himself nearby.

URINE FOR A SHOCK

Ramonito Yuson, a 37-year-old taxi driver from Manila in the Philippines, got a fatal shock when he made an illicit stop to answer a call of nature. Pulling up in a quiet street in the Intramuros district in the early hours of a Saturday morning in 2002, Yuson ignored local bylaws preventing public urination and began to piss against a lamppost. Unfortunately for him there was an exposed live wire at its base and electricity from the lamppost arced along the stream of his urine and electrocuted him. A local police spokesman commented that the death should "serve as warning to all those who pee in public".

SPREADING HIMSELF THIN

An engineer from Market Harborough, lost his cool after rowing with his wife over a slice of toast and marmalade at breakfast in July 1988. He ran into the road and lay down to wait for a car to run him over. Naturally, it wasn't too long before a vehicle came along and ran over his head. Should have had cereal.

ROLL OUT THE BARREL

Karel Soucek was a Czechoslavakian-born stuntman, daredevil and – some would say – a death-seeking fuckwit. He first came to prominence when he illegally climbed into a barrel in July 1983, was rolled into the Niagara River and was swept down more than 150 metres at Niagara's Horseshoe Falls. Soucek emerged bleeding but alive from the barrel, which bore the slogan "The Last of Niagara's Daredevils".

The authorities fined Soucek $500, but he used his appearance in court as an opportunity to announce he intended to build a stunt museum at Niagara Falls. Capitalising on his notoriety and in an effort to raise funds his museum project, he undertook to appear at the Houston Astrodome. The plan was for him to perform a stunt where he would be in a barrel that would drop 55 metres to splash down into a pool of water below.

Even legendary stuntman Evel Knievel thought the stunt was ridiculous and that Soucek was mad to attempt it. He tried to persuade him to abandon the stunt, but Soucek still insisted that the show should go ahead. However, before the barrel had been raised to its apogee in the Astrodome ceiling, it was prematurely released. Instead of landing in the centre of the pool of water, it hit the rim. Soucek sustained fatal injuries, ensuring this was the last anyone saw of the self-styled last of the daredevils.

HAIR-RAISING HILARITY

A widow, 72, from Birmingham, was visited by her two-year-old great-grandson to show off his new, cropped haircut in October 1992. Unfortunately she had just accepted a sweet from him prior to this revelation and found his barnet so hilarious she choked to death laughing.

WHEN HIPPOS ATTACK V

As we have already seen, hippos not only do not care for human life, they seem to hold a particular grudge for anyone riding a bicycle. In February 1988, a Kenyan newspaper reported on the death of George Kamau at the jaws and paws of a vicious hippopotamus. As the 38-year-old cycled home from his workplace in the Kwale District of the country, he passed a sewerage pond.

Walkers on the road behind Kamau reported seeing a hippo emerge from the stinking water and charge after the cyclist. Despite being on two wheels, Kamau was unable to outpace the beast, which crashed into him and brought him down. Once on the ground, the hippo bit into the injured man, before trampling him to death. A local police spokesman said: "These hippos will attack zebras and fierce dogs. A man on a bicycle is nothing to them."

TOP 10 TOILET-RELATED DEATHS

10. In May 2002, a 74-year-old man from Johannesburg bled to death from cuts received when he fell on shattered porcelain from a toilet bowl that had collapsed under his weight.

9. Jane Runchman, a 48-year-old woman from Louisville, Kentucky, died in March 1986 after slipping from a toilet with a broken seat. The primary cause of death was an injury sustained to the head, but she also suffered a broken leg and wrist.

8. A burglar attempting to rob a home in Los Angeles in 1992 died when he slipped on the floor, after entering through a bathroom window, and fell headfirst against the toilet.

7. On 1 January 1997, convicted killer Laurence Baker died while serving a life sentence in a Pittsburgh prison. He was electrocuted by a fault in his homemade earphones as he watched a portable TV on his cell's metal toilet.

6. Kenneth Matthews, a 58-year-old man from Moss Bluff, Florida, was beaten to death by housemate Franklin Crow in February 2006. The reason for the violent attack, according to Crow, was that there was "a lack of toilet paper" in the bathroom they shared.

5. A flatbed truck carrying several toilet bowls and tanks swerved to avoid a trashcan that had been rolled into the road in Clackamas County, Oregon. This led to several toilets falling from the vehicle onto traffic behind it. One toilet bowl smashed through the windscreen of a car, leading to a crash that killed its driver.

4. In 2001, a 32-year-old male camper died in Montabaur, Germany, when the campsite toilet he was using exploded due to a build-up of leaking gas from a septic tank.

3. Murderer Michael Anderson Godwin spent several years fighting the sentence of death by electric chair while being held in a South Carolina jail. In March 1989, he was sitting on a metal toilet seat on his cell as he attempted to fix his small TV set. He bit through a wire and was fatally electrocuted.

2. In 1956, Jacques Soulet, a Frenchman of restricted height, was visiting New York on theatrical business. He died from complications to a genital injury sustained when the toilet lid fell down whilst he was urinating.

1. SHIT HITS THE CLAN

Tragedy engulfed a small village in the Surkhonaryo province of Uzbekistan in August 2005. A father and son digging a 23ft overflow pit for an outdoor latrine fell into the sewage as the sides of the pit collapsed. Five neighbours and relatives who rushed to their aid died from inhaling poisonous gases after they lowered themselves into the sewage to try and rescue the men.

IT'S ONLY A METAPHOR!

A 60-year-old man from Bath took the old adage about ostriches to the extreme and was found with his head buried in the sand at Woolacombe, North Devon, in April 1982. He was wearing just his underpants, having earlier been seen heading for a swim.

THE CURSE OF THE KENNEDYS

It has to be said that the Kennedy American political dynasty is not the luckiest of families. Michael Kennedy was nephew of assassinated US President John K. Kennedy and one of the sons of assassinated presidential candidate Robert Kennedy. On New Year's Eve 1997, he was playing 'football' on skis with other members of the Kennedy clan at an exclusive ski resort in Aspen, Colorado. Not only was he trying to catch and throw the football – improvised from a hot water bottle – but was recording the fun on a camcorder. Obviously, Kennedy was not a multi-tasker, because somewhere between skiing, catching and filming he forgot to look ahead of him and went splat into a tree. He was not wearing any safety equipment, so not surprisingly he became yet another fatality attributed to the spurious curse of the Kennedys

PEEPING TOM, DEAD RAUL

Raul Zarate, a 48-year-old Mexican prison warder, died in December 2000 when he tripped and crashed through a skylight. He had been spying on a couple below who were enjoying a conjugal visit.

ICE COLD IN NY

1981 brought a harsh winter to New York City. As temperatures plummeted towards those you would expect to find in the artic, the poor of the city were especially vulnerable to the extreme cold. On 22 January, police in the Bronx were called to the unheated apartment of 47-year-old Jessie Smalls. When they broke down the door of her home at 65 Featherbed Lane in the Morris Heights district, they found Miss Smalls entombed in a block of ice. A pipe had burst, flooding her apartment. As the water froze it had entirely entombed her, forcing the police to use pickaxes to chip away at the ice to free her frozen form.

PLANE STUPID

Roger Wallace, a 60-year-old radio-control plane fanatic from Arizona died at the Pima County Fairgrounds in 2001. He turned into the sun and lost sight of his 3kg plane with a 1.5metre wingspan. It then flew into him at a speed of nearly 50kph.

SLIPPERY SISTERS

In 1991, Yooket Paen, a 57-year-old Thai peasant farmer, met her end while making her way across her cow enclosure. She slipped in the mud and dung, and as she fell, threw her hands out to break the fall, only to grasp a live wire powering an electric fence. The next day, Paen's sister was demonstrating to neighbours how her sibling was electrocuted when she lost her balance in the still slick mud. The Cosmic Joker seems to have been on hand, as she too reached out as she fell and connected with the same killer cable.

REVENGE OF THE HUNTED

In November 1994, Einner Dahl, a 54-year-old hunter from Canada, killed a buck dear while hunting in Saskatchewan. As he tried to move his kill, an antler pierced his leg and hit an artery, causing him to bleed to death before he could summon help.

DEATH PENALTY

Ghanaian footballer Patrick Gyan was playing in goal during a local cup derby when the goal's crossbar fell on top of him, crushing his skull and killing him instantly. Fans accused the opposition team of employing witchcraft.

BURIED ALIVE

In October 1980, the Indian mystic known as Pilot Baba – due to the time he had allegedly spent in the Indian Air Force – held a gathering of fellow mystics, who specialised in demonstrating their higher spirituality and concentrated meditation by being buried alive. Pilot Baba arranged for fellow mystic Baba Khareshwari to be lowered into a three-metre pit with only a few cubic metres of air in it. Pilot announced to hundreds of people who flocked to watch that Khareshwari would remain buried without food and water for 10 days before returning to the surface.

Pilot then collected all the rupees and other gifts thrown into the pit and disappeared. When, after the tenth day, the pit was dug up, instead of finding Baba Khareshwari demonstrating his attainment of siddhi, all that they found was his decomposed corpse, proving he had died of suffocation within 24 hours of being buried. It seems the only true mystic gift displayed was Pilot Baba's ability to charm money from the faithful and then pull a pretty good vanishing act.

THE WORST DAY FISHING

According to popular angling wisdom the worst fishing beats the best day at work. However, the experience of Daniel Wyman in 1995 might disprove the trusted folk maxim. In an effort to increase their catch of fish from Fox Lake in Illinois, Wyman and a fishing buddy decided, unsportingly, to throw fireworks into the water. Their chosen weapon against marine life was a bunch of illegally imported M-250s – large firecrackers originally developed by the military to simulate grenade explosions and known colloquially in the United States as 'quarter sticks of dynamite'.

All was going well for the explosive-wielding anglers until a sudden gust of wind blew their rubber boat directly onto one of the recently thrown M-250s. As it exploded directly underneath them, it holed their craft. Wyman's pal managed to swim the 100 metres to shore, but Wyman himself was not so lucky.

PURE WATER, PURE POISON

Health professionals are always banging on about how essential it is for good health to drink plenty of water. Unfortunately it was a message that 35-year-old Shaun McNamara from York took to heart a little too seriously. In April 2007, his body was discovered in the bathroom of his home.

The cause of death initially puzzled coroners until they discovered that McNamara had been consuming huge amounts of water on a daily basis. The intake of up to 20 litres of bottled water a day had caused McNamara to develop hyponatremia – also known as water intoxication or water poisoning. The rare condition is more usually seen in marathon runners who drink too much water during a race. It leads to a fatal disturbance in brain function when the normal balance of electrolytes in the body is pushed beyond safe limits by massive water intake – which is exactly what happened to McNamara. As one coroner said at the time: "He drank himself to death, just not with alcohol."

PUPPY LOVE

Fernando Poe Sr was a famous actor in the early cinema era in the Philippines. In 1951, he sustained cuts during a film which became infected when he allowed a rabid puppy to lick his wounds. As you do.

WHEN HIPPOS ATTACK VI

In March 2006, Norman Chingoka, a preacher from the Church of Apostolic Faith, led his flock away from the repressive regime of Robert Mugabe, the vile dictator of Zimbabwe. Chingoka directed his followers to follow him to the slightly more promising land of South Africa, despite the fact that in their flight they would not only have to illegally cross the border, but cross it via the flood-swollen and crocodile infested Limpopo River.

As they approached the banks of the Limpopo, Chingoka told the faithful that: "God has told me in a dream we are Israelites fleeing from Egypt and Mugabe is the pharaoh. God will part the waters for us and allow us to walk to the other side. No harm shall come to us." He then waded into the water and was attacked by a bull hippopotamus which bit huge chunks out of his chest and arms. Chingoka's horrified congregation then saw his bloody body pulled downstream to his death by the bloated tidal flow of the Limpopo.

ALL OVER FOR WANNABE WILLIAM TELL

Kentuckian Larry Slusher had been pals with Silas Caldwell since childhood. They had both grown up in the small town of Arjay, Kentucky, and were still the best of friends more than 40 years on. In June 1998, Slusher and Caldwell, both aged 47, spent the day drinking, eventually winding up at Slusher's home for a fatal reinterpretation of a trick first made famous by Will Tell.

Local Sheriff, Harold Harbin, told reporters: "According to Caldwell, Larry Slusher took hold of an empty beer can and placed it on his head. He then dared his buddy to prove what a good shot he was by shooting it off. Caldwell took up the challenge and shot at the can with a .22 calibre semiautomatic pistol. Unfortunately, he missed the can and hit Slusher's head. We don't think there were any arguments or anything, because everyone knew they were close buddies."

DOCTOR DEATH

It is all too easy to laugh at another culture's practices and deeply held beliefs when they seem strange and alien to us. It is especially easy to guffaw when those beliefs lead to a spectacularly stupid and ridiculous death.

James Numeni was one of Liberia's best-known herbalists and witch doctors. He had grown wealthy during the country's civil war by supplying magic bags and charms to both sides of the conflict to protect them from harm by their enemies. In June 1996, Numeni was employed by two high-ranking soldiers of Charles Taylor's National Patriotic Front of Liberia to cast a spell that would make them invulnerable to bullets.

Numeni brewed up some herbal medicine which he claimed would harden the skin to the point that no bullets would be able to pierce it when activated by a magic incantation. Having performed the incantation, Numeni then offered to demonstrate the effectiveness of his spell by shooting at both of his customers at point-blank range with a machine pistol. Not surprisingly, their heads and chests were reduced to a bloody mess by a stream of bullets that were still skin-penetrating.

BELT UP

As we have already seen, the belief that witch doctors have the power to fashion magical items and create potions that will make someone invulnerable to bullets is not exactly uncommon in certain parts of Africa. Unfortunately, if predictably, it seems especially rife in those countries afflicted by the horrors of war, where the possibility life will be ended at the barrel of the gun is a common part of many people's lives.

In 1998, 49-year-old Colonel Pascal Gbah of the Côte d'Ivoire army died when he was shot by his own service revolver. The gun had been fired by the 20-year-old son of magician Andre Gondo, who was testing a magic belt his father had made for Colonel Gbah to protect him from bullets. When the alleged protective powers of the girdle failed to save the life of Gbah, Gondo told the police that it had only not worked because the Colonel had not abstained from sex for a sufficient period of time before donning the belt.

ALL LIT UP

1982 was not a very happy Christmas for the family of Seattle man James Hoban. He electrocuted himself when he decided to water his Norfolk Island Pine Christmas tree with the fairy lights still on.

HARD TO SWALLOW

Barry McCabe, a real estate agent from Miami, Florida, died in 1986 while testing a nine volt battery with his tongue. It was not the electrical output that killed him, it was swallowing and then choking on the battery as he licked the electric terminals.

TIMBER!

To some, members of the radical ecological action group Earth First! are nothing more than green Nazis who put plants before people and want to see civilisation crumble back to the level of the Neolithic. To others of a more environmental bent, they are crusading heroes who are willing to takes risks to ensure the protection of the forests and other resources of Mother Earth.

Earth First! member David 'Gypsy' Chain was certainly willing to take risks for his environmental beliefs. A committed monkey wrencher, in September 1998, Chain was protesting about the logging of Redwood trees at Grizzly Creek in Humboldt County, California. He was part of a group engaged in tree-sitting in an effort to prevent the destruction of the protected habitat of the marbled murrelet – an endangered seabird.

However, it was while on the ground that Chain met his end. Loggers felled one of his beloved Redwoods and it crashed to earth on top of him, crushing his skull. His death was only discovered when loggers began cutting the tree that killed him into segments.

BANG PANG

Student teacher Pang Yang hid in the home of fiancé Benjamin Kult, made noises to attract his attention and then burst out of a wardrobe when he came to investigate. Unfortunately, he thought she was a burglar and shot her dead with his handgun.

LIGHTS OUT

On the hot Californian night of 13 August 1998, keen amateur astronomer Kimberly Millet was trying to watch the heavenly display provided by the annual Perseid meteor shower. Despite her telescope, she was having trouble seeing the meteor stream due to light pollution in Kimberly's West Bluff neighbourhood.

To try and help her out, her 20-year-old brother Scott decided he would turn out the streetlights in the area by opening their inspection panels and cutting the wires in the base of the lights. Before undertaking the act of brotherly love and extreme stupidity, Scott announced his intentions to sort out the streetlights on an internet chat channel frequented by computer hackers, signing off with the words: "I'll tell you if I'm successful. BRB."

Unfortunately for Scott, he successfully managed to open the light's plates with a pair of pliers, allowing him to attempt to cut through the 2cm thick insulated wire he found inside. As he cut the wires, Scott received a fatal shock of more than 4,000 volts, putting his own lights out forever.

PLASTIC PLONKER

A resident of Sao Paulo, Brazil, decided he did not need professional help or special protective gear to remove a beehive from his orange tree, just clear plastic bags over his arms and head to protect him from potential stings. His wife found his body after he had suffocated.

GAME OF DEATH

At a soccer match in the Democratic Republic of Congo in October 1998, all 11 members of a football team were killed when lightning struck the pitch. The game of death happened in Kasai Province in the east of the country. However, when none of the players for home team of Basanga were injured, suspicion arose that they had employed witchcraft to ensure the match – deadlocked at 1-1 at the time of the lightning strike – went their way.

With feelings running high about possible use of the dark arts to swing the delicately balanced game, opposition supporters spotted Benjamin Tshilombo – a witchdoctor known to supply fetishes to Basanga – at the side of the pitch. A screaming mob then chased Tshilombo from the football ground. In an attempt to evade angry opposition supporters, Tshilombo climbed up a tree, which the rabid fans then set fire to, causing the witchdoctor to break his neck as he made a desperate leap to the ground.

BROUGHT TO BOOK

Petite Florida woman Mariesa Webber measured just 5'3" and while her height had never given her any problems before, it proved fatal in 2006 when she fell into a space behind a 6' tall bookcase at her home. Her family thought she had been kidnapped and it was not until a police search 11 days later her body was discovered.

LOVE LIES BLEEDING

Love makes you do strange and ridiculous things, sometimes for good, sometimes for ill. Possibly the most dangerous form of amour known to man and woman is unrequited love. It certainly proved the undoing of 44-year-old James Dinardi from Columbia, Missouri.

In July 1999, Dinardi drove the 2250 kilometres from his home state to Topsham, Missouri, to try and pursue a relationship with a woman he had been talking to over the internet, and sending money to, for several months. When he arrived at her home and she wanted nothing to do with him, Dinardi took a chainsaw from his truck, stood on her lawn and began to cut into his own neck in a bewilderingly misguided attempt to prove to the woman how much he loved her.

Even with Dinardi bleeding to death outside her home, the woman would not open the door to him. Neighbours called the emergency services, but it was to late for the lovestruck fool, who died within minutes of arriving at hospital. A local police spokesman said: "Dinardi was distraught. He thought he had met the love of his life on the internet, had sent her thousands of dollars, and then she wanted nothing to do with him. It broke his poor heart." Yep, and the chainsaw did not exactly fix his neck either.

A STEP TOO FAR

Barbara Rock was a 54-year-old head teacher at the Highgate Preparatory School in London. In 1995 she was cleaning cobwebs from the windows of her holiday home in the Suffolk countryside when her husband surprised her, causing her to fall from the ledge she was standing on. The tumble was a nasty one and she needed to be treated in hospital for injuries to her pelvis, lower back and legs.

After 10 days she was able to walk on crutches and allowed to go back home. Following a strict regime of physiotherapy to help her recover, Barbara began to do step exercise. However, she slipped off her step box, crashed through a first floor window and suffered fatal head injuries.

FINISHING POST

Frank Hayes was a professional jockey. In 1923, he suffered a fatal heart attack while riding in a race at Belmont Park in New York. Despite his death, he stayed on the horse Sweet Kiss, which went on to finish first, making him the first dead jockey to win a race.

BULLET CATCHING CALAMITY IV

As we have already seen, in the annals of stage magic, the bullet catching illusion has been responsible for the deaths of numerous magicians or their assistants. Most of the fatalities have occurred when the magician or his assistant made the basic error of not exchanging live bullets for blanks. In the cases of Madame deLinsky who died in 1820, and 'The Black Wizard of the West' who was shot in 1922, the error may have been deliberate. Evidence suggests that both deLinsky and the Black Wizard may have been murdered by jealous spouses who just happened to be their magic act assistants.

However, one of the most ridiculous bullet catching deaths occurred in 1840, when stage magician Arnold Buck announced to his audience that he was "able to catch any bullet with my teeth of steel". Before he even had a chance to get any further with his act, one of those watching stood up, shouted "Catch this!" and fired at Buck. Unfortunately, his 'teeth of steel' and other magic powers failed him, and he dropped dead from catching the bullet in his forehead.

SUPERHERO SLIP-UP

As we have already seen, dressing up as a superhero seems to be a dangerous activity. Perhaps donning a cape or mask acts as a signal to the Cosmic Joker that a wannabe hero needs to meet their ultimate nemesis – death. Whatever the truth, dressing up as Spiderman played a huge role in the death of Barry Madden.

The 28-year-old from Cumbria in England pulled on the fancy dress costume as part of a stag night celebration in Newcastle in 1995. Complaining that he could see very little out his webslinger's mask, Barry walked into the concrete base of a streetlight. Concussed from the collision, he then stumbled off the pavement and into the road. Before any of his friends could pull him back, Barry was hit by a passing car and died two days later in hospital. Well, that is one less thing for the Green Goblin to worry about then.

SAVING LIVES THE BELGIAN WAY

The Belgian Air Force took part in a humanitarian relief effort in Sudan in 1995 by dropping crates of food to starving villagers in remote locations. Unfortunately, one crate scored a direct hit on a hut, killing three men. The Belgian Ministry of Defence blamed the error on "tall grass".

BARKING UP THE WRONG TREE

Some people just will not listen. Neighbours, friends and even the local branch of the Humane Society had all told Sandra L. Piovesan from Salem, Massachusetts, that it was dangerous to keep wolf-dog hybrids as pets. Even the fact that many US states and countries across the world ban them from being kept did not seem to give her a clue to the danger they could present. The 50-year-old, who lived alone with her pack of nine wolf-dogs, just would not have her mind changed. She told a neighbour: "You can think what you like, but they are the only things on the planet that give me unqualified love."

In July 2006, Piovesan was found in a caged rectangular enclosure in her back yard. An autopsy performed on what was left of her body showed that she had bled to death after being mauled by the beasts she had tried to raise as pets. According to a Humane Society officer: "Everybody told her this would happen, but she just wouldn't listen. She was a very likable person, but she was just delusional about their danger, and totally misguided." We could not agree more. If that is unqualified love, we think we will give it a miss.

DYING TO BE HEARD

Professional gardener Gabriel Gonzales-Ferrer was clearing trees at a property at Tustin, California, in November 2007. He was feeding branches into a mobile mulcher when he became caught up and dragged into its blades. Gonzales-Ferrer's screams for help were not heard by his colleagues, as they were wearing protective equipment to protect their ears from loud noises.

TOP 10 RIDICULOUS
UNDIGNIFIED DEATHS

10. Paul G. Thomas, the 47-year-old co-owner of the Thomas & Sons Textile company, met a ridiculously undignified death in August 1987 when he was wound into a giant spool of wool. He got caught up in a spooling machine and when his body was discovered, he had been suffocated behind hundreds of metres of yarn.

9. Before obesity became a modern plague, being ridiculously overweight held enough novelty value to make 486-kilo Robert Earl Hughes a minor celebrity. However, when his flab-related death came in 1958 at the age of 32, Hughes' despatch from the mortal world was lacking in any dignity. He had to be hoisted from his deathbed by a crane and buried in a coffin made from a modified piano case.

8. The body of a Romanian farmer, naked apart from a condom, was found in his pig sty. A doctor pronounced the farmer had died from heart failure, while his family tried to explain his unusual appearance at death was down to his fondness for "pig wrestling". Well, that sounds like one euphemism for it.

7. The naked body of Abelerd Hattensperger was found on the deck of his boat on Lake Biggesee, Germany in 1983. An autopsy showed he had been struck by lightning, but could not explain why his groin was covered in grease.

6. The body of 60-year-old Robert Dean Eaton was found naked and chained to an oak tree in an area outside Happy Valley, California. Police said: "He had a history of mental health problems. He was always doing this sort of thing."

5. Deiter Lörz, a 53-year old photographer, was discovered in his Stuggart apartment in 1985 with homemade electrodes attached to

his testicles and a cock-gag in his mouth. Police described his death as "an unusual but self-inflicted accident".

5. The body of Terrence Simmonds, a 49-year-old from Oxford, was discovered in a cocoon made of plastic bin liners. In a kinky solo sex game, he had used a vacuum cleaner to suck all the air out of the bags and suffocated.

4. The body of retired German electrician Manfred Lubitz was found in his apartment in Malaga wearing a handmade gadget he called the 'orgasmatron'. It featured a vibrating mat, massage pads and electrodes attached to his manhood. Police believe he died as a result of a power surge.

3. Alex Maines was found dead in 1989 on Hampstead Heath, a London beauty spot also notorious as a place where gay men meet for casual sex. When discovered by an elderly dog walker, Maine's body was naked aside from a Star Trek T-shirt and a condom tailing out from an orifice. An autopsy showed he had died from cardiac arrest possibly related to recent sexual activity.

2. When 230-kilo Patricia Mullen died from heart failure related to her morbid obesity in 1996, the first few hours after death were anything but dignified. Chicago police officers dragged her naked body from her house and left it on the curb, then told neighbours "The fat lady's dead. Want something to eat?"

1. OVER EXPOSED
In 1986, a woman was found in Dayton, Ohio, naked and trapped under the corpse of her lover. The couple had been making love in her car, which was parked on the upper storey of a garage. During sex he died, collapsing on her and pinning her to the back seat of the car. By the time she was discovered under his decomposing body, she was suffering so badly from the effects of dehydration and hypothermia that she too died within hours of her rescue.

BLOWN FROM HERE TO ETERNITY

The Halona Blowhole on O'ahu, Hawaii's third largest island, is a natural lava tube which funnels seawater up in spouts of up to 9 metres. Bounded by beautiful beaches and the secluded cove where the infamous love scene featured in *From Here To Eternity* was filmed, it is one of Hawaii's most popular beauty spots. On 30 June 2002, 18-year-old Daniel Dick was on holiday from California, and clambered over the rocks to straddle the opening of the blowhole. He told those with him that he wanted to "feel the water hit his chest".

With arms outstretched, and laughing as spray caught his face, he waited for a big blow. Dick got his wish. A jet of water thundered from the Halona Blowhole, hit his chest and blasted him more than 1.5 metres into the air. He was then sucked down head first into the spout. It took divers two days to find and recover his body. Dick certainly lived up to his name in death.

DUMB, DRUNK AND DEAD

Vlad Înecatul was a Prince of Wallachia between June 1530 and 1532. He died when, in a highly inebriated state, he rode his horse into the full waters of the Dâmboviţa River. Not surprisingly, his royal moniker in history books was Vlad the Drowned.

LIVING IN HARMONY

Henry Purcell was England's most famous Baroque composer. His compositions brought him fame and his musical talent secured him a career as the organist of Westminster Abbey. In 1695, at the age of 36, Purcell returned home from the theatre late, only to find that his aggrieved wife had locked him out of the marital home. Having to spend a night outside in the cold and damp, Purcell caught a chest infection and died.

LAST BEER, LAST BREATH

Texan Steven Brasher received a life prison sentence for the fatal shooting of his best friend Willie Lawson. What had Willie done to provoke such a fate? According to Brasher: "There were two beers left in my refrigerator and Willie took the last one."

OUT COLD

Overgrown kids Gerry Brewer and Mike Napper – both 26 – were throwing snowballs at each other in Vermont when Brewer threw a ball that knocked his pal out cold. In his panic, Brewer ran to get help, slipped and fell down an embankment to his death.

POACHED POACHER

Ukranian poacher Nikolai Stadnik used a live cable from a portable generator to kill fish in Lake Somin. When dead fish floated to the surface, he waded in to collect his catch without switching off the power and was electrocuted.

IN LOW SPIRITS

The Rev Graham Friend of Derbyshire became so depressed by having to conduct five funerals in one week in his small parish that he ran away to France and killed himself with an overdose of aspirin. His wife said: "Death and the language of the funeral service really got to him."

FLOWER POWER

A giant flower parasol was sent into the air by a freak gust of wind measuring 130 km per hour. Unfortunately for 83-year-old Cardiff resident Selena Andrews, when it came down, it struck her on the head killing her instantly.

WEEDING OUT NAZIS

No-one is sure how former Nazi solider Andre Richter mistook weed killer for vodka when he filled his old hipflask engraved with the SS death's head. Yet it proved a fatal mistake when he took a swig from it and then passed it around at a military reunion in 1981, killing himself and two former comrades.

BOWLED OVER

Carol Williams from Swansea drowned in her pet dog's water bowl when she fell facedown into it with the rim pressed against her neck. The subsequent inquest heard she was three times over the drink-drive limit at the time of her tumble.

DEAD AS A DOORKNOB

Frantisek Kotzwara was an 18th century virtuoso double bassist whose fame was such that he could tour across the whole of Europe. However, he has achieved a form of immortality not for his musical prowess, but for the ridiculous manner of his death.

On 2 February 1791, while touring England, Kotzwara visited a prostitute in Vine Street, Westminster, London. He paid the woman, Susannah

Hill, two shillings and requested that she cut off his testicles. When she refused, Kotzwara then tied a ligature around the doorknob, and fastened the other end around his neck. He proceeded to have sex with Hill. After it was over, Hill discovered that Kotzwara was dead, making him possibly the first recorded fatality from erotic asphyxiation.

SUMMERTIME BLUES

In 1997, 29-year-old travel writer Stefan Rosengren returned to England after four years touring Asia. He was so depressed by the miserable summer weather that he leapt to his death from the Clifton Suspension Bridge in Bristol.

SPIDER MAN

José da Silva Rocha, an engineer from Brazil, thought his mates were joking when they told him to stand still and not move a muscle as he had a huge spider on his back. Laughing, he reached behind him, only to be bitten by a Brazilian wandering spider, whose venom killed him. Shame his spider senses weren't tingling!

HOLY HANG-UP

In 1835, weaver Claude Geraud became so convinced he was Christ – despite a failure to manifest any miraculous powers – that he made a cross out of the wood of his bed and a crown of thorns out of nails. He died when he then lay down upon the cross and began knocking nails into his legs.

WHAT A CRACKER

Workmen called in to sort out a Paraguayan graveyard that had suffered a landslide in 1956 piled the bones together for reburial. When priest Luis Marti came to bless and reinter the bodies, he slipped on the mud, fell headfirst onto the bones and cracked his head open on one of the skulls.

HOT DIGGITY D'OH!

Tokyo TV company Channel 12 announced in May 2002 that it was cancelling the broadcast of its annual hotdog eating contest after a 12-year-old schoolboy from Tokyo choked to death after trying to repeat what he had seen in the contest at the school cafeteria.

DEAD AS A DOUGH D'OH!

A 38-year-old Japanese housewife from the Hyogo Prefecture died at a bread and noodle eating contest held in front of a public hall in Fukusaki in November 2004. The woman was scoffing bread during the food stuffing marathon when a piece of crust led to her death from choking.

CHICKEN WINGS TO ANGEL WINGS

In March 2003, JD's Café and Nighspot in Regina, Saskatchewan, in Canada held its annual spicy chicken-wing eating contest, during which one 36-year-old male contestant choked to death. The manager of JD's, who was in the bar when the customer collapsed, called his death "deeply unfortunate".

DEADLY IDLI

Idli are savoury steamed lentil and rice cakes, and they are a staple of both Indian eating and Indian eating contests. In 2007, Sridhar Shanmugham, a 29-year-old from Sathyamangalam, died from breathing complications after wolfing down 20 idli in under 10 minutes.

CHUBBY BUNNY CHOKE I

Chubby Bunny is a game involving stuffing as many marshmallows as possible into your mouth and still being able to say the phrase 'chubby bunny'. It sounds like a piece of harmless food fun, but 12-year-old Catherine Fish from Chicago died after choking on four marshmallows while playing it at her a school's annual fair.

CHUBBY BUNNY CHOKE II

If you thought choking to death on marshmallows was a one-off freak accident, think again. In 2006, 32-year-old mother Janet Rudd from London died in a Chubby Bunny competition at a Western Fair when St John Ambulance volunteers were unable to remove a marshmallow blockage from her throat.

GOOD DOGGIES?

South African pit bull breeder Charles Murray was mauled to death by four of his dogs at his Durban home in 2003. Murray was working on his car when it fell and trapped him, giving his beasts – which he sold as pets – the chance to tear at his throat, arms and legs. Good doggies? Yeah, right.

OVER THE TOP

Many idiots have attempted to go over Niagara Falls and some have even lived to tell the tale. One who did not was 39-year-old Robert Overacker who went over the Falls on a jet ski in October 1995. However, his parachute failed to discharge and his body was recovered by staff on the Maids of Mist boat tour of the Falls.

BATON-ED TO DEATH

You could be forgiven for thinking that watching a bunch of marching band majorettes give a display of their baton-twirling skills would be a fairly safe way to spend an afternoon. However, when 61-year-old Jean Miles saw a majorette performance at Weston-super-Mare in 1994, a mis-thrown baton spun through the air and hit her on the head, with fatal consequences.

BOY RACER

It seems some men have a hard time growing up. Michael Joseph Garcia, a 22-year-old 'kidult' from Sun Valley, California, was a member of the Illegal Soapbox Federation – members of which spend their spare time building soapboxes, illegally racing them on Californian streets and sending the resulting videos to YouTube. Garcia came a cropper when a soapbox car he was racing lost a wheel, spun out of control and crashed into a sports utility vehicle, killing him before medical attention arrived. Well that is one way to stay young forever.

PICKLED PRESIDENT

Zachary Taylor was the twelfth President of the United States. Elected in 1848, he spent less than two years in office, dying on 9 July 1850. After sitting in the sun for too long during Independence Day celebrations, Taylor gorged on cherries and large amounts of pickled cucumber, washed down with several pints of ice cold milk. This combination, combined with mild heatstroke, was enough to give him a case of gastroenteritis that proved fatal just five days later.

BEAMS – MORE DEADLY THAN A COMANCHE SCALPING

Josiah Pugh Wilbarger was an early Texan who lived for 11 years after being scalped by Comanches in August 1833, despite the fact that the brutal attack left parts of his skull exposed. However, he died at his home near Bastrop in 1845 after an accident in which he struck the exposed part of his skull on a low support beam inside his cotton gin.

TEMPTING FATE

John Sedgwick was a Union Army general in the American Civil War. On 9 May 1864, his corps were probing Confederate defences at the beginning of the Battle of Spotsylvania Court House. Confederate sharpshooters were about 1,000 yards away, and their shots caused members of his staff and artillerymen to duck for cover.

Sedgwick strode around in the open and was quoted as saying: "What? Men dodging this way for single bullets? What will you do when they open fire along the whole line? I am ashamed of you. They could not hit an elephant at this distance." At that very moment, he fell forward with a massive bullet exit wound below his left eye.

Sedgwick was the highest ranking Union casualty of the Civil War and upon hearing of his death, senior commander of the Union military forces Ulysses S. Grant repeatedly asked: "Is he really dead? Is he really dead?"

COMPOSER GETS CLOSER TO DECOMPOSING

Charles-Valentin Alkan was a French composer and the greatest pianist of his day. Alkan died in Paris in 1888 at the age of 74 in an outstandingly ridiculous manner. He was reaching for an overcoat when a port-parapluie – a heavy coat and umbrella rack – fell on top of him. It severely crushed him and left him pinned to the floor, where he died before help could arrive.

GOOD NEWS, BAD NEWS

François Faber was a Luxembourgian cyclist who achieved fame for his performances in the Tour de France – especially in 1909, when he dominated the Tour by winning five consecutive stages. It was a record that went unbroken for almost a century.

When the First World War broke out, Faber joined the French Foreign Legion. On 9 May 1915, at Carency near Arras, Faber received a telegram saying his wife had given birth to a daughter. On reading this, he cheered loudly, giving away his position to a German sniper, whose bullet killed him instantly.

WIZARD WHEEZE

Vaughn Bodé was an underground comics legend and the creator of Cheech Wizard. Bodé described himself as "auto-sexual, heterosexual, homosexual, masso-sexual, sado-sexual, trans-sexual, uni-sexual, omni-sexual". He should have saved some words and just said "kinky".

Although the legacy of his artwork prevents him from ever being forgotten, the manner of Bodé's death has also delivered a form of immortality. On 18 July 1975, Bodé was experimenting with the "auto-sexual" aspect of his personality by indulging in autoerotic asphyxiation. Bodé was choking himself with a noose while masturbating, in the hope that when he passed out, the noose would release. Guess what? It didn't and he died.

THE BIG ONE

Redd Foxx was an American comedian best known for his starring role on the hit 1970s TV sitcom *Sanford and Son*. One of his most famous routines on the show was to feign a heart attack with the lines: "I'm coming Elizabeth. This is the big one." In 1991, Foxx was making a comeback with the TV series *The Royal Family*. During a break from rehearsals on 11 October 1991, Foxx suffered a massive heart attack, felling him on set in front of the crew and cast. Instead of rushing to his aid, there was laughter as several people thought Foxx was performing the routine he had made famous on *Sanford and Son*. By the time it was realized that his collapse on the floor was not part of his usual schtick, it was too late to save Foxx.

EMUS CANNOT FLY

Children's TV presenter Rod Hull had achieved huge fame in the 1970s for his act featuring a vicious puppet called Emu. His TV shows often featured a mix of ridiculous slapstick stunts and anarchic behaviour, and helped make him a millionaire. However, by the 1990s, Hull was bankrupt and rarely in the public eye.

In March 1999, Hull climbed onto the roof of the ramshackle shepherd's cottage he lived in outside Winchelsea. A football fan, Hull was trying to fix the aerial on his television so he could get better reception for that night's Champions League quarter final, a second-leg match between Inter Milan and his own favorites Manchester United. In scenes eerily reminiscent of the slapstick Hull had done so well on television, the slightly inebriated entertainer stood on the roof shouting down to his son to see if the signal was getting better or worse. While doing this, Hull slid, bounced off the roof and fell to his death.

Hull should have remembered that emus are flightless birds.

GAME OVER

There are many arguments about who can claim the title of the first person to die due to a video game. Possibly one of the strongest claimants is Jeff Bailey. In 1981, the 19-year-old American died of a heart attack after scoring 16,660 on the arcade game Berzerk. Unfortunately for Bailey, he collapsed before he even had the chance to enter his initials at the top of the highest scores leader board.

AN UNUSUAL WAY TO SIP SHERRY

As many entries in this book have shown, excessive alcohol can be a killer, and so can some acts of a kinky nature. Therefore mix booze and the sort of kinkiness no-one usually admits to their friends and you have a sure-fire potential for a ridiculous death.

Michael Warner, a 58-year-old man from Texas, died in May 2004 after receiving an enema full of sherry wine. An inquest showed that Warner had a blood-alcohol level of .47 percent – more than five times the legal limit – when he died. His wife, Tammy Jean Warner, was initially charged in connection with his death by alcohol poisoning, but those charges were dropped as full details of Warner's fondness for booze enemas came out. Tammy Jean told the police: "Michael was just addicted to getting enemas. He was always doing them with alcohol to get drunk. There was no stopping him."

LAST BREATH

Of all the ridiculous religious ideas which have killed people that we chronicled in this book, the one that really takes the biscuit – or rather does not take the biscuit – is Breatharianism. Those that believe the patent nonsense that is Breatharianism think it is possible to live without food and possibly water. They believe that are not humans and can be sustained solely by mystic prana energy or sunlight.

The claims of Breatharianism proponents such as Jasmuheen, an Australian who advocates 'pranic nourishment', might seem like harmless hokum, but some of those who have followed them have ended up dead. Among them are Timo Degen, a 31-year-old Munich kindergarten teacher, and 53-year-old Melbourne resident Lani Marcia Roslyn Morris. However, probably the most notorious Breatharianism death occurred in 1999, when the body of Australian-born Verity Linn was found naked in the Scottish highlands. She had died from starvation and dehydration while practising her Breatharianism beliefs. Jasmuheen's book, *Living On Light*, was found in Linn's possession.

Jasmuheen said she had no knowledge of Linn, but described her as "a spiritual warrior whose work was complete". She also said she had spoken through cosmic telepathy to one of her ascended masters, St Germain, who assured her that Linn had found "a very nice way to go out". That's OK, then.

STOPPED IN HIS TRACKS

E. Frenkel was a self-styled psychic healer from the southern Russian city of Astrakhan. In 1989, the man who many thought was a mentalist began to announce that he had the power to stop cars, bikes and even trams with his "amazing psychic-biological powers". Not surprisingly, most people did not take him too seriously, so to demonstrate his psychic-biological power, he announced he was going to stop something really big and impressive – a train.

On the day of his death, the driver of the train saw Frenkel step onto the tracks. Frenkel then raised his arms, lowered his head and tensed his body. The driver immediately applied his emergency brakes, but it was too late to stop the train thundering over the man with 'amazing psychic-biological powers'. Not so much a superhero mystic as a super-twat.

TOP 10 RIDICULOUS WILDLIFE-RELATED DEATHS

10. Franc Filipic, a 47-year-old from Slovenia, was described by friends as a "passionate fisherman". In August 1998, Filipic was last seen alive as he waded into a lake when the sheat fish he had landed proved hard to reel in. His last words were "Now I have him!" Police divers found his body two days later.

9. Two fishermen bled to death in 1999 when their penises were bitten off by fish in the river Sepik, Papua New Guinea. It is thought the fish were able to detect the urine streams of their victims, allowing them to home in on their genitals, which were chomped of with razor-sharp teeth. Government environmentalist Dr Wari Iamo blamed the attacks on pacu fish from South America, which had been introduced into PNG.

8. In 1995, a Chinese hunter from a village in Shanxi province met his match – and death – when he trapped a snake by placing the butt of his gun on the back of its head. As his brother tried to place the snake in a sack, it thrashed its tail and accidentally connected with the trigger, blasting the hunter who was holding it down in the face.

7. In 1985, a villager from Syamtalira Bayu, Indonesia, decided it was a good idea to pick a fight with the bull elephant that had been raiding his crops. Swinging punches and slashing at it with a machete, he was surprised when the elephant responded by hurling him into the air with his trunk. When the injured villager fell to earth, he was then trampled to death by the other elephants in the bull's troop.

6. Deaths by attacks from bears are still so frequent in the 21st century that most of them they are commonplace rather than bizarre. However, the death of 67-year-old Barry Campbell from Alaska is more than a little ridiculous. He was so shocked at seeing a bear on

his porch trying to get into his home he ran up stairs to get his gun, slipped and cracked his skull, killing him.

5. Everyone knows that a swan can allegedly break a man's arm, but it appears they can be a lot more deadly than that when they set their minds to it. In 1982, Louis Hestroffer was riding his motorbike near the town of Assenoncourt, France, when he was repeatedly buzzed by a low flying swan, causing him to fatally smash into a stone wall.

4. Elephants can be deadly at the best of times, but mix pachyderms with booze and you are asking for trouble, as residents of the Indian village of Gauhati discovered in 1999. A herd of wild elephants came to the village, stole rice beer and went on a drunken rampage, trampling four villagers to death.

3. A cartload of angry chimpanzees living in a Tacugama Chimpanzee Sanctuary in Sierra Leone turned on the construction workers building an addition to their home. The chimps – some of who armed themselves with the worker's tools – beat two humans to death and hospitalised five others before escaping from the sanctuary in 2006.

2. Jeff Cowan was so shocked to see a wallaby hopping along the road in the English countryside when he was driving towards Henley in Oxfordshire in 1986, that he lost his concentration and crashed his Volvo into a wall. The passenger in the car with him survived to tell the tale.

1. OUT FOR A DUCK
Leon Resnick was a 31-year-old worker for a boat dealership in Fort Lauderdale, Florida. One morning in November 2001, Resnick was testing a jet-propelled water bike on a lake at Deerfield Beach. He was monitored by a co-worker with a radar gun who was clocking him at speeds of 88 kph. In the moment it took his co-worker to adjust the gun, Resnick was apparently struck in the face by a flying duck. According to the sheriff's spokesman, when they found Resnick body it looked as if he had been "smashed in the face with a cinder block". They also found the carcass of the duck and feathers all over the handlebars of the water bike.

GETTING THE BOOT

James Berry, a 42-year-old from Watford, became furious when he discovered that his car had been clamped and he would have to pay £240 to get it removed. He was so furious over the 2005 incident, that he kicked the clamp. Bad move. His burst of anger caused an injury to his foot that sent a blood clot off into his body that killed him three days later.

STRIPPER SLIPPER

Dutch stripper Anne Marie Comstock died after slipping off the stage at the Bananenbar strip club in the Netherlands. Her act – which featured innovative uses for everyday objects – saw her walk on stage in six-inch high heels. Unfortunately, the previous act had left the stage slippery with vegetable oil. Poor Comstock took a tumble and smashed her head against a stage light, which killed her instantly.

DICK IN THE LION'S DEN

The Rev Harold Davidson was a Church of England priest who became known as 'The Prostitute's Padre' when he was defrocked in 1932 for providing more than ministry to various ladies of the night. Trading off his notoriety, Davidson went to Blackpool and made a living by being an attraction – either fasting in a barrel on a pool or being apparently roasted in an oven while a figure dressed as a devil prodded him with a pitchfork.

In 1937, Davidson had found work at Thompsons Amusement Park in Skegness, where he was billed as "a modern Daniel in a lion's den". For his act, Davidson would enter a cage with two lions – a male called Freddie and a lioness called Toto – and give a speech about how he felt the Church of England had done him a great injustice. All went well till 28 July, when Davidson accidentally stood on Toto's tail, causing Freddie to leap on him, bringing him to the ground and mauling him. Although he came out of the cage alive, Davidson died a few days later. More than 3,000 people attended his funeral. Less a case of Daniel in the lion's den, more a case of a right dick in the lion's den.

CAPTAIN OVERBOARD

Captain Matthew Webb achieved international fame when he became the first person to swim the English Channel. While most people would have been quite happy with this claim to immortality, it was not enough for Webb. Basking in the celebrity which saw him launch everything from a brand of matches bearing his name to commemorative pottery, Webb kept himself in the spotlight by doing a variety of stunts.

The most ridiculous of these was attempting to swim across the Niagara River in the rapids below Niagara Falls for a prize of £12,000. Most people thought the feat was not only impossible, but clearly suicidal. This did not stop Webb. At 4.25pm on 24 July 1883, he jumped into the river from a small boat and began his swim. Within 10 minutes he had become caught in the current and was dragged under to his death by a whirlpool. It took four days for his body to be found.

TEASE ME TIGER

Hannah Twynnoy was the first person in England to be killed by a tiger. A barmaid working at a pub called the White Lion in Malmesbury, Wiltshire, Hannah was a popular girl. In 1703, a travelling circus arrived to set up in the pub's grounds. The circus contained an exotic menagerie of animals, including a tiger. Hannah was fascinated by the striped beast, but was warned against upsetting it. However, she ignored the advice and took pleasure in riling the tiger by continuously poking it with a stick and throwing water over it. Unfortunately for Hannah, somehow the tiger broke free and mauled her to death.

EXTREME IDIOT

Let us not beat around the bush. Most extreme sports are actually extremely bloody dumb. Of all the extreme sports, possibly the most ridiculous is train surfing. It involves riders climbing onto the outside of a moving train to 'surf'. Aside from the basic problem of trying to stay on a moving train while it is accelerating, added deadly dangers include avoiding collisions with bridges and tunnels or being electrocuted.

Among the many idiots who have died train surfing, the name of Martin Harris of Denmark stands proud. On 12 May 2007, Harris decided that instead of travelling back from a football match inside the train, he would surf on its outside. Climbing on top of a train heading to Ringkøbing, he managed to survive travelling under his first viaduct, but forgot that another one – with a clearance of just 74cm – was coming up.

Harris had posted several clips of his train surfing journeys on YouTube. He had even given a TV interview about his 'sport' in which he said: "Danger is a rush, but I always know the route. I always know when to duck."

HANDS OFF THE STALLIONS

Kenneth Pinyan was a resident of Gig Harbor, in Washington, who had a sordid secret. He liked to be sodomised by horses. Pinyan filmed his bestial acts with stallions and distributed them to others sharing his kink under the name Mr Hands.

In 1995, while a friend videoed Pinyan having sex with a horse, 'Mr Hands' unsurprisingly suffered a perforated colon. His life could have been saved, if he had not been too ashamed and worried about the consequences of explaining how he got the injury and gone to hospital earlier. However, not wanting to admit to being buggered by an Arabian stallion, Pinyan wasted the vital hours in which he could have been saved and died in agony. Somehow it is hard to feel much sympathy for a man who believed that animals could consent to sex.

HISTORICAL HILARITY

Somehow it is reassuring to realize that ridiculous deaths are not restricted to the present day, as the discovery of an old parish burial register listing deaths from 1656 to 1663 in the parish of Lamplugh, Cumbria, reveals. Among the causes of death listed in it are such gems as the following: four people were "Frighted to death by faries"; another died after he was "Led into a horse pond by a will of the wisp"; 11 people died after catching a cold from "sleeping at Church"; two were done for by "Mrs Lamplugh's cordial water"; a further two met their end "By the Parsons bull"; a couple of "Vagrant beggars were worried to death by the Squire's housedog"; one man died after a drunken duel "fought with frying pan and pitchforks"; while another life was claimed when a man died in a fight "between a 3-footed stool and a brown jug".

If nothing else, the register reminds us that death and the ridiculous have always been – and always will be – a part of life.

ACKNOWLEDGEMENTS

Matt would like to thank:

My wonderful girlfriend Laura – so accident-prone I'm surprised she's not become an entry in this book – thanks for her support; my ever-reckless pals Andy and Warren, who'll have to be careful not to appear in Volume 2; and David for both his friendship and the privilege of working alongside him.

David would like to thank:

Surreal Girl, who despite the five broken ribs, falls down stairs and death threats is always there to hold my hand and make the world a better place with an atomic sun smile and a cup of tea; Tim, Stephen and Sean – brothers by other mothers; and Dickon, the only man I know likely to die a more ridiculous death than me.